Kintsugi

William F. DeVault

TO MY FATHER

ISBN: 979-8-9995232-0-4

Preface

Lord Byron was referred to as "mad, bad, and dangerous to know" by some contemporaries. I like to think I am not bad, although the other two adjectives are certainly in play when discussing me, or at least my poetic side. Who else would write a crown of a crown of sonnets in a month (my book *liaison*). When the fit is upon me I write…nearly constantly. I have been known to carry pads and pens with me to suddenly pounce upon at 2 in the morning when the inspiration strikes, and when running out of paper writing new works on the willing body of a lover, to be transcribed later (a few in this volume started that way)..

And once the spark is struck, it sometimes goes for hours or days or years.

I write from passion, I do not rewrite, as my process is that once written, a poem or passage is like a photograph, a capturing of a moment, an instant, and to alter it defiles and counterfeits the art. Needless to say, I throw out a lot of poems, as I treasure those that resonate with me, but not everything written is worthy to be given to the audience, The poems that have made it between the covers of this volume represent survivors, regardless of the inspiration that kindled and sparked them.

Here you find pieces of me, shards of my thoughts and emotions, my hopcs and fears, desires and instincts, that are not a complete picture of me in their individual existences, but when soldered together give a more three-dimensional view of me, my psyche, my soul, and my talent. On one of my passes through I noted that every major and most minor muses and totem-muses are represented, for what is a poet without inspiration. I stand by my definition of my process that states I am a lens that focuses the light upon the page. A lens in a dark room is useless.

My thanks to everyone who influenced me, some by merely existing, some by encouraging me, some by seeking to thwart me. From the woman who taught me kitten kisses to the night blooming jasmine in Venice Beach. From the pain of betrayal to the unexpected flirtations from a protégé. To quote myself, I have fallen and have risen, and taken penance given, every mile.

This is not the end of my story, my narrative, at least I hope not, merely the transition to my next arc. What is will be, I am uncertain, there are thousands of flashes of light in my small corner of the universe, and many adventures and misadventures yet to live and to share. Consider this merely a clearing of the table and a cleansing of the palate.

I am grateful for the life I have lived, grateful for those who touched me and inspired me, and I thank God for the opportunity of my existence and the will to persist.

There are many rumors and legends about me and my poetry. Many are true, many are not. When in doubt, ask me, The truth does not offend me or frighten me.

With love, hope, and poetry.

William F. DeVault

Foreword

Desire is the essential mystery of Creation.

It permeates longing leading to disruption, bliss, satisfaction, the act of creating, and preponderance.

The nature of desire is to penetrate like a curious reader studying an ancient, cryptic text.

William F. DeVault's *Kintsugi* culls from the poet's faith the art of deciphering the depth of love and order from the vaults of chaos and confusion. These poems restore the order of love while traversing the complexities of definition through history, personal experience, death, sexual grandeur, beauty, and political and religious misunderstanding; witnessing love can be hardship, and experiencing it is tumultuous, doubtful and even sagacious.

These paradoxes are illumined by the Romantic Poet of the Internet's clarity of emotive description, adventuring throughout the stars and the cosmic bounty of life experience.

One may think DeVault has mysteriously vanished into astral travel to share the unity of Creation with us, his readers. Penetrating, insightful, yet descriptive and allusive these poems are bursts of quantum uncertainty at length.

By sharing these reflections, DeVault invites readers into a world of primordial quantum foam where the seed meets the egg through bold action and consent. Love invites, seduces, informs, teaches, instructs, pleases, and grants burdens while shouldering them faithfully to enrich our experiences with depth and mystery.

Life may have no absolute and ultimate solution, and the quest for certainty is its own riddle.

In *Kintsugi*, we are part and partisan of a joust with the Creator and Their mad impulses.

-Dustin Pickering, Love's Philosopher
author of *The Ophelia Prophecies* and *Salt and Sorrow.*

wasting time and temperament

a second gong sounds in plastic and metal and glass
the roadway littered with sharps and shards
while I clear my head
no one injured
but a familiar process grips me

like that time a lifetime ago
when God had gotten tired of me wasting time
and temperament
slowly sliding out of the darkness
to find the grey way of desperation

waiting for the worms
maybe next time I won't be so lucky
maybe next time
I shall be in the grace of a lover
who gives me reason to pick up my bed and walk

not just talk about the memories of jasmine tea
a sea I sailed upon once for endless nights
when the lights were not brighter but newer
the gong awakes me
to reconsider a life in lower gears

Cracking the Gimcrack Artifices around the Burning Bush

Intro

driven to the brink
we think ourselves competent
competent to contemplate our very nature
nurture future impure and unsure
fragile standing stones
easily corrupted by the tides of history and herstory
our bastard ores melting at varying heats

Transition

the thinnest veneer shades fear from madness
the best beat bestiary hermetically sealed
in congealed wet spots on the satin sheets
where all promises are in the moment

Third Movement

caesurae fury in the darker corners of a sphere
tears that tear the fabric of our perceptions of time
crime to the dreamlords who do not have to wake
breaking dawn unpatched unmatched and thatched
hatches against the rain and stain, memory made
laid across the chasms of orgasms and suffering

Sotto Voce

tinkling tingling bells in the distance, persistence rewarded
with the medium stuffed bear, the big one only for winners
not just dogged effort and sporting propositions, positions
learned from a sideshow slideshow wordplay bloodspray
evidence of our history made in dark rooms when alone
atoning for our solitude in gratuitous gratitude, deep
sharing of our most intimate revelations in nerve endings
electroconvulsive therapy that seals our secrets within

Fifth Movement

the dichotomy of the erotic and the sacred
is not dichotomous. they are one and the same.
blame the Creator whose name we invoke
in goad and overload, flesh becoming metaphor
as our communion is at a higher temperature
and the warm wine is white, aperitif withheld
until after the body is consumed to nourish
the coexistent consecration of lovers' faith

Crescendo

I will look into your eyes if they are open
to enter you on every level possible
there is more to the coit than the copulation
of lip to hip to slip a grip in various orifices
to the solemnification of treasured pleasures
sacred in the religion of poets and lovers
where the transfiguration is replayed
as many times as necessary to your joy

Epilogue

I remember everything, dammit. Everything.
the texture of your lips, the taste of your breath.
the words you whispered then recanted once
it was too late to take them back and stack
your denials against my memory, imperfect
but full of you and the sound you made
as we parted at the airport and you wept
as doubt crept into your heart that there would be
another christening into our generate dreams

you never danced for me

as I cast sacrifices
offerings
promises

in accordance with your wishes
and the strange scriptures
recorded in texts

ancient
recent
scrimshaw
glyphs

kissed and denied
like every time
that I lied to myself
out of charity
and hope

pretty parasites

freedom is not just another word
for nothing left to lose.
you still, at least, possess freedom,
which is a terrifying and mighty place
to find oneself.
even if the bedclothes are not as warm
and you miss the pretty parasites
of passion and peace.

Anno Domini 2018: The Great Cat Gives Birth

labyrinthian fires

in from the ashes and against the wind
fire and desire are the sire of memory
cracking like bones beneath the boots
worn by conquerors and their toxic children
no surprise the lies as we all seek survival
even at the expense of love and truth.
squeezing the last few drops from the seeds
after the flower and the fruit is consumed.
whispers blister thin skin and within we die
to be reborn the next morning one less life
to barter like a feral cat, in labyrinthian fires.

buried alive

love is not a barter, but a gift.
grifters sift the dust of our trust and lust
to gather pretty pennies and peonies
to place on cold cataleptic eyes and graves
where we are buried alive
breathing the same breath
over and over
until the last of us dies in agony
but grateful it is all over

survivor

the heart that was left behind remembers
walking in scatter-step lame sameness
as in a thousand other betrayals
you get out alive
but the cripple has an intact soul

kindness

soft as snow in the darkness
falling in infinite repetitions of unique
instants and crystals of lives that dance
like children born and buried by indifference

the ghost of incongruity

we are known by the imprint we leave on the faces and traces
of the people we knowingly engage
the panhandler in the grocery store parking lot
begging money for her kids while she drinks her Starbucks
makes an incongruous impression

saying the word without comprehending it
like a toddler having heard a curse word
repeating it because it gets a reaction
the false lover who leaves a Judas kiss
as a mark of an affection shallow
barely wetting the surface
while looking for a graceful exit

hangman's hangover

do not mistake the warmth of the shelter
for the heat of the blast furnaces
you would not survive such immolation
unless you were of the highest metal
or your purposes was purer than silver
burned from a meteor's core
to be fashioned into legends and icons
in the hands of heroic Hephaestus

a greater heat, a truer coit

Mythology and theology. Kissing cousins
in the motivation of the breed and brand
of human considerations and expectations
capped when slapped to expand
our lungs and bring us into the world.
Belief in self as a mantra and a trust,
dust crusting on incinerated sins curled
around a serpent's tongue once thrust
into the very genesis of the human soul.
The argent sergeant gives final command
and we must follow or hollow the hole
into which we crawl, transfigured or damned.

we kissed as criminals

touched
we touched the aching sky
and told our truths in sighs and tears
defending pain, decanting love,
we were all we needed be
but we were fragile.
agile and asleep
to rising tides.

I cannot set back the clocks
that cast the rocks
we could not evade
our hearts and fleshes pale parade
was just a target for the stones
that tore our flesh and broke our bones
and all the kitten kisses
faded amber.

the walnut shells
in which we hid did nothing
but make illusions of our hope
as we clattered, scattered seeds
down Newton's slope
gathering speed but moss
declined to join.
and we kissed as criminals

into the void

I have found that when I shout into the void
anticipating reciprocity
on the part of strange and beautiful creatures
I am ultimately (so far) disappointed

in my mourning I contemplate
whether it was my expectations
as to the nature of those
that dwell in shade and shadows
or if my words were inadequate
to capture the focus of eldil
that dance in four dimensions
mesmerizing me and drawing dreams

there are times in recent times
where I have even begun to doubt
whether or not I am not heard
because I am not articulating
in a manner that penetrates the void
or perhaps I am a delusional mute
making not noise aside from within me
imagining that I have spoken or been heard

the void drains my soul and senses
making me a martyr to the heresy
that love is more powerful than dysfunction
the failing of flowers to bloom not guilty
when there is no earth or water or sunshine
to pound profound pulses of renaissance
offering my dreams and warm wines
as sacrifices to cracked idol pantheons

I have found that when I shout into the void
anticipating reciprocity
on the part of strange and beautiful creatures
I am often disappointed

intimacy

fit to flow, I know.
emotions like a confetti stream of dreams.
distance adds persistence
doubling down on wagers of soft sin.
imagining where your fingers are
right now.
wishing they were mine.
your spine is the rough racetrack
as I trace sensations
eclectic and electric
from lip to hip to tip inward
cured of pretense
until there is no memory
of you and I as
separate...

the religion of poetry

I am called to prayer
air thin with remorse
but the course is mine
and wine turns to water
daughter of creation
father of memory
the convocations call
invocations to tomorrow
built on frail yesterdays
and the band plays on
the melody forgotten
but the words resolute

The Samaritan's Empathy

another shepherd shot overseas
in the name of a disease called fear

grave men send brave men with bullets bought with your taxes
while the inner city is full of hungry babies
but it's okay because neither the babies nor the shepherds
are white enough for the Samaritan's empathy

another Hispanic child sold into the trade
to earn passage to a promised land full of hate

the Rio Grande runs red with American dreams
fears manipulated to conceive, achieve, and relieve
in a placebo pharmacology paid for by billionaires
who want more than money to line their caskets

history is written by the victors. dirty footed poets
and the spurned, learned prophets will have the final say.

in the movement of light

as the season of apple harvest draws to a close,
there are amomancies in the air.
the scent of jasmine and roses.
the slightest breath against the softest hairs.
the clarity of the charity of the heart,
light made white then bright until radiance dances
on the very edge
of the event horizon of time sublime.
the soundless scream of understanding and acceptance
as the dance begins again,
the pirouette of memory
and the frail blasphemy bound and found in the religion of a kiss.

wonderlust

I shall lock away my heart
tattered battered shatter scrap it is
within a box of a strange metal I spat out in furious curious doubt
when I saw nothing of value remaining
in the faux stain of passion
worn like a cape of legendary beasts and hung on hooks of glass
I shall pass into the evening sky and never die
for Ka Latil is everywhere and nowhere
the ciphers on the doors are based on a religion
forgotten by the strange creatures that pass for mortals
out of a sense of misbelonging
valuing that fell from broken towers
like splintered tears on a morning pillow
rich with the scent of a woman's tresses

in the beginning

the age of.
the rage of
poets
is upon us.
the sad glad madness, badness in Byronic whispers.
a religion beyond the mere fleecing of desperate believers.
in the beginning was the word.
we are the words.
the incantation.
the incarnation of the divine.
sacraments of warm wines
from the vineyards of the blessed and cursed.
the thirst for absolution
burning away the pains of
the chains of
the stains of mortal mediocrity.

Malevolence

the desire never really goes away. it sleeps beneath the skin
like some alien parasite
waiting for you to sleep
so it can feed
with ragged mandibles that ooze curious acids
dissolving memory and willpower
lapping up the trace prayers
that never really helped
and now that it smells blood through thinning skin
it is ready for the next round
the final round
all life ends in tragedy

light

that which we care to love
dare to love
ennobles us
enables us
disables us
destroys us
illumination or lasers
light is fundamentally the same

02/17/2018

I.

ten million miles from nowhere
twelve thousand miles from you
five thousand one hundred and eighteen days
without a proper improper resting place
the feast is famine and the damn sham has drawn
the window syrup taffy to threads measured in angstroms
but still unbroken
for the most elliptical orbit
remains an orbit
even when you are so far from the light
and the sweet heat
that you are forgotten for generations
returning only as a portent of the end times
every time

II.

life is written in red ink drawn from the veins of those
brave enough to capture the rapture in impure metaphors
five or more times, recounting crimes uncommitted
but spitted out in watermelon seed celebrations

III.

will you ever believe me to be as gullible as you need me to be
or can you comprehend a detached sense of charity carried
too far for most to grasp, the rasp of a kitten's tongue
the long game is not a con, merely beyond your frame of reference
penance in a poor of unremitting tears remaining to string the pain
with a sense of an elegant grace, face to face with the abyss
in every kiss. playing with a deck of infinite suits and numbers
where every draw is a suicide king or the queen of hearts.

IIII.

we must step outside of the rationalizations that lie to us.
like a lover trying to get what they want and give what they want
never surrendering to the pretend perfections and confections
served in a hall of molecular mirrors, letting the light the blinds
that binds us at a dark matter level, outside of the measurements
pleasured and treasured like a child clutching a teddy bear in the dark
a false sense of security and purity a relative term to the firm standards
measured in tolerances that only the just and honorable can waive.

V.

the disease progresses.
a touch of numbness as nerves wither.
decades of slow descent into the relentless nature
of life that circles the drain in a spiral dance
to escape the final fall is illusion born of fear
I measure the degree of defeat and know where this ends
embracing all aspects of my time in the proving grounds
as I move towards a distant door, distant no more.

VI.

I miss kissing. I was good at it and if they gave out trophies
I probably would have several on my mantle, along with the weeping Buddha.
I never kissed a woman I was not willing to sleep with
and never slept with a woman I would not be willing to wed.
one must have standards and earnest affection plays well
on the stage of life stages turning like pages to rust and dust
like the crust of a once-familiar bread no longer sold at the bakery.

VII.

to be wanted instead of needed.
not a counselor or sage, or a living ATM machine.
just a man, wanted and haunted not by every lie
accepted as truth to keep the fire kindled and caught.
it is so much simpler than the formulae of Solomon,
prayers passing for incantations, the cantata of night song,
just another illusion like dancers on a television screen.
not really there, wearing on weariness in a vague and vain
attempt to relieve the bludgeoning ennui of sentience.

desire on a sea of hotel sheets

even in the oppressive darkness I am aware of you.
your warm body heats the air as you scent it with your attar.
sweat and jasmine. a call to be fed upon, feasted upon,
consumed without burning, the sign of divine revelation
caught and held taught in your laudatory thighs, your curved back,
your infinite tousle of hair, a snare for my fingers and adoration.
the curve of space-time wrapped in linens draws me nearer.
pulls me into orbit, but not to my fiery immolation. not yet.
my blood roars and either you are oblivious to my craving
or brave enough to tempt a knave's ravishment in fresh feralities.

confession of irrelevancies

the light shall fade, subsequent to promenade
in darker shadows wound unbound to confound
the mythos of the mysteries we trace embrace.
I do not clutch titled entitlement, ego spent
in unrelenting echoes of self-denial, the trial
proves what twelve people think, and a wink
removes an instant from the chronology. we
do not exist, for all are singularities...seizing
the trailing traces to catch a ride with Apollo.
every outcast cast out to the gods of the desert.

anthem

the age of the dreamers is never done
for in the dark we find bright shadows
reflections of what is yet to come
revolution in what we suppose.
the time of poets is yet to pass
for words pierce deeper than any blade
transforming hearts to raise and surpass
most eloquent mysteries displayed.
the renaissance is ever rising.
old truths rediscovered and new light
filling stale corners, energizing
generations to raze lies of night
offered up by the tradesmen of fear
bartering chaff for the immortal.

misplaced kairos

in time the pain fades.
never truly gone
but diminished
by hours and days and month and years and decades and lifetimes.
always willing to leap up
laughing cruelly
to remind me of your touch
your kiss. your voice. your attar. your sigh. your taste. your smile.
the salty-oily texture of your tears.
the illusion of the forever
that I imagined in your arms and
tasting jasmine between your thighs.

shower

listening the glistening of warm water on your skin
the next room a purification portal, binding the fingertips
that ache to press you to me. that ache to stroke you
in comfort and into feral combustion. the heat rising
against the walls of solitude. the etude of vanilla lovers
practiced against the wet frets of your heart and loins.
your breasts sweet as maple sugar, comfort and silence
that crests in a symphony of colors and flavors and favors
granted as wishes from a precious vessel rubbed to summon
to invoke to provoke and to bid you join the joyous jeremiad
of lovers come and gone as they feared the sacred bed
would consume them. they did not understand the nature of fire.
desire is not a conscription, but the jasmine taste of liberation.

scrip

words traced in warm wine on the curve of your back
words you will never see
absorbed into your living flesh as sacrificial runes
completing the ardent spell

perfumed and consumed, the faint trace of jasmine
ananas in saline rain
barely holding back the blossom of divine flashpoint
anointing the covenant

filling the well, then drawing out the waters of life
in selfish charity
rituals of the love gods of a forgotten religion
sanctifying this moment

more than mere acolyte

the priest must allow for their doubts and diversions,
entertaining painful questions of faith and reason
that may challenge closely held beliefs, subversions
of the gospels of life and love and finding no treason
in the earnest desire to know profound the nature
of the faith he has bound to his immortal soul.
lost in the mysteries and the histories, nomenclature
becomes semantic lie and dodges pervert the whole,
the narrowing necessity of the cult of one, shunning
discordant heresies that may be whispers of martyrs
to the purest intent and path, the wrath of cunning
calculations that lack the purest of motive, barters
born of utility in surrendering to a life as penitent
on an indistinct road, parched lips seeking an advent.

past lovers, fallen

light without heat.
distant stars.
luminous with great and nuclear incandescence.
so far away, only their light reaches us.
we decline, die in the cold reaches.
warmed by only memories of passion, fire,
the essence of desire and memories
that themselves are foreign photons.
what was. a million years ago.
gravity calls a new sphere.
the fire is summoned. bartered for.
trading mysteries between muse and supplicant.
hoping. demanding fusion's heat.
settling for nothing less than conflagration.
immolation.
echoes of distant stars blotted out.

on altars spread

there is a welcome comfort
in the arms of a lover
when you believe in their heart
and you have taken the time
to learn more than just the geometry
of their erogenous zones

nothing against erogenous zones
they are shrines to a fire goddess
places of diligent and playful worship
where the sacraments of flesh
and blood merge into transfiguration
the joy of surrendered souls

every sense set to burn in turn
and all at once to hear the liturgy
in sighs and soft groans of pleasure
revelations are drawn out, taken in,
the internal curves of your body
how best to make throbbing sacrifice

the altar within you, veils penetrated
while the study of your lips and breasts
with hand and lips and fingertips
slipping mysteries into a rapture
of my mythology that demands confession
of all the nights I dreamed this

draw my offering out and into you
breaking the seal with your own prayers
leaving scars on my heart and back
as evidence beyond faith and memory
allowing me the blasphemy
of entering a goddess with lust and reverence.

Triptych for Agnia

Hunger

I want you to burn me alive,
consuming me over decades of unfaded affection and passion,
our glory a story of hypergolic conceits,
sweet and crisp like burnt sugar.
The taste of polite touches turned to feral kisses
that browse the entire map of your sweet skin,
heated with the need to have me enter you again
in any and every way you can find pleasure in
to release the demons of cold doubt and despair.
Therapy for creative hearts that self-immolate
In the darkest places to light the corners of karma.

Tongues of flame

The fire is not extinguished by the dark warm licking of the tongues of flame
but kindled and fanned by warm breath and guttural sounds
that feed and bleed and seed the coming conflagration
I want to breathe your heat and with patient persistence
feel your resistance melt away like wax before it boils
then catches fire. the better to immolate me
as you engulf me in your arms and legs and lips and hips
and burn me with a soul-deep brand consummating and illuminating.

Kindling silk

I am not afraid of the fire. I crave the consummation
to be found beneath the kindling silk and tindered lace.
I will leave nothing between my touch by lips and tongue
and fingertips and cock as I search out the greatest heat
to be sparked in arching back and cries of release and peace
won in the war between the stars, where light is an illusion.
But the heat to be found unbound beneath your kindling silk is not.

collision with the morning star

captured in slowly deteriorating orbit
of your Venusian plains
the hellish acid of your atmosphere
will burn brighter as I descend
in final fall to be consumed
doomed
by having been captured by your nature
to draw me in and spin me to
a cataclysmic finish
a sound that tears apart the ground and sky
as I am absorbed into you.

the aftermath of a passing flirtation
not oblivion
but the witness of those creatures
who saw my descent
and wondered at the nature of my origin
as my constituent elements become part
of the hard sulfurous heart
forming the sphere of legends of light
love
and the scrimshaw of my fragments
that, even unobserved, are proof I once was.

I can't be your lover

in fantasies bright and dark, I park my senses
on the very edge of what you inspire in me.
deep, plutonic desire to share an immolation
a fictional friction between bodies and spirits.
I dream in lucid arrogance of the dance you dance
with your lover tonight, lingering in the shadows
like a metaphysical incubus, my words weaving
frail and fierce fires in your mind and thighs
such that for a flickering moment, an instant,
or even later, as you sleep. it is my touch.
my hands. my lips. my tongue. pleasuring you.
measuring you as a muse of lambent incandescence.
I cannot be your lover. but I want to be your hero
so that, when the facade of proprietary and taken vows
splinters with a moment's weakness, you feel me
inside you. and you are unashamed. and I am yours.
my devils at levels you would scarcely admit to yourself.
but you feel this and seal this with darkened kisses.

Feast of Echoes

Prophecy confounds me. I do not know the truth of the shadows
I see dancing on distant walls, as the clock counts down. Evidence
is not a part of the future, but of the past, and memory shows
the unreliability of lovers who came on their own terms, a sense
of doom and desperation demanding a sacrifice of blood and seed.
I am not your lover, yet, and perhaps never will be, like the elusive liars
who danced away in the morning light, mourning that feed and bleed
on my words, but that want nothing more than a feast of echoes, fires
burning in memory and hopes that were dashed by a second thought
caught upon the turning wheel of stone that ground grandiose song
into whimpers of a wounded animal in the shadows of the night, bought
and sold with the IOUs of deceitful paramours, their right to make wrong
the amomancies that others will read over my casket, and curse their name,
each muse that flitted like a moth around a campfire of a passive fame and flame.

dance with the one who hung you

cross of cards

a cross of cards regards
and speaks in pantomime
the colours fade unmade
by memory and time

the shadows dance askance
suspicious of your whim
indifference suspense
illusions gone to grim

there's no dharma karma
kisses in the distance
your path of least persistence.

mango

like a mango
my heart is not a freestone
and you will find it complicated
to feed
to fill your need
but I bleed ambrosia and magic
in ink and photons

Poitiers

there is an intimacy beyond the mere intersecting flesh.
but no one is ready for it. steady enough we bravado our ways
through our days for the sullen nights in languages preverbal
and conveniently hardwired from the ancient brain.
you were a lousy lover, as liars always are, too far from the truth
to be able to transmit the synesthetic delight on the oversight.
the only person I lie to is myself, not wanting to have wasted
the years and faux passions like a hungry man eating dirt
when that is all he finds at the bottom of the pit he is chained in
by his own expectations and insurrections against the beauty of life.

expatriate

exile and the inclusive banishment
vanishment behind a cloud of magician's prestidigitation
and the puff of smoke and fire
like a bullwhip made of dreams and broken glass
invocation. coronation. theocricide.

Tempered glass that passes for the lens of the eye of God

I do not recall in perfect clarity the taste of a woman's lips.
the currency of seduction. the toll into the palace of Aphrodite.
for I have lived my appropriate years in the desert where slips
the shards of self-delusion out, away and the darkness so bright we
conceal ourselves that we cannot burn away to the crust
we have folded within to guard and ward as we conceal
the resplendent truth that is evident by the ashes and dust
that coat our feet and fingertips as we crawl to the well to kneel
in confession to the love gods of forgotten religions, with my psalter.
praying they will forgive us, for that is their principle of redemption,
that everyone deserves a second chance to dance before the altar
and proclaim their faith in tongues of flame and the fool's exemption.
love is too feeble a word for the transcendence of pyre and desire
I have seen through the eyes of stained glass and fire.

idolatry

the argent sergeant gave the order
and we followed in our line
over the cliff
for no purpose
other than evidence of faith

ripping the stitches

don’t move too soon, too much, or you’ll tear the wound
open again
and again
sedentary goes from temporary to the way of the nosferatu
just slowly
but inexorably

in common words

I want to hold you, to comfort you,
like a father to a frightened child
when then wind blows too fierce
and the night lingers too long.

I want to sing to you, in common words,
that lift your heart and feed your dreams,
when the world is stupid and uncaring
that you are in it, to make it more perfect.

I want to stay with you, wherever you are,
and wake to the sound of your breathing,
watch the way you fill the room with light
share with you the sound of my heartbeat.

I want to lay with you, every night,
and allow you to drift to dreams in pleasure,
your every need fulfilled in lover's joy
at peace with who you are and who you are to me.

Waiting for the Wyrms

planted in holy soil, toil to the tempest,
best of the wrested slices of time, prime
moments in the indifferent counting of instants.
intricate runes written in the air to dare breath
to freeze and fall, shattering on the stones
when our warm feet find cool solace in the night.

I have read the prophecies, seen the tapestries
and caught the disease of ennui. on we march,
slower and our shoulders lower under our burdens,
burnt and bitter as little as possible, but even pig iron
runs in the core of stars running red and rosary rogue.
the heat is sweet but defeated we are by our hungers.

somatic components of a very complicated weave.
believing in something by second hand evidence.
present tense and the tension winds the bindings
until we are captured in the webworks of whims
both surrendered to and pretended to have seen,
the light delights us when we fear the dark.

from the backstab to the cold slab the distance
is in the insistence in making utility of the futility.
a very beautiful woman once kissed me, then twisted me
until I was drained and stained with my own faith,
wraith of a ghost hosted in a virtual promise forgotten
when it was no longer a convenient concept.

arabesque in red and gold

flesh woven together in intricate confessions.

fingertip ministrations.
words in arcane, ancient languages
that lovers shared
before there were words or languages
other than the cadence of breath
speaking in tongues
and hands reaching
for an uncommon commonality

I dream this with you
even when awake

the dances we improvise
rather than repeat the lies
of pas de deux past
new and urgent urges
purging our pretense
purgatorial passions

unsilvered reflections

even in the perfect core of a star
the fires eventually fade and cool.
heat and light are surrendered to the night,
infinite night, cold as vacated hearts
where once the champions of dreams held sway
over the crushing grip of gravity.
life itself anathema to reason
the savour of luminescence pure born,
consequential to the very nether
in which it exists, through which it passes
forming warm eddies in the dark matter.
defining the very engine of life.
walking to the window to observe it
while photons dance upon your naked breasts

April 2016: a cycle

on the nature of poets

I once tasted a petal of clover, but that does not make me a honeybee,
merely a curious seeker unable to restrain myself from the moment
where I could imitate, faintly, the actions of the bee, aping the apis
to try to understand from where comes the honey, the nectar.
it was revelatory as the scale of the essence I partook of shook free
the magnitudes of mortal man from insect. imitation by rote of role
constrained by nature and the Almighty is not the same as transfiguration.
I am not the clover. not the honeybee. I draw my sustenance in inspiration.

the undodged curtain (for my Mother)

I did not watch them shovel the rude earth over your mortal remains.
for that is not how I would remember you, celebrate you.
how many times had you dodged the curtain? more than I knew, no doubt.
but it comes to this, a separation of mother and children
by the very ground we walked upon just weeks ago,
laying flowers on my Father's grave you now lay beside.

to an eager lover's religion

brighter than the fractured morning. she calls me with her kisses.
too far away to feel then, to savour her breath or the texture
of her moist lips, slipping into a transcendental trance to dance
across my skin and soul like faerie in the absinthe, green and greedy.
I am ready for the rapture, theologically or held within her.
worshipping as an earnest acolyte to the delight of the night
when she sheds clothing in a disarray, like a torn veil in the temple
where all mysteries are to be revealed to the patient pilgrim.

a soft pink ghost upon the wall inside my skull

I thought of you and all the promises you meant at the time you made them.
I admit, I still miss you, kiss you in dreams heated and sweet, holding nothing back
as I embrace the blackened corners that are foreign to me, for you are not there,
merely a simulacrum of your beauty, your fire, the feral desire that was light without heat,
bone without meat, even when cracked open for the marrow in desperation.

biscuits

the rain reminds us all that we do not
control even the soft fall of heavens.
it speaks to us words of a held tongue, caught
expressionless, yet eloquent, leavens
the pale and dry biscuits of our conceits:
powder and salt and lard, concealing taste
only in the baker's skills, the bland treats
seeming as more unto punishment, waste
of our attentions and intentions. lips
split and bloody as our cursed thirst damning
to a revelation of lives' eclipse
as we watch the kitchen timer turning,
mysterious clockwork and alchemy,
our lives measured by hands we cannot see.

measuring disaster in decibels of laughter

measuring the steps to the ledge, then running to turn
and leap
and fall
with practiced panic and the graceful disgrace
that saves face in the last instant and inches
before disfigurement and death
the breath of god and the occasional kind goddess
giving life at unexpected instants and instances
dances of the dreamers
that I will am still able to perform
even in my hermitage and hermit's age.

when all is sad and done

will you stay with me
will you lay with me
until all is sad and done
and the sun reconsiders rising
for just an instant
out of respect

when I leave
will you grieve
briefly
then remember
that I was about celebration
and dance barefoot on the kitchen floor

eloquent madness

the gentle glide of hands pressed against
the smooth spiral of your emotions
as they feed you need you bleed you
for an extended moment's pleasure
measure by measure touch by touch
such sensual light burning a tattoo
of invisible runes deep into you with every
lap and kiss and penetrative trace
of fingertips as heralds to a deeper thrust
into the puzzle box of your body
lips touching in every sense and tensions
tightened and let in increasing
unceasing releasing wet and fevered
as you draw out my sacrifice
exchanging passion for passion
as expression of earnest peace
until the feral chaos of the next
hungry consummation

weltanschauung

well, well,
the weltanschauung
is a dark place.
no surprises.
the mysteries were meant to be
complicated
and with a mercurial flow.
questions born as oft as not
from prejudice and memory.
but history
is only an echo
and echoes are just words
even when preconscious
and warning us of intended
consequences
that may never be.
the ebb and flow.
the ebon, below
the surface
measures itself
against the bloody flood
of passions.
and there are no strangers here
tonight.

Transcendent hummingbirds

Warm
no
hot blooded

iridescent breasts

sparks of transcendent beauty
guiding me in
framing the hummingbird flutters

I hear your song
transcendence
as the heat becomes light
between us

we shall share sweet nectar
that will fill us
and drive us

to a higher and deeper
state and sate

demarcation (pause)

the demarcation between the lemon meringue of your hair
and the pink meringues of your flesh
whipped into peaks by my attention and intention
leaves me little room for error
and little time for wiser patience
as you call me in.
in to the garden of your beauty.
petals dew-swept where they wept
in colder nights
but by the rights
granted me
when you enchanted me
you do not sleep alone tonight
if sleep is on the agenda
at all.
or just a feverish

pause

when the claws you left in my back
won't grow back
as quickly as I shall
and the sacrilege of your prayers
murmured when I kissed your shoulders
on the path to enlightenments as to the color
and the taste
of the fragrances
inherent in your blossoming
and my release and surrender
deep inside you
as requested
and unprotested
throughout the night
that lasts beyond the Bavarian tests
of your passion and fashion for pleasure.

Paris is not Palmyra

Paris isn't Palmyra.
They have survived more bullshit bullies
over the centuries
than you can imagine.

Do you think your shouts of false allegiance
to a Prophet and a God
you defy and lie about,
indiscriminately killing
and defiling,
that you are something
new and scary to anyone but the most naïve?

Your unpardonable sin
is claiming to be an agent of God
when you are just using
the veil of lies
to promote your agenda.

Parisians rise to the occasion,
like bubbles in champagne.
They will mourn, then laugh again.

God is truly great.
But you,
hypocrites and criminals of Daesh,
worshipers of false idols of pain and fear,
are not.

A Psalm of Thanksgiving, 2015

Praise the Lord, in all things.
In times of great prosperity and adversity.
We are not born to live
but to take this life to prove our worthiness
for a life beyond imagining.

Praise the Lord, in all things.
In an attitude of gratitude show honest thanks.
The gifts we have received
are beyond barter or compensation
as they are gifts of divine charity.

Praise the Lord, in all things.
For the first fruits and the final bone
are all because we have a loving God
who gives in a patient rain
that washes away our disobedience.

Praise the Lord, in all things.
In the silence of your dark corners
find the inner light and fight,
fight against the inevitable to show
that you know you are never alone.

Praise the Lord, in all things.
Dance like David before the Ark,
in celebration and without inhibition.
Taste the vinegar and contemplate Laozi,
for in the bitter there is yet beauty.

Praise the Lord, in all things.
Selah.

your garden calls the serpent

I feel your fingers
snake through my hair

clutching me to you
as I run the serpent tip
of my warm tongue
over the pink meringues
of your breasts

triggering electric sparks
in your mind
between your legs
as your essence begs
for a deeper violation

you convulse in pleasure
and measure the heat
that radiates from you
your body and heart and soul
as I trace an arcane language

I listen for your sighs
and for the inevitable tug
as you force me down
between your legs
to continue my hungry tracings

subtle smile

Dark eyes in subtle smile,
unassuming but lovely
like wildflowers.
In a field of lemon hair,
a bright bouquet that speaks
a language of charm
that disarms
me
such that words seem
frail tokens of respect
and desire.

Cupid's Rosewood Bow

Draw back the subtle curve that unnerves me
and let fly the arrows of desire, unleashed in
elegant arc to spark the stars to bid for light
kindled in the rosebud smooth texture that vexes
as it hexes and steals will and resistance.
A dance of soft invitation, accompanied
by word or whisper inarticulate unless drawing near
to be caught in the tender threads of your smile.
I would taste a rare and sweet venom, laid soft
at first blush to crush against the cold night
and bid a game of dancing fantasies to start
and part like lips of a wicked innocence.

Eyes of the Moon

Pale eyes that light the night like the moon.
Lambent and luminous, framed in sky
of pale skin and cascades of cocoa hair.
Windows into a soul posted with signs
that there may be a safer route to heaven.
But perhaps not one so beautiful.

necessity

for now
let us do what is necessary
laying groundwork for the future
until you are strong enough
to be certain what you want

then

whether or not you choose
to send me away
to build my life elsewhere
without you
or
allow me to stay and give
my everything
to you

I will at least have done
what love requires of me

with a patience
and tenderness
you will not find
with anyone else

but that will be your choice
and your voice
shall be my gospel

suitor

measure my heart, my will
against all the faery tale romances
sold to you for ten dollars a ticket
and a bag of chocolate candies.

I am not Prince Charming,
by some measures I am less.
by others, far greater, and I possess
the virtue of being solid to the touch.

if my words seem too eloquent,
that is the nature of my station.
but each word is true and earnest,
meant to make you smile and dream.

I bring you legend and magic.
for who does not need more beauty,
hanging like stars in a midsummer sky,
spoken not just to you, but of you.

grim ballet

beaten.
undefeated.
the penance met and meted.

a vagabond. a priest.
roadkill and a beast
inviolate
at the unhinged gate.

you will find your way
into the grim ballet
of my herds of words
the immortal
portal
into my perception
of your deceptions.

or the other way around.

delicati redux

So pale, so frail, so vulnerable to the cruel whim
of the world and to unworthy lovers, liars and thieves
who would steal your heart to wear as ornament, trim
on the mottled cloaks they wear to mark their station, sleeves
worn and stained like their souls, as broke as fallen glass, grim
and unsuitable to hold the barest trace of the nectar that is your
tender passion. That I would gladly trade blood and words for.

precipice

there is nothing for the taking.
sharing is all there is to staying the night.
I see you, and am forsaking
all the others, this seems so perfect and right.

I am not one
to fall out of love
you fit like a glove
my heart is won.

dreams in colours that tumble down.
rain that floods the tears and fears that I have known.
tender madness consumes, I drown
in all the sacred sins I've yet to atone.

I am not one
to fall out of love
you fit like a glove
my heart is won.

graveside

fifteen degrees below zero
(windchill at graveside)
sound doesn't penetrate.
the family is here.
(blessed are they that mourn)
I and Josh are windbreaks for my mother.
the honor guard waits nearby
waits patiently in the cold
to take their turn and fire at the sky.
Dad's lucky
he is beyond the cold.
Mom is not.
I am not.
(Josh is not).
I am uncaring.
not apathetic.
ambivalent.

ours to give

pretend, if you must
that this is just
a random meeting.
meaningless, yet,
as wet as you are.
as deep as I go.
there is a binding.
the way our skins glide
as we slide against
one another.
into a single
entity, not
what we had thought
would happen tonight.
or, in honesty,
we knew all along
that you would wrap
yourself around me.
drawing essential
nourishments from me,
more than physical.
but pleasurable.
gratification.
then again. again.
into the bright morning.
when we awake.
and take yet again,
what was, ours to give,
and by our choice.

captive

Nothing good can come of this.
Nothing good at all.
I feel you pierce my shadowed bliss.
Now in my sunken hall.
You've overrun the battlements
where I had made my stand.
And now cut deep inside my stones
I'd marked with sacred brand.
You're everywhere at once, and yet,
you dance, you dance away.
You've toppled walls in sacred halls,
you drive my thoughts astray.
And what would you, my conqueror,
demand to ransom back
my sanity, my vanity,
my soul on which you snack?
Benign malevolence you are
and beautiful, beside.
You've broken my defenses, token,
and in my heart, abide.

Overture and Underworld: 59 and counting, surmounting the sublime and divine

It has been a rough year, a tough year.
Heroes falling and lovers stalling
(waiting to see if they can make a better deal).
Seals cracked and blistered, insistence
shading into ambivalence, future tense
and the dollars and sense of best laid plans
making mock the monk and the steamer trunk
where the metamorphosis used to occur,
hinges now rusted shut and air running out.
Shout and the audience cannot hear, as they cheer
the lights and legerdemain, vain pavonine flourishes
nourishing nothing but overstuffed egos.

My father passed a day after the new year turned,
quietly and with dignity.
Awake to the end, aware and reassuring
that he was okay.
I don't think I will slip away in peaceful acceptance.
I will not go gentle into that good night,
the light is too bright and I have work undone,
a daughter and a son or two to look out for.
Wars and whores and spores and sores and scores
unsettled and fine kettles of fish to bring to a boil
as I toil in twelve dimensions at once.
The solemn somnambulances going catatonic.

On the first day a girl shaded her fade and stayed
just long enough to create the illusion of permanence.
I saw the mirrors' edges well in advance but the dance
must be danced in keeping with the probabilistic
prophecies, ballistic hearts spinning from rifled shots
that catch on the wretched illusions we accept
as they tear more that flesh, flechettes of briny bone
forming patterns on the far wall as we seal and heal.
As nerves rework themselves, there is knowledge
that the pain feeds the machine it bleeds, deep inside,
a pride of leonine nobility. Ignorant and arrogant,
a flesh in the pan that can span the decades' dance.

Pulling in the skin and finding a deeper understanding
in words that cannot be taught, armies march in arch
abominations as nations that are and were and would be
see the extent of their spent hatreds and currencies
drawn to evidence their sacrifice of the first fruits.
Roots and leaves, the trunk of willful ignorance.
Steel jacketed elegance, we take pride in snide stutters
as we utter the words of our own damnation.
This life is not the point of life, but cowards cower
and the flower overpowers us with a perfume
that we consume in puffs of smoke that choke
our shallow awareness, less grief in relief.

Dance the amomancies, make straight the way, play
a game that is never the same. Quantum chess
where every piece embraces chaos theory, pawns
spawning kings and queens and the occasional princess,
whether or not she accepts the golden slipper I slip her.
I am afraid to put my back into it, afraid of being dismayed
and disappointed by the end result, for I know the nature
of the nurture of the world is a complicated thing
and Bragi only brings the nuance to the dance.
He does not choose the band or the playlist,
the twist of the wrist required to channel the fates'
river of molten sulfur across continents. To awake.

waking

In the light
are you tethered to the fire
is the high wire of desire
all you crave?

Like a dream
fearing only the waking
in the aching to be taking
you tonight.

the scent of jasmine

for hours after we talk, the scent of jasmine hovers.
a welcome memory, too soon faded, but never jaded
by the doubts and discouragement of faded lights.
the constellations shift in time and I'm facing nights
needing met in lovers' cries, a celestial symphony serenaded,
each earnest note a glissando of surrendered lovers.

The Feast of the Night

I make myself a sacrifice, the price of loving is precious.
To give all. Flesh and heart and strength. The rage of quiet affection.
Perfection a path, not a citadel. Hell fears my words. Hush. Hush
and listen to the roaring silence, imploring a moment, shun
the japing mockery of those who cannot understand that love
is both divine and diverse, perverse and pristine, between the seals
the veils fall and we are left, surrendered, feast to raven and dove
who will both feed on the seed of our coeur rage and what it reveals
about the nature of our barefoot hearts, dancing the patterns found
in the mysteries of our histories. Kisses in kairos. Breathe.
Breathe and find my breath in your lungs, an intoxicant. Hope, unbound
and tied with a ribbon that unwinds where we dare our wills to sheathe.
Accept me for what I am. All I am. Lover and acolyte.
This, a holy day commemorated in the feast of the night.

early morning

lay before me as my feast.
let your hungers be released.
I shall feed upon your need.
you shall swallow all my seed.
in the night I shall impale
your willing body without fail
deeper yet until you scream
this shall be your perfect dream.
we shall see how far you'll go
not just to fantasize, but to know.

Revelation in satin and silk

face me and trace me.
my blood, both red and white.
night for night in a light we share.
I am inside you.
and yet, part of you is inside of me,
purifying me and defiling me.
driving me to heroic efforts
to make you understand
just how beautiful you are.
and how much I need to leave a part of me
as fluid offering to the goddess you are.
a religion of passion and intimacy.
beyond words.
beyond worlds
we kept to ourselves
for too long.

the legacies we design

hollowing out human experience to find
the seeds are not at the core, suspended throughout,
dancing dandelion puffs, significance signed
in carefully coded chaos, they spin about.
understand the wind and you understand the sky,
where man hangs heaven for convenience and dreams
weigh heavy on the diaphanous clouds, we try
to capture them in flutterby nets as it seems
we can, if we try. but this riddled universe
is more than a puzzle. unmade by mortal hand
we capture what we can in silver and in verse,
glad for the moments we can recall as we stand
on various ledges at various incline,
daring gravity with legacies we design.

gold and violet

gold and violet, godless and violent, the colours kiss
and the hiss of the creation overwhelms the light of stars
that are but gaseous scars in the dark matter of dreams.
love is the quintessential fabric that sustains us between
the flicker of conception and the cold embers of death.
the breath of a sated lover that hovers just in front of you
before you say something earnest but too heavy in times
that are measured in a false gratitude of platitudes, graceless,
faceless like every name that fades in the charades.

time slows. then stops. for how long, no one knows,
of it there is no measure when the cosmic egg rips through
the quantum foam and we roam only within ourselves.
life is a dream and death is the waking, taking us away
from the other dreamers who may not even exist
if Democritus is to be believed and we are so deceived
by our own need to not be alone that we invent bent
simulacrums that carry out the ragged rhythm
of our solitude that intrudes in our illusions, in the moment.

stir

violins.
I hear violins late at night
when I think of you.
sweet strings bowed
to express the emotions
you stir within me.

the stars.
the stars are electric white
in the midnight blue
of a sky like a road
into eternity, resurrections
you stir within me.

deeply.
deeply you set your barb,
harboring few regrets
I follow your lead
as you swallow the seed
you stir within me.

The Celestial Rime

We shall burn with an heavy light.
This phage. This cage. This graceless age.
We'll not go gentle into that good night
that poisons all with a cowards rage!
This will not endure, will not defeat us!
Still on our feet, though battered, sure,
we will ensure the dawn shall meet us
in principles and purpose pure.
Refined and cut to meet the task
that seeks to drag us down and lost:
To give e'en more than challenges ask
we fight for more, ignore the cost.
We seek ascension to the prime.
We march to the celestial rime.

Playing in Another's Garden

differences in the most dread sense, no defense.
bloodlines divergent and convergent, all one species,
pushing agenda as we befriend the darkness, tense
to the pretense of our worst, our cursed disease.
greed that bleeds in currency and power, flowers
trampled in our search for beauty, duty empowers
all sorts of inhumanity. the vanity of a selfish goal
that washes away in the saline rain of the martyrs.
the crime is revealed, the documents unsealed, our role
exposed and our sins branded in tears and fears.
the lie of leaders or the peoples' cowardice, genocide
or burying truths deep in the search for a national pride.

The Conqueror Wyrm

drink the blood of the conqueror wyrm,
mingled crimson and alabaster.
draw it out and take nourishment
that you may be granted your truest wish.

drink the blood of the conqueror wyrm,
warm and fresh on your tongue, and
you will comprehend the dusky night,
speaking the language of fiends and angels.

drink the blood of the conqueror wyrm,
turning lovely quicksilver into radiant gold.
the alchemy of the soul, a single draught.
you will perceive the most arcane secrets.

drink the blood of the conqueror wyrm,
made a communion of madness, no chalice
can hold this thick venom, you must drain
the very beast in a feast of unleashed desire.

mysteries

mysteries of life are more.
more than mere histories.
histories of what we have done.
done and left behind, finding.
finding the diamond in the stones.
stones, cool to our tread and touch.
touch me. I am more than my mysteries.

dangerous women...

I am no stranger to dangerous women,
long legged angels of devilish regard.
haughty, naughty attitudes who exude
the pure allure of those who know passion
is a two edged sword and have the scars
to show for it. but are, nonetheless, irresistible.

Courtship

This is the time where caution becomes paranoia.
Fear of falling. Fear of winning. Fear of the unknown.
Like tasting, blindfolded, something placed on your fork
as a test of faith. I don't want that just-like-chicken taste.
You intrigue me, and I am not one to be easily intrigued,
having spent many years searching for someone
is not a near miss, bright and sensual, funny and kind,
a first class mind in a form like mortal sin, devastating
to the fears of inadequacy the abuses of frail imitations
have ground into me. For my religion is my love,
and I have had too many idols fall when I tear the veil
and find the arrogant and cowardly impostors,
looking only for the quick fix of literary immortality
and an anticipated lover more worldly than their sphere.
If you are here for the right reasons, the sublime blend
of selfish desire, curiosity and an ennobled heart,
proven in darker, starker times to be a banked inferno.
I would welcome your fires. A steampunk boiler,
full of heat and wetness, screaming in release,
driving us to ascend the barriers we would challenge.
I am ready for that. I have been ready, waiting,
a patient impatience wreaking havoc on and in my path,
but always ready for the opportunity to fall into joy.

haiku: 24 hours later

yesterday morning
you did not ask for kisses
I was not there yet

sepsis

souls and hearts, like wounds, fester in the darkness.
silence is violence against them and the imagination
seizes us with displeasing thoughts uncaught by defenses
we have built over long years of betrayal and deceit.
defeat is the result. the soul withers, a septic whim
poisons our days and nights, waiting for the sunlight
and the oxygen that can cleanse and bind hope.

temptation

what ingenious God conspired to drive me mad,
placing such a woman in this graceless world?
placing such a mind as to enthrall me
in a woman so beautiful as to court my desire.

fire in a core of fusion. I am not unmoved.
the heat is sweet and beats down my doubts,
shouting them down in tongue of flame,
calling your name in restless dreams.

fly far and fast and when at last you find peace,
I would look to my secret prayers that I
was among them, my words surviving the heat
long enough to meet you in the sun's core.

lover's taunt

dreams bend and we befriend
whomever shows up before morning.
it makes sense in the present tense
to be with those who make us feel right.
we need to bleed our seed in fields
where we stand, revealed to the first light.
night is gone. but it will return, we burn
lumps of coal dug from our souls
and made into a secret symbol for sins
we think we will never commit, we split
heirs and hairs and stare into the fires,
waiting on the call that may never come
before the lever is thrown and we pass
through the glass with nary a scratch.
patch me up and put me back into the game.
I won't tell anyone your name. that's your job.
if you have the couer rage to share the stage.

cleave

short of my soul,
which God holds,
I am yours.
if you would have me:
human and bent,
sent to Hell and back
on more than one trip
for water for the burnt.
still with a few trips left
and a desire to inspire
one more heart
to feel something
honest and beautiful.
to make children,
whether of paper and ink and light
or flesh and blood.
to be for you
all you ask of me,
want me to be,
need me to be.
that I can be.

red leaves of autumn

stranger danger. I know you won't give birth in a manger
if anything comes from what happens next. no problem,
I've got a few miles of cobblestones up my back, the crack
of my spine is like the wind in the red leaves of autumn.

your soul is black cherry, but your essence runs even sweeter,
your shades and shadows, ghosts and demons all play well
with the monsters from the id that I keep chained and restrained,
just enough silver in the alloy to keep them compliant and silent.

I want to see if your quicksilver and mine could make a wine
that flows into our lower selves while leaving a shine sublime
that glitters like a pop diva's ignorant pentagram, mad facades
notwithstanding, branding us of the same cotillion as we dance.

the honor of your flesh

Bend your strong and supple limbs
and wrap me in your angel wings,
singing songs of forgotten sorrow,
misplaced by grace and a face
I would look upon while you take me
into you. Sliding into smooth curves
and bringing you an unsubtle pleasure
as you measure me for your kisses.
Draw me deep and drinking me in.
Swallow me with all manner of lips,
and I will feed you more than seed,
but my observations of your kindness
and the tender way you curl about me,
a comfort and conundrum.
Exciting and alluring, but ensuring
that I will recall these nights and afternoons
when you invited me into you,
and allowed me the honor of your flesh.

the value of faith

the shadows are electric.
you just can't see
because
your eyes are far too small
and used to fragile visions.

the clockwork kiss will unwind
and we will find
answers
to misstated questions
that we don't, won't understand

the priest utters mysteries.
the histories,
obscure.
pure and unsure he prays.
then lays down still confused.

but my confession

I own my soul.
This is not defiance,
but a confession.

It burns like hot coals in the pit
of my stomach
to know that there are people
alone in the madness
who don't want a little company
in the pit.

Do you understand
that this violates all I believed
in the nature of love?

God is love.
And we are to emulate God.
But we can't agree
on what is love.

How can I explain
that which is mystery
when the concept of light
confounds the blind.
The taste is dry and bitter
like a long forgotten kiss.

I own my soul.
This is not defiance,
but a confession.

The Damning Darkness

Every day I feel the rust encroach.

No more.

Let us burn the bright towers and awaken the golems
for one last season in the fields of anguish and delight.

Night is coming for us all, all the tall children of Adam and Lucy.
And none shall escape the rape of the clock. Passions fading.
Limbs withering. Memorizes glazing over to grey mists.

No more.

Roar into the storm and threaten theocricide, dare fate
to grate its brittle teeth, pocked with the grind of other bones.

Night is coming for us all, loping an uneven gait of pursuit,
sniffing the wind for evidence of our decrepitude. I will feed
on your essence and extend my vigor into the damning darkness.

petals, bright and warm

open to me, your petals bright and warm.
inviting to my touch and fragrance not sensed
since Eden was a garden not a lost paradise.

I will drink, softly and deeply, careful to show respect
and not resurrect the memories of cruel harvests
where you were just another random flower cut down

fallen angels covet this pollen and nectar,
for in their taste is the secret to immortality
and a sacred joy unknown by those lost and gone

I will feed here for a season, hoping you are perennial,
and that you will let me inhale your attar and kiss
your soft petals until time itself is irrelevant

tasting quicksilver

lay back in the black and feel my hands
as I follow the elegant curves of your body.
close your eyes and focus on all other senses
as your flesh tenses to my caresses.

I will kiss your sweet breasts, drawing your
peaking meringues between my lips
as my hands stroke your hips
and fingertips dance between your legs.

your body begs for penetration
but the consummation is delayed, denied
as I slide kisses down you and you feel
my warm breath between your legs.

strong hands part your thighs
and the darkness is full of the touch
of my lips and tongue, teasing and tasting
as you strain and moan, clutching the sheets.

you are sweet and musky, I feed
relentlessly, made more hungry by every taste
and you feel my fire and desire rising
as I pleasure you to the point of madness.

your legs wrapped around my neck,
my tongue inside you, lapping, trapping
your desire for me alone, you groan
and call out my name as you convulse.

a beautiful dance in the heated darkness.
a perfect release that never ceases
until you are spent and satiated
and I lay beside you, your taste on my lips.

invocato

share what you care and dare.
for I am hungry for an earnest lover,
fearless and evocative, whose body
is an instrument of her art and a voice
of ten thousand words beyond
the most guttural of vocalizations.

although, I do like the pillow talk.

open in all ways and stay , stay
more than the night, if only in spirit,
and leave me in the morning knowing
that the heat will return to burn your brand
deeper into my soul with every touch
and tremulous kiss that explodes in fire.

for, I do like kissing, very much.

teach me the unique topography of you
as you trace my desire and place my hands
where they will do the most damage
to your already thrown down defenses.
I want to be lost, and found, inside you,
and know you know I know your secrets.

and I will make you an altar of madness.

quicksilver is better than fool's gold,
it moves and snakes and makes rivers of sweat
and leper's blood that you may take me
to the edge of all reason and rapture,
captured in your eyes, your hands, your lips,
and between thighs that whisper my name, tonight.

preying mantissa

how many times can nine go into one
such that there is no remainder
but sweaty sheets and deep breaths
hearts pounding in sounding out
the memory of equations
where I found several solutions
to the problem of where to enter
the sum of our parts
and, with hearts pounding,
found three deep answers
to a riddle we will recalculate
once we have untangled enough
to see if there is yet another result
we have yet to find, lost in our calculations.
as you impale yourself again,
hungry for more answers to questions
we will keep resolving to the last
decimal place, and again. and again.
just to be sure of our proofs.

lovely

Lovely.
It suits you
like white lace on tanned skin.
Graceful.
Your soft ease.
exotic, erotic, with a quick mind.
Charming.
Disarming
a poet or two along the way.
Lovely.

rough and incessant ruttings

shells of antique denials of our own vulnerabilities.
hazy, brazen defenses torn down in an heated ascent
to the peaks of tender passions, manifested in rough
and incessant ruttings. whisper to me what you mean
when you cry out from the sensations of my cock,
buried inside you, my lips taunting your pink meringues
and your body lost and adrift somewhere between sky
and the ocean. motion and emotion consummated.
and you know my goal is more than mere flesh.

resonant hungers

would you trade for me your fire, desire,
quicksilver touches and the tempest
that comes from an imperfect understanding
of why we are here.
both thinking that we are clear with our needs
but that the other wasn't listening
as glistening skin and unresolved pain
finds a way, like magma under the earth,
erupting in the moment
but never promising a sustaining.
which is, in the end,
what we both need even more
than the moment when you cry out
and your beauty drains me,
stains me with memories of you
when I want more
more than your perfect curves
and the faint scent of your lips and hips
as I slipped into you
one more time
hoping that it would not be the last
that this poem would convince you
that we have more than
resonant hungers

resurrecting the golem

grey light tonight we fight a mighty right
in our passions and prayers, layers of hope
piled and plied and styled to ensure solemn bight
binds us blinds us finds us a braided rope
entwined, defined and mind over matters
that scatter our patter as in truth sealed
we are revealed to be, as time batters,
stronger than sum of our partings, revealed
as cinnabar and wolfram, alien forged
and hammered in the soul of the earth, birth
just movement, water to anvil engorged
with the sweet heat that proves our mettle's worth
in the mirth of an afterbirth of dreams.
with waking eyes, lies shed for true extremes.

deep and perfect

closer, I call you, closer to me, until our bodies touch.
long destined by the thick impalement that joined us
when you gave your permission for me to enter you.
centered inside you, I feel the pulse of your heart
and the graceful, rhythmic movements of your body as you slide
down and over me, swallowing me to fill your greedy need
to contain and control me. your warm flesh in my hands.
your animal curses in words I will have to ask later
what they mean, but I understand the essence of them.
ride me until you are on fire and let me feel how deep
you dare to let me by the loo in your half-closed eyes,
your thighs wet with sweat as I lose myself inside you.
the perfect heat of your inner skin enfolds me
and I am found at peace within you, kissing corners
that have a strange familiarity to my aching ram.
seal me away with your own kisses and teach me all,
all you are and want and need and bleed in tears
of pleasure and surrender. look into my eyes
and take my offering of white blood that I would give
as claim to your sanctified body, making it mine.
as I am, and forever, already yours. deep and perfect.

from thousands of miles away

your tears are like diamonds
precious expressions of stress and fire.
and all I can think of
all I can think of
is that you are not happy
and I wish I was there
to touch your hair
and kiss away the diamonds.
turning pale to vivid colours and life
like alexandrite
found deep within the earth
and brought to the surface
by Orpheus
wanting only to raise you up
and earn your love and respect
and passion.
how I want to turn the diamonds
to rubies of desire
strewn on a bed
when you confess your hunger
to be in my arms
and to stay.
first, the night,
then, for as long as the sands run.

Comfort

let the pain drain away
the stain remains
but the ability to breathe
returns
even after the sharpest ache

wake and shake off the night
like fallen petals
of an indifferent flower
pretty
but lacking fragrance

I will watch over you
the warding fires
flickering in my luminous eyes
solemn
and certain of my purpose

stories of and for another time and place

Hard to conceive,
but for decades, four, I believe,
I have kept my mouth shut
and never uttered word
and no one has heard
the secret you sealed with a kiss
and more.

I will carry
it, and a few others, with me
as engines of passions.
Soft memories of you.
Echoes of a time.
The secret you sealed with a kiss
and more.

I wanted to
say something solemn. Sweet. But you
were gone into the night
before more than stray smiles
reconnected us.
This brand of tender trust is mine
and more.

But I wonder.
In your own midnight conjurings,
if you ever summon
a time and a place known
but to you and me.
And ask yourself if it was
magic.

brave and honest hearts

brave and honest hearts
never scare me
always dare me
to find as much love as I can
and set the firmament afire
desire burning through the wire
like an electric kiss
that misses the mark but parks
in orbit around your soul
elliptical and sometimes shaded
but never faded
I'm not afraid of love
what are you so afraid of
more than ghosts in the graveyard
where I'd gladly dance with you
anytime, anywhere
even at midnight
so that all our old lovers can hover
powerless and flowerless
they made such a mess
and left us to clean up afterwards
but I'm a fast learner
and my afterburner
burns beyond blue white light
and in the night
that's better than a few words mumbled
when thoughts get jumbled
and it is time to see
if lips are for more than spit and kisses
as the steam hisses
and the jasmine tea you promised me
dries up
like poetry on a page you ignore
until you get to explain to the children
what you were afraid of
because I'm not that scary
dancing in the graveyard
and calling out the hesitation constellations
that die in the sky
brave and honest hearts
live with bare feet on the cool grass
and never pass
on a brass ring

Mandela's Chariot

In silence your chariot approaches. Bright light, a piece of heavens.
A man of destiny, a prince, grandfather of his nation, returns home
to the heavens that birthed him. A moral authority, of grace and peace
who helped lay aside the chains of oppression with a soft laugh and guiding hand.

Your ride home is here, not to the village where you took first breath,
but to the heavens where your soul was forged to change the course
of a people, a nation, a world and the history that is to follow. Relax,
enjoy the ride home, knowing that you have sown well the seeds of peace.

Madiba, you are a leader who did not need a gun or threats of terror,
but lead by simple moral authority, not so simple in this graceless age.
Twenty seven years in the stone belly of the apartheid beast, released
to forgive his jailors for the betterment of all, rising above fear and hate.

Once around the sun and then back into the heavens, Mandela rides proud
and the angels line his route home, his chariot carrying evidence
that we are better than our worse intentions, our worse inventions.
Enjoy the ride home, knowing that you have sown well the seeds of peace.

afterburner

in mysteries of histories not yet written
I am held, fast, last of my breed
first of my species,
to a path on which few travelers dare.
a girl with dark hair passed me by
then wandered off to live or die
in distant lands
where I rule
but am not afforded vision
or even rumours.
each night I sit in my chair
where I promised I would wait.
hating the wait.
but never her.
never her.
my passion and my promise
are not ephemeral.
even in this graceless age.

the sound of gears and stone

born in steel and clay
rising to press back the clouds
and scattering them with a wave
of hands and arms made for
other things

the sound of gears and stone
shifting and grinding
shifting and grinding
walking towards the edge
of the world

pocked with the mark of times
when hungry beasties fed
and took me to their bed
if only in their minds
not their hearts

the horizon is never closer
and entropy betrays me
but not yet, I say,
but not yet, I say,
and I move through the night

history

There is a time for more than mortal men and women.
Epic heroes. Gods. Small gods, certainly;
but gods nonetheless, wisely offering obeisance
to the one true God, but aware there is more
than the grey mediocrity of the blood and bone
that rose from the red clay of the ancient lands.
Aware that they are more than frames of shame
on which to hang our doubts and jealousies.
We can transcend the entropy of our clans and cultures,
we can bend the paths of fate and mate our martyrs
with the rugged juggernauts of change and the arts,
creating legacies that will echo long after footfalls
of armed armies and wagging tongue tattoo slogans
of chanting, canting crowds are laid silent
by the violent inevitability of time and truth.

telishment

lay thick and hard the lash.
I am not guilty, even by association,
but merely by the necessity of telishment
for all men and lovers who have failed you,
jailed you in their gilded cages
bartering for your affections with wages
carved of soap and wood.

lay thick and hard the lash.
grow angry if I cry out as dies out
my empathy for your sorrows, beat me blind
then grind against me and never quite apologize
for the clotted trickle you drew
as a dowry of the damned, slammed
for being the earnest suitor.

lay thick and hard the lash.
I bleat and retreat into the unforgiving desert.
deserted, in spite of momentary vows.
for my sins, I have earned this,
but not from you and we are more kin
of the descendency of our makers.
but someone must bear the lash.

thick penetration

My hands in your bare flesh
feeling the sweet heat within,
that I will explore with more than words.
Fingertips and lips and tongue,
and, when you are ready,
I will curve into you
to seek to thrill and fill you
with thick penetration
and a sticky memento of me
left behind to remind you
that there is more to me than words
and I like the taste of you
when you writhe, afire, and cry out
as I enter you. For the third time, tonight.

killing with whispers

words

tiny crystals of thought, spit out
as venom or in a purging of the soul
marking the trail back home
to a place you've never been
but read about
and would like to be from

words

a currency of variable value
depending on the merchant engaged
some keep their thumb on the scale
then try to tell you that you can't afford
what you're craving
starving in the midst of plenty

words

shadows that are tricks of the light
or spheres of star-born neutronium
and the density and truth is set
in the ear and heart of the listener
not in your truth
killing with whispers, unheard screams

words

dream of elegant beauty

In my mind you defy gravity.
Floating in silent beauty, high,
the wind kissing your bare skin
and cooling your flesh, your limbs, thin
and graceful, moving in a dance
of subjective seduction that drew me in
and lifts my feet off of the ground to follow
as you merge with clouds and myths
of a long-haired star, riding the skies.

not in the moment

I've heard a lot of promises
I've heard a lot of lies
can't tell one from the other
they often wear disguise

truths aren't in the moment
the proof is that the stone
not wear away or tear away
once the moment is gone

Pascal's wager played it out
and I must stand, be on my way
a lesson learned in brands that burned
at least for me, I say

open

lay open to me.
take me in and I will not fail you.
for my purpose is pure
and my passion is sure.
I want nothing more
than for you to speak my name.
lay beside me.
lay open to me.

through the night

for hours through the night
I would like to
I should like to
find comfort in your presence
sometimes in gentle words
sometimes in restful embrace
sometimes in passion that burns
scars into our souls

holding nothing back
and worshiping you with thoughts
and honesty
and curiosity
to see just how many ways
I can make you smile
and call my name
as we surrender to each other

brazen in winter

perfect snowflakes
unique
and like you
beautiful beyond dreams I had
when I was a child

I watch them flutter
and land on your hair
your shoulders
your bare breasts
as we make love in winter

brazen with desire
your hands
on my chest and dancing
like a snowflake, melting.
perfect, unique and beautiful

Chastushka

He dreamed a dream of tender thought
of a woman-child with slender thighs
and found, instead, that he was caught
inside her soul, behind sweet eyes.

tempted into truth

Waste not, want not.
Taste not, taunt not.
I want more than a kiss, bliss released,
the priest of passion serves the sacraments
with a renewed faith. A baptism of dreams.

Dreams to the awakening.
Shadows fade and beginning
to believe in the morning, an iconography
of silver emulsions and digital thoughts.
Caught in the veils, the memory remains.

just grateful for the time

there have been questions
asked by time and space
that I have no answers for.
but I know that I'd like to see
what I can discover
before I walk out of the door.
I'm not the nicest person;
I can be selfish and irate,
but I want for you before I want for me.
just let me be your companion
on this unpredictable road
for as long as you can want my company.
it may seem kind of strange to you
that I want to walk your path
asking little for myself, if anything.
but it is in my nature
and polished by experience
to share all that with me I bring.

have faith

I cannot see behind your eyes and find your dreams.
Or know my place in them.
I can only go on the wisps of words you have uttered,
which tell me little beyond
"have faith"
as I am a creature of faith, believing in time
that all things are revealed
that were concealed, that were hidden from me.
But time grows grey and thickens.
"have faith"
I wish it were that simple, but too many lost wisps
have whispered to me
endearments and encouragements, giving me a rope
of hope to hang from
"have faith"
seems more dust than trust, a crust to entomb me
while they ponder their desires
unconcerned with the blood they drain from me
in their delicate thirsts.

the heat and the darkness

I have seen you sweating through silk on satin sheets,
the scent of your heated flesh sweet and sensuous.

I have tasted your lips, your hips and every curve that serves
only to make you more beautiful, even in the night's chaos.

I have heard you whisper my name in ceaseless release
and cry out in dark shame and burning tongue of flame.

All in my dreams.
All in my dreams.

pulchritudine in veritas

this is truth.
this. you.
the smooth sooth of your legs,
warm to my touch and serving
as chalice to desire.
fire more cleansing
than all the altered altars
of history, their purposes
obscured by the words of men,
worthy and unworthy
to touch you as I do,
my hands worshiping
the curve of hips that slip
into my grasp, like a bottle
filled with a perfect vintage.
full and rich and created
to be made a Dionysian mystery.
unveiled to a proper impropriety.
I will place hands on you
and drink deeply, inhaling heaven
and feeling the complexity
of your sex upon my tongue.
until you are drained.

I will sleep tonight and dream

I will sleep tonight
and dream of you
whether you are beside me
or ten thousand miles away

you are inside me
a piece of me
a perfecting prayer of life
I barely dare to touch

I await your will
and imagine
a world where you and I
are always together

Venice Beach, revisited

The empty basketball court.
Not fifty feet from the pot barkers
calling out "we got medical weed"
and asking if you'd like to come in
for an assured and predestinate diagnosis.
Venice Beach is a different planet.
But the exobiology of stoned vendors
and tentative rollerbladers
doesn't change much.
The sand still feels the same
and the seabirds hop closer
as if to challenge you
to an arm wrestling match
for the last bite of the last pretzel
the world will ever see
if the homeless guy
with his apocalyptic cardboard
sandwich sign, smeared with cheese
and ancient ketchup stains
proves to be right.
And the pot barker keeps selling
the modern snake oil
to the kids and the tourists.
While I watch the Leyden jar
in a string bikini
flash by on foot-borne wings
no less synthetic
than her breasts.
But her teeth are perfect.
And there's the approaching thunder
of someone dribbling a basketball.

the chair

a sweet and sticky fleur de lis.
a dance of passion on your knees.
binding me to your release,
I ache to enter you this night.

hours pass and we transform
through heat and darkness, we are reborn.
veils we lay now pierced and torn.
we strike the scales of flight and fight.

you wake to find I yet remain
deep inside you, peace and pain,
giving all, no poseur's feign,
you whisper wonders of delight.

nevermore but always there, the chair,
where hearts dare care and fleshes bare.
conspired to fire back against despair.
my love, you know my vow and sight.

flutter

pretty wings beating against the wind.
wrap me in their beauty. draw my nectar
out in metaphor and more, sustenance
to ensure you know the nature of delight.
night blooming jasmine. the taste of you.
I want to hear the wisp whispers that keen
in intimate moments, caught in sticky webs
of desire and expressions of tender surrender.
pause on my petals for the moment to feed
and I will bleed my sweetness into you.

the cage, the phage, the rage

broken is a poor word for shattered.
tattered remnants of a dream,
burst like ripe fruit held tightly
until it explodes, juice and pulp,
mocking the hungry pilgrim
who meant what he said, beyond the moment.

there are lessons here, to be learned,
burned in flesh and memory, the knell
of death, the smell of catfish, the pain
of an intercepted fist that kissed me
with an not-unexpected confession.
the resurrection of the games of children.

the cage. the phage. the rage.
I do not respond to any as anticipated.
the calculus of the soul is rudimentary
and does not take into effect dimensions
where you have not seen or been, I endure.
unsure, not of myself, or the virtue of love.

do not think

do not think
that because I am silent, I am unthinking
or unfeeling
or that, because my wounds do not kill me
that I am not wounded
and bleeding, every day.

do not think
my heart is like a stone, or a pinwheel,
or any other
of ten thousand meager metaphors
for the complexity
of the human heart.

do not think
that I judge you. I do not.
I judge myself for not being what you wanted
and for being less
than what you needed,
when I needed you, in the end.

elf

there is a method in your melody
but it is not in a Western scale.
nor kabuki. nor any other music
common to the sphere of men.
your mind works in magic and mysteries.
you scream in silence and violence
is an allegory for another story
that no one around here knows
or cares to listen to, except, perhaps,
an ancient poet who knows the alchemy
and understands the significance
of your slender form and pointed ears.
so sing your song for me and I will learn
your elegant truths as you reveal them.

elf II

you dance away in patches of light
on the floor of a forest made up
not of trees and leaves
but the memories of our species
and our own, sweet and brutal, times.
fallen about us in metaphor for leaves,
no longer alive, but mulch for growth.
and yet.
and yet.
there is an intoxicating scent
that rise from the fallen times
and fills my heart with longing
and memories of moments that linger
like the warmth of an earnest kiss
on alien lips, returned at length
to make logic of mystery.

enfold

enfold me in your wings.
brazen membranes of a spectrum
I dreamt of once
in a world before the pollution
of false idols.
I would worship at your altar
as I search for a true faith,
not one built on artifice
and idle curiosity.
I am a pilgrim
I deserve truth.
I am a prophet
I deserve respect.
I am a poet
I deserve the vision
to see what lays within the chrysalis.
warm me by your gypsy magicks
transform me by the power of desire.
find fire enough to kindle
a dwindling heat
still un-nourished
from when your spread your wings
and spun your silk
and told me
that you'd be back.
enfold me in your wings
and teach me your miracles.

the grass in Autumn

I wish the grass in Autumn
would sing to me more
soft winds on yellow stalks
remembering the Spring before
and the one to come
like seasons of our lives
perpetual and perfect
if you listen close enough
and believe.
your hair in the wind
makes me believe in God
and perfect moments.

I'll see you on the mountain

I'll see you on the mountain
where the mulberries grow thick and sweet
and the grass beneath your feet
betrays no stone or sorrows.

One day.
But for now, run ahead.
I will catch up later.
We have forever
and your friends are waiting
to share cups of tea
and stories you haven't heard
in the longest of times.

I'll see you on the mountain
where the blueberries lay fat to pick
and you eat your fill before
you lay in jam for winter.

One day.
But for now, run ahead.

blaspheme

cold carotids leak little or nothing,
our pulses fading to blue
then grey
and we are so involved in our deaths
even the forgotten joi
tastes wet

set upon our paths by others' evils
we make cat's cradles of webs
left back
so that we can tell ourselves the lies
we take as our sustenance
and prey

Mariya

I do not mind
the wicked curve and swerve
of your hips
your slender limbs and tender lips.
But the sexiest part of you is your soul.

near San Juan

I like to watch your eyes and see
what the windows to your soul reveal
of what you are thinking and how you feel,
the night wind off the beach
across your bare skin.
the curtain waving ambivalently.
and your exquisite curves softly sheened
by sweat of many sources,
reflecting the voyeur moon,
sad to not be in arms' reach of you.

marking territory

tender are the kisses
that leave no sign of their passage,
but memory
sweet and warm

blessed are the kisses
that make message and mark flesh,
reminding me
I am yours

Queen of Black Hearts

I envy your fingers
subtle stand ins for my touch
and tongue and more
stroking in emphatic rhythm
to feel your legs tense
and wrap around me,
deep inside you. the taste
sweeter than any wine.
the sensations, divine.
the taut, hot tunnel into you
as I kiss your sweet face
and listen to your urgings,
wanting to feel me
deeper
even though it is already
excruciating to have me
fully inside you, your lips
to mine, your breasts
against my chest and you
swallow me up inside you
as I ride you to the edge
of limits of my sanity.
before I swear your name
and lay sharp teeth
to tender flesh
to take my fill in your blood
as you feel me flood
you with my warm, white wine
of surrender as we dance
convulsions of joy and damnation.

feedback loop

I want to hear your soft sighs
as I kiss the back of your neck,
follow the curves of your bold, bare hips
with my hands, warm with an intimate heat
kindled in your eyes and the scent
of your flesh and breath on my skin,
thin fabric melting away that we may play,
not as children, but lovers, in this sphere.

I want to know that you are feeling warm.
then hot. then charged as if lightning
exploded inside you, sending light and delight
through every muscle of your body.
I want to hear you grip the sheets
with hands that moments before gripped me
and slipped me into as tight a wresting place
as I dared imagine, to steal and seal pleasure.

I want you to put into words if not action
all the fire and desire you conspire
to share with me, your perfect thighs raging
as they are caging me between them, afire
and yet, running with your sweat and more
as you find corners of your flesh untested
by other lovers, who were satisfied
to be satisfied, not to worship you as I do.

Show me your shoulders, your lips, your back,
and tell me what would please you the most,
what would make you convulse with releases' peace
as you swallow me up, more than flesh and heat,
an hard, curved key to fit the hungry symmetry
of your most wicked and tender needs and greeds,
shared with me in confidence and concupiscence.
Our fleshes' feedback to our souls, and we are sated.

on the tip on my tongue

you linger
on the tip of my tongue.
the taste of your kiss.
your shoulders
the taunting meringues of breasts
kissed not often enough.
shall I tell you what
the small of your back
tastes like to me
or can you tell enough
by the soft sounds
in the depths of my soul
I make when I am testing,
wresting control from your soul
that I might go further?
you linger
at the edge of my thoughts
and I am caught in your trap,
struggling only to move further.
deeper. to bury myself inside you
by whatever means you desire
and let the fire consume me,
doom me if need be.
you linger
on in the scars in my heart
that part, unhealed,
to let you in
when you let me
and allow me to feed
on your intense beauty
and the joy of your joy.

impossibly warm

I find your flesh
impossibly warm
to my touch.

I did not imagine
such heat, rising,
your perfect attar

filling my senses,
me hungry to feed
deep and insatiable.

you know you stir me
you know what I want
and your heat summons me

ready to warm myself
by your lambent beauty
and in your lithe form

sharing my heat as well
as I swell to your touch
and penetrate your whims

I find your lips
impossibly warm
as I kiss them, insistently

I find your body
impossibly warm
the deeper I go, and faster

I will leave you
impossibly warm
and immolating to my touch

I will return
impossibly warm
and ready to make you burn

stonework

passing through the eye in the stone
fractured by the persistent drip and rip
of the acid of the tongue,
the unrepentant dung
of past illusions, digested
as, to spit it out, would be rude.
the mouthful of cheap champagne
on a wedding night, uncelebratory
when the story remains...
a story, a fabulous fable I am able
to carve in my flesh in one of those spots
that remained yet unadorned after I'd sworn
forever in exchange for a pocketful of mumbles
that I suppose were meant in the moment.
the fermentation of hearts that never were
aware of the specific gravity of the stone,
pale pink and sunshine orange
like the dawn over distant lands were words
are held in higher regard
and the shard only cuts so deep.

still pristine

I have manses you've never seen.
roses red and grasses green.
places I never let you in.
flowers grow and bloom and die.
again.

you never asked for what I am.
just what you could see behind the dam.
the rivers rage another course.
hollow pockets overfull.
again.

a prayer uttered in the night.
has the same answer as in light.
for all you knew you had it all.
but even Atlas had to fall.
again.

unconditional

unconditionally given. never retracted.
the light may be refracted but the photons
go on and on and on. light is immortal.
even more so the light of the soul,
born in the incandescent desecration of self
when you barter away yourself. there is pain
and the occasional doubt, without that
it is a blind faith, not a real belief
that transcends the grief of fractured life.
I have not wept, but kept to myself the rain
of saline and sorrows. Life borrows and repays
in a karma that curves and swerves and unnerves
those for whom the eloquence is craft,
not the draught of white blood and sacraments.

the rite of favour

kiss me

once

and command the seas to fall silent for an instant
so they are not embarrassed by the crashing
of my blood in my veins

wake me

again

like you did hours ago, and days ago and years ago,
demanding sustenance and pleasure, owed to you
for your existing in so drab a world

favour me

forever

for my strength is malleable and I will bend
as you require of me, to comfort you
and fulfill the rites of a lover.

desire

have you ever been wanted so completely
that the heat of kisses and the vaguest touch
burned you like the taper of an arcane candle
doomed and damned to summon the demons to release
and to compel me to ravishments I would regret
were you not to smile the next dawn, sighing
and whispering you enjoyed yourself, and me.

I should like very much to place my hands
on the curve of your breasts and rest my body
on yours, feeling you curl your arms and legs
around me like petals of a carnivorous flower
seeking to draw nourishment from all you consume
in the next hours, as the night's delights melt
and run away, inside you, surrendering my flesh.

would you let me see how deep the dream goes
and if it flows past nothing more than the moment
that leaves dainty scars on your memory
would you accept the fact that, in the moment,
I wanted and needing nothing more than you
and the comfort of your darkest kisses, taut
and hot and feeding on me as I feed on you?

do you want me to desire you, to inspire you
to the revelation that passion is more than games
played by children in a drunken haze, that lovers
and courtesans and poets still exist in this world,
struck graceless with faceless sorrows we borrow
from the hollowness of lives we will regret
is not allowed to share, even for a night, the fire?

final sunday

I am cast out.
orphaned.
left for dead by the side of a wide road
so that others can swerve
to miss my fading form.
nothing warm
comes from this.
another legacy of ashes
left on my tongue
the taste of dung
and vinegar
from an apple orchard
I had once considered
a sanctuary.

the colding feat.
I am incomplete
and competing for sustenance
is not in my nature.
I will drag myself
into the dark
that I may not offend
those for whom
pain
is too intimate.
and I will find
myself. unbroken
once I fit
all the pieces.

drinking stagnation.
the hunger unabated.
but I will bind my wounds.
plant fists to earth and roar.
sore in a thousand places.
it is good you do not
have to see me like this,
the tattered, battered man,
the orphan of Aphrodite.
but I will not change
my coat of arms.
I will still be a priest to your divinity.
and I will love you
every time I feel my hollow soul.

dragons

There be dragons you have never seen.
I have been one
and may yet return.

It is a conundrum, for I forswore
that form and norm
for a woman's love.

When that grew cold an un-nourishing
and she walked away
I was fractured.

I heard the voice, within, as thin
as gossamer
offering to return.

I have laboured so long to live as man
and not the arch
that exceeds me.

This morning, as I lay in bed,
hollow and aching
I felt the scales rise.

Flecks of grey now mark their ebony.
But the voice is fire
and the wings, sturdy.

I have much to contemplate, for now,
whether to rise
or to resist the call.

There be dragons you have never seen.
I have been one
and may yet return.

the fighter falls

the fighter falls
down to his knees
and shakes his head
and sighs

he feels the pain
but won't give in
he clears his head
he rises

indulgences

stripped
of my indulgences
I am driven into the desert

where the test continues
where proof is demanded
and faith is commanded
to endure, ensure and to be pure
enough to enter a promised land

the sands of time burn my heels
and every step feels like acid
eating me out from the inside

the rattle of the wind in the dry brush
makes a threat of my sweat and thirst,
cursed only if I repudiate faith.
better to live, to love without doubt
than burn forever, a fool

Empathy for the Lovers

Movement One: Sonata: The Lovers.

The theology of passion bests the ecology of innocence.
A martyrdom to achieve transcendent life, bound to freedom.
Love. Life beyond life. Immortality in this transcendence.

I am not anyone you have known before, no evidence
exists that I would treat you as they have, where I am from
the theology of passion bests the ecology of innocence.

My words are my music, trouvere of the meme's persistence
that will make of you legend, priestess and queen of my kingdom.
Love. Life beyond life. Immortality in this transcendence.

You have my faith and fealty, my dreams fade my reticence
to leap from high parapet, you are my blood and martyrdom.
The theology of passion bests the ecology of innocence.

Do not mistake my manners or kindness for hesitance,
I am vested in the Gotterdammerung. I am bound to what is to come.
Love. Life beyond life. Immortality in this transcendence.

All issues beyond the ken of any, even the poets' eloquence.
Love is like the ether, even to those deaf to their heart's thrum.
The theology of passion bests the ecology of innocence.
Love. Life beyond life. Immortality in this transcendence.

Movement Two: The Death of Illusions

The theology of passion. A bold assertion,
that affections and lust might be a religion,
Aphrodite and Venus and Jesus spun into a cloth
of conflicting aspect. Catching the light in reds
both crimson and scarlet. Purifying and a branding
of sin and sanity, the vanity of daring to love.
I have faith in love, if not the lovers,
for we are frail and fail to fulfill the tale
we told ourselves in bolder times of hope.
The rope runs short and our feet still dangle,
with no way to see how far the fall but to let go
and risk everything. Even our belief in those
we chose to love, unlacing the traces to let fly
with wings of amber and of fire, graceful lies
unwound as the ground falls away and we play
at the phoenix. We make our own legends.
Fallen angels. Risen prophets. And the space between
the hallowed hollowing of our hearts to make room
for the opportunity of a real moment. Patience.
There is virtue in the long painful climb of the hill
where we know our persecutors would kill us
to prove nothing but their own powers.
And yet, love abides, resides and provides
a portal into the immortal wilderness of the soul.

Movement Three: Lyrical Variations on a Dream

Love. Life beyond life. Immortality in this transcendence.
In this world we are curled around our own cores.

Fear is the great disabler. Fear of loss. Of gain. Of the stain
of blood and more fel fluids that we drip out, rip out
in moments of surrender, pretending nothing for the instant
when tears are shed by more than eyes. Making a connection
in more than affection and drunken fumblings, stumbling
up the stairway to the altar when we are to be sacrificed
into our own deification. Releasing into one another.
The solitary soul is an illusion. A starving man eats anything
he can get his hands on and dies, poisoned with a full belly.
I want to see you sated in and with this life, wife to contentment.
You are like fractured gems set in the night sky, illuminated
by a mythology we ourselves wrote and sugar-coat
when all along we nod at the pain we will still have to endure.
The purity of you is in your darkest doubts. I have them, too,
but I have spent too long on the battlefield to accept
the conqueror wyrm as my better. I will kiss your scars
when the stars are aligned in keeping with your prophecies.

Movement Four: The Chaos of Erotic Innocence

Tears are wept. Promises kept except those to ourselves.
A final muse, a tacit refusal to embrace, for now, a future
with only a few certainties, for we are not yet there.
Care if you can, dare if you must, trust what is proven.
We need not play this game so badly or madly, sadly
we have proven ourselves from time to time, incompetent.
I have only faith to support my suppositions, not a thread
of a promised sackcloth and vestment has been offered
without being snatched back by the black hand of fear.
I am here, I am near, it is clear I would not make this walk,
speak this talk, dare your mockery if I was not sincere.
I have wandered the world to find you, and to be kind to you.

We are reborn in the shadow of our own illuminations.
Innocence suffuses us as a choice, a voice of passion
that we can fashion into whatever we want to taunt
the fates that so often have left us, broken and bleeding,
needing more than the nothing we discovered,
but could not bring ourselves to disavow because
we thought pride would protect us, direct us to something,
something more than the dust of lust tasted and wasted
because we couldn't wait for the banquet being prepared
for us in the presence of the enemies of our ascensions.
The chalices of change arrange themselves left to right,
each brew made only for our lips, our tongues, our nourishment.

The smallest sip that touches the lips of my love, I taste.
Cut and pasted to the tapestry. Not out of weakness,
for I can bend the very winds to my command if needs be,
but because I have taken a solemn vow and am damned
beyond this life if I break it, not to the whim of a deity,
but to my own memory of perfidy and the tyranny
of pale poisons let into the wedding cup. I acknowledge
that I may stand alone at the end, my passionate friend
having deserted me for less perfect purposes, and this as well
is a definition of Hell, to live out my hours, days and years
with only the screaming winds, drawing from me every thought,
caught in the maelstrom, as company, as I slowly fade.

I would not be changed for the experience, for my love
will remain, in my words and memories and my blistered heart,
beating on until it can no longer find time to bend, to spend
in an eternal passion for you. There are those who would
consider this a wasted life, but we are not measured by love
that comes to us, but by the love we give, unconditionally
and freely, praying in silent corners that our words are heard
and are palatable enough to feed the needs of our paramour.
It is a hard conceit, to walk the line between the divine
and the defiled, seeking subtle seduction through true words.
But anything more or less would be disrespectful of you,
and if I did not feel such awe I would not dare to love.

music for my sunday girl

silence in all ways offends me
I want to hear the music
the voices
the sound of your feet on stone and wood
communicating joy and life

nothing is more essential
than to know that you are laughing
and dancing
and the music is there to make you glad
that there is music in world

there is time enough for sackcloth
and the rough edge of sorrow
this is life
at its highest degree, and my sunday girl
has life enough to draw the venom

dance. dance with your flesh and heart
and wake the dangerous angels that
they may see
the beauty of the woman I love, transcendent,
even in shadow, but for now, luminous

sacrilege

what need is there for gods or odds and ends
when your flesh is altar to my sacrifices.
sins within that rise to meet the perfect curve
as every nerve fires with a desire to be sanctified.
I want all I can barter with my soul and prayers,
daring to be burnt by your perfect immolation.

the truth

the truth is never complicated.

we add our own neuroses and lies,
and often those of others,
as we all but smother it
because we are afraid of the aftertaste.

there is an elegance to honesty,
the e equals m c squared perfection
of being open and free. I'd rather
taste bitter wind than not breathe.

speak the truth to someone.
anyone and everyone. for this life
is too short for needless complexity
and I am not as young as I was.

dawn in East Los Angeles

hot winds off the desert
an annunciation of morning
with the skies going pale, then alive
with colours that shift from blue
to red and sickly green and back again.
the blinding glare of the sun
reflecting off of unnatural surfaces
erected irrespective of purpose
just to intimidate
like a poem in steel and glass

Resolve

twisted ankles and blistered feet
the heat gets to you
the elements assault you
and the gnats grow fat on your annoyance

this is the road, the path, the trail
we find is not always paved
with thick carpets or springtime grass
or gold or even yellow brick

it is bare feet on flint
it is the relentless sun
or drenching cold rains
or our own infirmities

but it is life
and I will walk
or run, to my purpose,
as long as it, and I, endure

beyond the black

the sky is breaking
ghouls partaking
in the blood and souls we are forsaking.
running faster.
quantum caster
runs you through an abattoir in alabaster.
burning so bright
heat without light
I'll pretend it's you with me tonight.

pretty trifles

Random night memories
a sign of time
spent on pretty trifles.

legacy

I do not know what my legacy will be:
A cautionary tale of failure
or a soaring epic of love and destiny.
It is sometimes troubling that the future
is not mine to command, but I handed
all my fate to you, sealed oils
of arcane visions and herbs, blended
to make pigments for the patient toils
of one who loves, without condition,
without doubt. For I know my soul.
But my legacy will be permission
from what you alone control,
your heart. Fragile and fierce, blind
am I to your purposes and mysteries,
but bound by words both selfish and kind
to remain a part of histories
that you alone have the freedom to write,
for I am given and gone, I have leapt
into a space between the day and the night
and the vision of my fate is, in your hands, kept.
I know no way to love other than this.
I am a mighty soul and a powerful mind.
But I have released it all to you, a kiss
of urgent, argent dreams, I tie my bind
and satisfy my yearning in silent cants
that may never see the eyes of anyone,
except for you, but in this trance
of fire and blood, my hardest work is done.
For I have chosen a path to follow,
rendering and surrendering my desires
in a manner that peels flesh and makes hollow
my soul to receive your fires.

And I pray, with a pilgrim's pain and stain,
that I one day I shall receive them.

opus 23

the smell of fresh linen
and that peanut butter sandwich
asked for
but never eaten
splinters
from a favourite toy
and always at least one present
at Christmas
that you could never have guessed

moments upon moments
days upon days
years upon years
and lives you have touched
or merely waved at from a distance
that go into who
and what
you are
and are becoming

hip hop ballerina
warrior and hostage
to her own best intentions
my friend
even when one
or both of us
don't act much like it
because. ultimately,
we are human

drink the dreams
take a crisp bite
out of experience
but don't chip a tooth
because
I like your smile
the way it is
and would like to not need memory
to see it again

blossom

spread your gentle petals
and let me find my way
deep
until I am lost in the radiant attar
of your blossoming.
the scent. the taste.
the heated release full of
inarticulate sounds
and clutching fingers and arms
as you draw me in
and feed on me
to my perfect delight.
your eyes, expressive and bright.
your lips, full and warm.
your flesh, an elegant comfort food
that I will take many more courses from.
feeding until we are both sated.
then, later, feed again.
for I cannot get enough
of your impatient curiosity.
and the ways your petals
draw me out, and in.
into you with tender violations
and an acknowledgement
that you are beautiful.

the morning walk

every morning I rise and
before all else
I walk the quiet road to the apple orchard
to see, in this season,
if I will find you there
or at least some token of your will

nothing yet

but I am, if human,
a patient man and
will wake tomorrow and walk
the path to my personal Golgotha
where history
and your whim
may mark me a martyr
to something greater than flesh
and orthography

the people watch me
as I climb the hill and whisper
oaths and prayers and
wish me the best
but know that I may
never find anything but the wind
and may pass
like thistle, my seeds impregnating
only memory

Defying the Fates

Scarlet. Crimson. Blood, red, we shed to mark our sacrament.
Effigies of memories. We shed thin skin to evolve our vanity.
Ebon. Stygian. The black tar scars of all we've underwent.
We know our constellations of sparks and marks, prayers sent
Into obscure ethers to save our souls and sanity.
Scarlet. Crimson. Blood, red, we shed to mark our sacrament.
The coinage of our coeur rage is lost or was spent
Trying to buy safe passages of a scripture of profanity.
Ebon. Stygian. The black tar scars of all we've underwent.
Pinch back the pain and tears that smear the battlement,
Our odd façade defending us and our frail humanity.
Scarlet. Crimson. Blood, red, we shed to mark our sacrament.
Scream your dreams so loud and proud, as testament
That you retain the stain of your identity!
Ebon. Stygian. The black tar scars of all we've underwent.
We are not slaves, we are the malcontent!
We are the lovers! The poets! The whim of God's insanity!
Scarlet. Crimson. Blood, red, we shed to mark our sacrament.
Ebon. Stygian. The black tar scars of all we've underwent.

roadkill

yeah
sometimes I do feel a little like roadkill
not knowing what laid me flat on the two lane blacktop
well
I know it was you
and I'm not dead, just mortally enamored
but the feeling is comparable,
even if the metaphor needs some work

Elysium

lovers dare to care and stare
into the blackest of voids, excited and annoyed
that the world does not promise a happy end.
pretty felicities and the loom of doom notwithstanding.
I won't pretend that loving you is an easy course,
but force of arms and charms of another
do not dissuade me from the agony of uncertainty
as you are what I want. and need. and believe in.
even when you yourself shout doubts.
for, love you I can. and do. and will,
even when you do not love yourself.

fallen

who would mourn the fallen?
the shadow of the hand that once fed
and bled and led the meager, eager dreams.
we are the forgotten orphans,
the cast off, the roadkill. martyrs
to our own religion of love and memory.
the fallen are remembered
but rarely saved from the end.

afterglow

Let us lay here in the merged airs and aurae
of our sated, naked forms. Warm and tender,
as the love we made moments ago, honest and pure
and sure that our emotions are not wasted on illusions.

fearless like a dream

she provokes me to imaginings and soft
feral
desires that burn from taper to bonfire
then ebb down to coals, white and patient,
until the heat is upon us again.

she is a stranger to me at times.
distant.
and I wonder if I have lost her love
and what can I do to reawaken her heart,
faded into the grey mediocrity.

she is all I want, and her voice haunts me.
taunts me.
words she hasn't said in so long, too long,
but I bend the fulcrum of my life around her
and surround her with my dreams.

unbroken

you are unbroken.

bent?
yes, of course.

resiliency proven
and there are a few little

cracks
where the fates hit too hard
too swift and you barely

barely

kept it together
even feigning madness
but you are more complete
than you realize
and I love every
bend and twist and angle
that life has compromised
in you growing
so strong and wise and beautiful

little voices

little voices
so loud
as bare feet hammer tracks
through the house
sticky doorknobs
and the sudden awareness
that you just heard the sound
of a whipped cream fight
breaking out in the kitchen
nothing bruised but pride
nothing broken but the rules
and the world re-engaged
through the eyes of children
who think of you
as perfect
because I told them you were

barter for legend

as through our dance I go
it's not an easy row I hoe.
you're worth it, though.
you told me so.
and of such barters are legends born.

was Aphrodite as beautiful? were her eyes explosions
of light and life that summoned metaphors of distant stars,
in a scale and tale of rebirth beyond the ken of men
who see nothing of the truth, as a fool cannot tell
diamonds from broken glass. you are worthy of song,
of poetry, of blind artists weeping their limits that such a muse
can only be derived in the words and works of others.

I have taken myself away from the butterflies and banshees,
frail delights of colour and dark creatures of prophecy and sound
that once abounded in my tapestry. I am content to have spent
nearly a decade in a prison of self-immolation, waiting,
if not always patiently, at least purposefully, for your tongue
of flame to make flow the blood in ancient veins again,
giving flesh to the golem and fire to the phoenix.

as through our dance I go
it's not an easy row I hoe.
you're worth it, though.
you told me so.
and of such barters are legends born.

glassine

membranes thin as skin begin to wear to clarity.
light passes through our flesh, our pulsing celerity
peeling back the onion skin, the fabric and veils,
revealing all we would conceal, when moderation fails.

be my lover, be my queen, my goddess to possess.
let me seize you, please you, appeasing nothing less
than the demons buried deep, that call my name
when you sleep, seeking sanctity and shame.

peel away the final threads, the binding, blinding patch
that covers eyes and lies and thighs, the better to detach
us from the cursed thirst we bear to taste the wicked flowers
from which we draw our sustenance, and all our pain and powers.

dwell

dwell with me in this, my temporal realm.
be my goddess, be my slave, be brave enough
to speak my name in public, without fear
that you will lose more than you gain
by making my passion for you public.

I am not alone by my own choice,
but my voice is shackled in silence, that you
might find your peace and purpose
released and given bright feathers
and the eloquence of flight in the light.

I am of some consequence, not only to you,
but to a world that waits my fiery arc
as I launch myself high above the walls
to land on two feet in the courtyard,
ready to bring down the walls of sullen pain.

allow me the right to die in your grace,
having looked upon your face and realized
that life is but a tapestry woven with skill
by those unafraid of the collective confederacy
that elevates us to the launching into love.

villanelle for White Sunday

I will pour my love out like a sacrificial wine,
surely purifying all manner of histories and mysteries.
Pure passion is transcendent, achieving the divine.
We are our own little hangmen, twisting the crucifer's spine
as we delve into that which our original sin frees,
I will pour my love out like a sacrificial wine.
The dove and lamb may fall to the lion and his kine,
the mindless hunger as natural as any disease.
Pure passion is transcendent, achieving the divine.
You are an angel, whose feet were bound to earth in sign
that the dust of man is your path, through cities and through trees.
I will pour my love out like a sacrificial wine.
Whisper my name, then speak it with couer rage so I'm
acknowledged before God and man, if you please.
Pure passion is transcendent, achieving the divine.
In my journeys, I am burnt by the sun and drowned in brine,
but I have found you. My perfect angel. And before the reaper flees
I will pour my love out like a sacrificial wine.
Pure passion is transcendent, achieving the divine.

legendes

Je m'accroche à la tête de lit,
avec les doigts raides et la résolution d'un titan,
de ne pas être digne de vous,
car ce serait impossible,
mais pour être digne de moi
et l'héritage de ceux qui se souviennent de nous,
des rumeurs et des légendes.

en exil

Dans ma solitude, la nuit douce
sensation de froid et amer
comme le vin chaud gaspillé.
Un goût simple refusé
comme la pierre précieuse ne voit pas la lumière
et la beauté est perdue.
En exil, en contemplant
les ventres froids
et des promesses creuses.

la pluie avoue peu

la pluie avoue peu,
des trucs et des indices de mystère.
les larmes d'anges
laver mes impuretés
et me rappeler pourquoi je suis né.

trouvere en court

would the royals and their loyals
call for my head and life
if they knew the words I'm singing
were to an obscure wife
who goes about her days and plays
as she sees fit to live
but I retain each blessed refrain
as blood and flesh to give
in sacrament offerings
in some facet of my sphere
a world not yet made visible
but holding every tear
and every kiss and passion
I humbly would express
as I lay down my destiny
in defiance of noblesse.

Libra

how curious that you are meant to be
the balance to my passion
when so often it is the other way
as the aging lion gives counsel and then, against his nature,
stands back and waits for you to see
he is not an illusion or a fool,
but possessed of gravity enough
for all the stars to circle, even when he bows his head
and swears incessant fealty
as you weigh his suit
against all the prettier baubles
the world has to offer.

you laugh

you laugh and the rainbow becomes more prominent
the colours of life ignite and brightly burn into the night,
awaking the voiceless angels, trapped by silent vows
such that they cannot express the joy except with touch.
not for aught of heaven and naught else I would trade
a moment of your happiness, for it is the amber sun
rising in the grey morning to chase away malevolences.
you have power of me. and through me, power over
the mysteries and histories that are to be written
when the veil falls and the walls of glass and grass
shatter and their remnants scatter before the winds.
I am not between you and your dreams, but sent
to make straight the way, a prophet of your purposes.
I draw my power from your tender smile and hope.

belongings

I know to whom I was given
and I know where I belong
more than a moment unforgiven
more than the lyrics of a song

bind

you blind me
bind me
to your needs
a hungry soul
out of control
that ever feeds
I want to satiate
as I desolate
my colding world and soul
my last moments
be as your demons
lick the bowl

the fallen angel

for God so loved this world, you were conceived,
to both create your art and inspire art
in those who find the spark divine, relieved
of doubt and uncertainty that the part
of the Creator is diminished, light
in the darkness, dreams in the shadows, black
as a statement of intensity, bright
memories to be made, imagined, crack
open the shell and find the beating heart
that pumps blood and quintessential purpose
in a beat that does not resign its part,
guide past pretenders that would usurp us
in accomplishing the impossible
with grace and rise of the fallen angel.

epitaphs and cold stone

perhaps my love for you
will be one day recorded in cold stone

words, cut by hand,
by someone who knew neither of us

but, for now, my love for you
is a living thing, measured in warm skin

I am mindful of my legacy
and I want it to be a celebration of you

you are easy to love
if not always easy to comprehend, to grasp

but I reach for you,
mindful only that you asked of me, and I am here

and not a stone or threnody
can capture all the aspects of your glory

witness

your light persists, even though bent a bit
by the refracting forces of history and mystery.
passions like a thousand fires on the face of the sun,
you run light and bright into the night, immortal.
I am but an observer, your witness to the world
that might otherwise rest dull and dumb, uninspired
by ignorance of the fires that dance across your skin.
you are, by any measure, remarkable, perfect padparadscha
regardless of the wit and wisdom of those who see
and do not comprehend your worth and wonder.
you are memory and prophecy, beauty and truth,
the one I have waited for, and will wait for,
even until the end of all things. all things.
for you asked me to wait, to linger, to learn patience
that I might be there when you whisper my name.

noctem

the night suspends my disbelief, the grief
of the knowledge wrested from firmament
in which the blithe and lithe spirits make brief
the eternal questions of trust once spent
on ill-perceived odds that even now cost
the currency of joy, of love, of peace
that hides in the hollows beneath the lost
city, pity a pale treasure measured in fleece
that once was gold, now mould and memories
that mock our hearts. we offer now the cup
in which we mix impatient alchemies,
seeking to drink the wine divine and up
to some celestial union ascend,
a place of peace where no friend is pretend.

wake the night in crimson

stealth in silent dark
creeping catlike through the night
slivered almond eyes
remembered prey that never dies
cool the stone to tepid feet
treading purposefully
necromantic catalepsies
the essence of the lie
liquid spine to guide along
silent and serene
fixed on hunger burning deep
feral as the dark

summer snows

snowflakes.
petals of a white rose.
I can only tell the difference
on close inspection
or if I feel them on my skin,
testing their temperature.
is Sunday the day of rest
or the rest of my days?
king or knave of hearts
is difficult to discern
until you know the nationality
of the deck
the fates deal from, stealing
and sealing from us
a few clumsy secrets.
I play my cards face up
to a veiled challenge
and hold my tongue
when I want to cry out in joy
and despair.
where I am is irrelevant
next to where I will be
in a few moments
or scores of years,
tears of regret
tasting different
than those of joy.

fasting

I am starving
carving myself from the inside out.
doubting myself.
waiting for the morning that may be denied
for pride or memory.
wanting so intently
to break the fast
and get past the barriers,
carriers of our own suffering.
inelegant and cold,
like an all-too familiar headboard.
but I will prove my stone
my steel and seal a kiss
with more than words.

the page

channel it to the page
and rage!
burn away your inhibitions.
I want in ink the stink
of sweat!
fear, lust and the dust of desolations

Pentecost

fifty days
still waiting for the first
to end this thirst
for ambrosia and wine
divine and intimate
not looking for a miracle
because I found it
just trying to hold on
with both hands
but not so tight
looking for a sign
that I'm walking a path
that gets somewhere
where we share
more than an intimation
of a life, hidden away
in the upper rooms
where tongues of flame
descend
and we pretend
we know the repercussions
of surrendering
to a higher power
I'm not denying
I'm speaking in tongues
to hide my bride
behind a veil that tears me up
while it sanctifies me
as it denies me
the rest of my life
as it gives me purpose
the latest of these
and the greatest of these
is on the downside of Golgotha

confirmed

I admit
I am weary
and the cold iron wears grooves
in the flesh of my back and arms
but I am
committed
confirmed to a religion
sworn to a passionate quest
no matter
in moments
when the sun is hidden
I will still believe in the light
and the night
will pass by
as I wait for you, as promised,
as requested, my faith tested
and tasted
not wasted
for even if as paramour
in bare bones left as artifact
I endure
never sure
but always so certain
that this is where I belong

rusting

the playground lays flat
as the rust overtakes the bars
and spires
the metal posts and chains
reverting to rust and crust and dust
the children long

gone

apogee

the high side of the arc
parking orbit for the obit of my doubts
I am well and even though
from time to time the cold and rarefied atmosphere
is not what I had hoped
I have learned to cope
with the elliptic of your moods
trusting for no better reason
than you asked me to
staying when I feel alone
straying...never
because I am not afraid
ever
because eventually
gravity reasserts itself
and the fiery reentry
is all the Promethean glory
I will ever need
knowing that it is you
I orbit around
whether I die tonight
or in a hundred years
your name will be
the last in my lips
and the first in my heart
even in the cold womb of the night

warm caramel

the cracked curve of a childhood toy
found years after it escaped notice
and slid and hid
behind the old dresser
so massive it hasn't been moved
since before the modern age

sharp plastic
unfaded by sunlight
unjaded by the night
when promises were meant
to be broken
like the once treasured toy
rediscovered
with a faint nostalgia
and enthusiasm
like the taste of warm caramel

canniboli

after the hollowing
following the sound
down to the bottom of the well
and finding
silence
a mirror in a dark room
reflects only the dream
patience
strength without fulcrum
a wasted pavonine display
played out
until the cloying night
raises disturbing questions
of mortality

an appreciation of her mother

you could not have known
how you would transfigure my life
and, indeed, the world,
with the gift you gave

life

messy, imperfect
sometimes loud and rebellious

life

to the woman that I love
and that the world, in its own way,
loves
and I just wanted to make sure
that you were shown proper respect
and gratitude
for so great a gift
so great a

life

(conceived within you
nourished by your body
raised under your protection and direction)
that words fail me as I try
helplessly, hopelessly,
to express my thanks
I will never write a poem
or turn a phrase
as full of grace and hope
as what you gave the world

leisure

in leisure I write
sometimes
not the burning churning yearning
in and out
orgasm of light and words
but a slower, gentler,
more tender, perhaps,
expression of passion
and affection
that measures control a virtue
and gives me
a sense of wonderment
that you still here
considering my heart
with an excruciating uncertain stare
but, nonetheless,
considering my heart
at your leisure

wed

I married you
while you weren't looking
because love is
not always bilaterally symmetrical.
I took my vows
and now can just wait
and see if you
show up, a little later, to the altar.
it's not that I
expect anything more
than a soft sigh,
profound and perplexed, from you and the world.
I married you
while you weren't looking
because love is rare
and I want you to know where I stand.

the cage

no promise of release
or even when I will be next fed
or allowed to lay my head
to sleep way the pain
I volunteered
and both as I hoped and feared
it has lived up to my imaginings
bars of cold iron
that I could rend apart with a thought
but that would defeat the purpose
for I am not bound by bars or whim
of anyone but myself
and I choose to be here
for my own purposes
it is that thought
that perfect awareness
of the nature of my cell
that liberates me
as I know
I could walk away
at any time
but for now
I choose not to

spill my wine

I want to slide between those lips.
while I kiss between your hips.
make my intentions more than dreams.
fill the room with feral screams.

spill my wine

drink it down, there's plenty more.
you know what you came here for.
see how deeply we can merge,
then deeper still with hungry surge.

spill my wine

cocoon you in my boiling seed.
make of desire an expressed need.
every corner and curve I'll claim,
exertions beyond pain and shame.

spill my wine

dark inventions

click clack
click clack
boots or bolts
the sounds of dark intentions
dark inventions
made to kill, not cure,
impure purpose

click clack
click clack
perdition
the lies we tell ourselves
dark inventions
to justify our murders
murmuring tattoos

click clack
click clack
kill me now
before I speak more truths aloud
and you are caught
between your handspun gods
and the real

pillow

Though you may not always need it
refuge is yours to take
I will not withdraw my promises
for a broken moment's sake
The life I offer up to yours
is mine, and mine alone.
And as long as I am regent here,
I'll lay pillow on the stone.

We've mysteries and histories,
some we wish were long forgot.
And I am fine as wine with that,
on the past I am not caught.
But I'll be bastion against the pain
when it comes against your throne.
As long as I am regent here
I'll lay pillow on the stone.

The tempest and the tumult rise,
the unforgiving fates
Hold in store for both if us
barbarians at the gates.
But I will stand with all my might
and for both our sins atone.
As long as I am regent here
I'll be the pillow on the stone.

Polyphemus

souls glow near critical mass as they pass
miles apart
and the new clear dawn fades with distance
persistence
is something of a virtue in half a relationship
misnomer
a one-wheeled bicycle, a cyclops made of man,
half blinded
with a pointed stick, sharpened in the fire,
held in wait
that words alone will spring the trap
the blood runs
and I am free to go, free to escape to my next
adventure
but the fates weigh me down and I made my choice
in a time
when this cave was not quite so empty.

winter

the wind in the bony white birch branches
speak an alien eloquence
to ears that listen for more
human
language of love
as they would define human
and love

faux trouvere just smile
and skitter like 2 am rats
trying to get out the door
before they have to admit
ignorance
and a certain subtle abuse
and fear

poets are not taught their craft
but are born to it
like lightning to the storm
or the taste
of a woman's heart
torn open and left on the altar
of hope

snow is late this year
but it will show itself
if you look away from the
misdirection
and into the low riding sun
as it mourns the loss of mystery
in dreams

forever

I can't conceive of forever
especially
if it is without you
and, yes, I know
you have a certain attitude
about long term things
turning to shit

but I want to show you I am
here for a Stonehenge
kind of thing and even
without a ring
will stick around and share my love
as much as you say
you will accept

I need your forever, ten
minutes at a time,
if I have to hold my
breath over and
over and again and again
until skies go red
and you believe

acceptance

I accept you as you are.
yes, even those things i do not know
but have long suspected or assumed
if only as intellectual exercise to see
what I would do if the worst were true.
it is not a rational thing, this love.
it is a heart unto itself, full of blood
that has the miracle cleansing properties
of the latest washday miracle solution
or a cup of sacramental wine, defining life
on my own terms. defining you as mine.
you have asked me to claim you with passion
and patience and an understanding
that you are who you are and you now
must accept that I do. and can. and will.
and now shadows of doubt are invited.

fluff

you dream of feral undertaking.
the raking of claw on flesh and fur,
and the occasional stray object,
as you demonstrate benign ambivalence
to anything not really relevant
to the bon vivant who turns nose up
to a new brand of cat food
but still cleans each nook and cranny
with tongue and teeth, glowering
if interrupted by lumbering
two-legged servants wishing only
to demonstrate a worshipful delight.

from a weird, dark place

if not you
then no other
will lay as sacrifice
to the dragon

for I will not play false priest
to an unsuitable sacrifice

or see the horror in her eyes
when I whisper your name
and the dragon breathes
inside her

and we are all damned

White Sunday: 290-299

290

the glass
s h a t t e r s
and I am left
holding holy water
in a bloody hand
only a titanium band protecting
even a tiny sliver of my flesh
such as it is lovers
unexpected
flechettes
and as long as some part of us
survives
we spin ourselves a fresh cocoon
and rest
long enough to be reborn

291

grip tightly the headboard
the iron posts that dig into your hands
as I show you the intensity of my hunger
plunging blindly into you
claiming everything
laying scars on top of old scars
that I may own it all
and bathing you
in the sticky sap
risen from my root
hanging on for dear life
inside you
as you grip the headboard

292

I will fetch the water
when you are thirsty
and give you my blanket
when you are cold
I will not grow old
but stay with you
probably longer than you
will care to have be around
but I will not disappear
just fade back until
you remember why you love me
in the first place

293

I want to fill my lungs with your breath
that every molecule of oxygen
inside me
was first yours and given freely
to my life and sustenance
I will give you my air as well
and feel your body rise and fall
with the rhythm of the poetry of life
as you speak volumes with your eyes
but perhaps a bit more eloquently
with your hands and thighs

294

there are places you have been that I cannot go
for they are gone
likewise in my life
roads I would've reconsidered
if I had known you were somewhere down another path
or just a matter of time
but I am here now and would be a fool
to not celebrate your presence in my life
every day and night and mile I have left in the journey

295

I am an anachronism
of a future yet undefined
there are parts of me like a millennia clock
that will not move for years to come
even as you will not comprehend
certain things until you have lived as long as I
and I only wish that when the mechanism
manifests itself, that you are there to witness
the craftsmanship and the aftermath
in my life
and that when you are striking the times
you do not look back on me
as a lost opportunity

296

there's a chair waiting for us
waiting for me to lay back and let you
curl up
in my lap
and whisper gentle words
and fall asleep in my arms
and know that when you wake
I will be there
in that chair

297

there are profundities that defeat me
expressed in the way you smile
sometimes with just your eyes or voice
or a curious bit of punctuation
that is more eloquent than a thousand pictures
but it is all a part of the mysteries
that are a part of my religion
in loving a sunday girl

298

I want you to be satisfied
if only in the moment
that you are making the right choice
and that you voiced it
with clarity and passion
and awareness that I take seriously
the sort of promises you have made
but wherever you go
and whatever you choose
you will not lose my love

299

be Sunday every day
and save for me the night and light
of the rising sun and setting moon
and challenge me to keep up
with the chariot of Apollo
and the wings of Hermes
and the apples of Atalanta
and the labors of Heracles
and I will not disappoint you
for I speak with the tongue of angels
and Hephaestus requires his Aphrodite
even when he is drawn
from the blood of a poet god
to lay all he is, all immortality,
at your feet

light and air

I'm past my prime, no doubt of that
there's flecks of grey on this black cat
yet all my passions run intact
you own my heart, this is a fact
and I will not desert you when
you slip, you fall, you cry and then
you turn to me to ease the pain
I'll take the blow and not complain
for you are want I want from life
as friend and love and even wife
if that is what you can accept
one day, I'll shoulder without regret
the burdens that I can foresee
and even more, if the needs be,
to be for you all that you'd ask
and make your smile my sacred task
in memories we've yet to consecrate
I'll cross the tapestries of fate
and through it all not hesitate
to live for love, not fear or hate
for here, with you, I've found a place
to place my back when I must face
the horrors and the fading light
and take and give my true delight
in you with you and through your eyes
I'll see the world and find surprise
in catching wing to sail above
all tragedy in patient love.

occupy Valhalla

the war-torn countries and the war-porn media
conspire to inspire a sense of desperation.
war-born, unshorn of the Nazarite's trappings,
and we justify ourselves with broken math.
and we justify ourselves with broken math.
killing sixteen people because a friend was wounded.
humiliating the dead by their vacant lives lost
were not worth one quick Sunday morning hypocrisy.
and a well-regulated militia being necessary.
and a well-regulated militia being necessary.
we are not the harbingers of evil, we are the evil,
retiring on pensions built on death merchants.
they were driven from the temple to the Beltway.
and we wrap ourselves in flags and kevlar.
and we wrap ourselves in flags and kevlar.
fat cats feeding on the lambs and the carrion
left behind when we can rip a pregnant woman apart
at a distance with napalm fire and fiber optics.
and we put In God We Trust on our currency.
and we put In God We Trust on our currency.
all the poor people's taxes and the widow's mites
spent on contraband goods and Viagra.
treason against reason and the nature of charity.
and the old men sing about the good old days.
and the old men sing about the good old days.
and eight thousand miles away, sightless corpses
pile high in the name of a merciful God of peace,
target practice for the bent and broken souls.
and every coward gets his gun.
and every coward gets his gun.

amotation

Beloved, you have said that these poems,
to you, are love letters, amotations
of my tender, tendered heart, imparting
all my hopes and passions in poppy-red
daydreams and exhortations to love me.
This is so true, for I have nothing but
my words and their power to melt your heart,
to make channel for my flood of bright blood,
flood of red and white and light to delight
and give you back your innocence and life.
I want nothing beyond your joy and peace
and am so often frustrated that I
am bound to the punishing stone to atone
sins of others, until you can love me.
I am given, if not taken, my love
is an exquisite prison and prism
of all the light that shines within you.

Joshua Tree

you are like the rain
that pays visit to Joshua Tree
too rarely
too rarely
to be considered a presence
except for those moments
when the need is great
to part your clouds
and share life
upon the parched soil
reawakening me
as I lay face down
amidst the bleached branches
and the hollows of sand
at the point of death
to your own purposes
but not unwelcome
I rise and will wander
infinite scoured lands
waiting for the next kiss
or death
as the high desert winds
play songs of devotion
in the branches
of the Joshua Tree

illusions

allow me my illusions
as an act of charity
that you feel for me
the same
vector
and
magnitude
of human devotion
smoke
and
mirrors
of my own design
may be giving me
inaccurate information
and, indeed,
your feelings may be more
pity
and
puzzlement
and
revulsion
than you have let on
allow me my illusions
if this is what they are
and I won't even
ask you if you love me
anymore

muse

you're not the sort of woman
people would expect me loving
as your hair and frame and attitude
are obviously different
when comparing you to those
people think of me with

but you have a soul of diamond
even with a fracture here and there
and you love me even when that word
gets stuck in your throat
and I understand.
I get that way sometimes too

hovering

it is the most painful of times
knowing you are in pain
or ill
or turmoiled
and I am set away
unable to comfort you
to reassure you
to stand between you
and all the avalanches of the world

but in truth
I am there
maybe not allowed to manifest
and that is difficult for me
a man who always likes
to wear the cape and save the world
but I would rather fall
guarding you from darkness
than stand
anywhere
in the light

and maybe
just maybe
you draw some small solace
from my devotion to you
reasoning that I am not
someone who wastes his time
on lost causes
but simply
and earnestly
loves you
and wants you to be
happy and safe

gash

the best wounds, painful,
bloody
with a smooth entry
but enough tearing
of the deeper tissues
that it may most easily
fuse
with the presented poultice
of another's wound

how foolish we feel
when our wound is
unconsidered
or even
rejected
and we stand
uncomprehending
that somehow we were
poor oracles

someone
didn't like the colour
of our blood
or the sound we made
when we ripped
ourselves
open to expose
our offered flesh
cleaved for cleaving

so you stand
there
holding open the gash
waiting as you bleed
playing Ouranos
incapable of death
but feeling the burn
of mangled flesh
and broken hearts

a bed

a bed of rose petals
and ashes.
nothing tragic in the magic
we weave with our sacrifices.
I will touch you in ways
you have made me vow to.
I will accept you
as you are, dark and burning,
our yearning earning us
our own liquid heat.
no defeat.
no defeat.
no defeat.
the power of your full lips
draws out of me
an emergent history
a mystery
that you alone
have the right to resolve.
consume me.

patience

I have kept my word
even in the most difficult of situations.
It has not been easy,
every time I am mocked by the trace
dangled before my face
then yanked away, with no explanation
beyond a gentle request
that I remain patient. So little to ask
and yet the task
in time will have its way with my sanity.
I am slowly changing
into something that you would not want,
bent by the shadows
you leave to entertain me, while you play,
elsewhere.

Escher flesh

Escher flesh
topographic impossibilities
and yet, we manage
to make the connections
in urgent purging surges
of urges
to find some way to stay

connected

intersected

unprotected hearts
that pull apart in pain
staining the sheets
with sweet completions
that start again
like a pounding pink palindrome
Escher flesh

Phoenix dreams

I want to wash your gentle scars
and kiss them dry.
denying nothing that you may want
or need, bleeding with you
when sorrow comes on crooked legs
and begs another long night
of doubt and recrimination.
I have my sins, as well,
and I understand how broken apart
a heart can be.
but you give me the dream of the phoenix.
and I will share it with you
one day, if you ask.

packing for Avalon

travel light.
a stray memory. a scar
barely healed, but just in time
it sealed what was left of my soul
away from the vicissitudes
of this obstacle course,
this proving grounds
we call life.

such are the lovers.
such is the nature of love.
travel light. hijacked hearts
litter the street paved red
with kisses and near misses
that define us, fitting tributes
to misprint Mandylions
where grave and graven images remain.

the stain of sweat.
of regret. the wet whetting
of appetites beyond comprehension.
carving ourselves up as feasts
for the beasts we released with a word.
cunning, running messengers
of heaven-sent contentment.
the obvious defeats the village idiot.

maybe room remains
for one more hand me down heart.
one more tribute to Hephaestus,
who we find the greater romantic
than even mighty Aphrodite, deluded
as she is by the power of her loins,
pillars that Heracles never set,
but serve as goadsigns.

the ship sails soon.
and I must be ready.
I must find a way to take everything.
or nothing. it works that way.
I think I am already past the point
where the ladies lay me on satin
and soothe my fever
and bear me somewhere safe.

The One

whatever cages keep us apart,
my heart is resolute and purposeful.
I can give you a thousand reasons
why we make no sense, but in my defense,
I know you are The One.
and, as a pilgrim in the desert
would be a fool to pass
by the oasis of dreams
and cool water,
I would be wrong, despite hardship,
to not crawl or walk as far
and as long as is required
to drink from your beauty.
your soul captured me first,
and the thirst rediscovered
in the shade of your heart.
I bound my rogue wanderings
into an eternal orbit
and I am held here,
because you are The One
I looked for in the wrong places
and the wrong faces,
finding only traces of what
makes you so perfect a fit.
because you are The One.

in sickness

faint cough
discarded tissues
and half-drunk cups of weak tea
petulant pouts
protesting vile medicines
and the aching joints

in sickness and in health
you are the wealth of my soul
and I'll keep watch tonight
while the sniffles do their best
to make you miserable
against my best efforts

only you

for you
only you
will I bleed the white wine
whether to your touch or taste or trace
to lay life
and pleasure
deep within you
only you

I have not walked
a sullen path
to waste my flesh
where it does not belong
but will wait
a bit longer
until you are certain
of your need

for you
only you
will I lay in solferino currents
to be swept away
with tears and joy
and the consecration
of love
neither of us expected

I will fill you
with all manner
of dark and pleasant
reveries and riddles
and give you the answers
even as my last pulse
goes, unwasted,
into you

only you

flesh fails

it has been
so long
since I last heard you say
what you wanted of me
too long
flesh fails
and I am damned to my path
crawling
on bloodied fingertips
that ache for something
more than jagged flint
and the coarse stones
of this crater on the sun
it is hard to keep
faith
in a world where
the deities are inconstant
and their scriptures
are ghostwritten
flesh fails
but even when
the wind and rain
wash away the last of me
my spirit
will endure
bound to the horizon
forever

Orphean descent

I did not descend to rise again.
The nature of flesh is to fail,
and so, I sail off the edge.
Down the rivers of forgetfulness
and eternal sleep, no Thasian thread
to mark my path, for I am not returning.

I tread the darkness, listening
with discerning ears for every turn.
The brimstone and sulfur burns
my eyes and nostrils and I hear,
clearly, the screams of the damned,
and the muttered threats of Hades himself.

Plato himself called my prototype a coward,
and there is no fear in my quest,
to test the very definitions of life,
of wife, and immortality. I will sing
a song that will echo to the stars
from the deepest pit of the underworld.

I have no plans to return to the surface,
for even the furnace, with you present, is cool
as the gentle breeze in Thrace in springtime.
I have brought my cithara and earnest heart,
weapons enough against time and temptation.
I am not come to pervert the nature of life.

Ever deeper I descend, for I depend on you
to be my world. Eyes like twin morning stars,
voice like the song of sirens, thighs
my own personal pillars of Heracles.
I will follow my soul into Hell itself,
with no expectation but to be with you.

altars

your thighs part and my heart
blossoms like a blue rose.
clothes already shed, the bed
is an altar for our raging fires.

I will worship you tonight,
the tight sheathe that breathes
the qabalah of demons
summoned from my darkness.

I am here to possess you,
to confess you my religion
is you, and you alone,
swallow my seed as I bleed.

no trace or place upon your warm form
will remain unconsecrated
by the living baptism you urge
to surge from me, bridging souls.

I dream of your scream
when the spirits connect
and we intersect our expectations
of ceaseless release and love.

yes, love. even in the immolation
of our surrenders, we remember
that we are needful of the hearts
and minds that bind us to one another.

perform the ancient rituals.
swallow me and all my soul,
I will trace wet sigils on your body
that will transfigure our destinies.

corners

when you step around the corner
to confront me
with your heart
I find myself
walking on light

you elevate me
with your touch
even if only words
escape to my space
they shake me to the foundations

you will always be slipping
in and out of my sight
but always I will welcome
your visits and trust
that you are well and strong

eclectic circuitous

I'm the monkey that unlocks the door
to pour the immeasurable treasures
in rivers of warm, white wine, divine,
to come to the cascade of Amontillado.
shackled here for fear of victory
too soon, too soon, and the moon rises
so high, so high, and the sky is cold.
all my gold is sold to buy your baptism,
rebirth of worth in self-doubt shouted.
pouted against petulant petals
that wilt in the silt of runaway run-off.
there are forces here at play and work
more than a tear, a sigh, a smirk
that speaks volumes in a foreign tongue.

dance of death

I begin now
although perhaps I never needed to
the dance being implicit in life
the dance of death is upon me

I begin now
to weigh my moves in the passage
between other couples on the floor
listening each to different music

I begin now
to understand why I hate funerals
and why I will dance and die alone
for there is naught but sorrow left to me.

Apollonia

where there are gods
there are goddesses, as well.

beautiful, graceful, gifted beings
born of the necessity of imagination

full of pain. and doubt. and hope.
mothers of us all. lovers of us all.

you are radiant, dark and perfect,
your flaws bending light and life.

soft skin. eyes of wisdom and innocence.
lips soft and sweet. drawing out warm wine.

princesses and courtesans. pawns and queens.
muses to the amomancers, dancing death.

the complexity of parallel lines
without beginning, without end, bending thought.

comfort. surrender. more than the sum
of her much desired parts and natural arts.

woman.

mason jar

the mason jar
I caught fireflies in
one summer night
the sound the lid made
as it was unscrewed
then clapped shut quickly
so the existing prisoners
did not escape
as I added a new capture
to their ranks

the tricycle horn
that didn't work quite right
so I made medicine for it
from mud and grass clippings
expecting that it would
be all better
because medicine always works
if you truly believe in it

the strawberry blonde
in the denim skirt
eating cinnamon hot candies
as she waited for sociology class
to let out
sitting on the hall floor
at Oglebay Hall
and she smiled at me
but I never asked her name

the feeling of immortality
when I'd take my sled
down the hill
at Duke's Lake
and slide out onto the thick
midwinter Michigan ice
braking with my feet
dangling off the end of my sled
as the wind whipped through
but I ignored it

the first kiss
between us
is every bit as real to memory
and every bit as essential

to who and what I am
and will be remembered for
when all the cotton cotillion
of this life fades with the music
of all the unforgettable moments
know that you are not tears in the rain
you are the rain

confessor

do not make me say another three hundred Hail Marys
to purge my urgent sins and urge purgatory for my soul.
I am making my confession of my blasphemy, contrite
but right in my own heart, for truth is an higher order
than the mere bowing before divinity. and so I confess
my love for you. expecting nothing, praying for a miracle
that somehow you may see in me some virtue worthy
of your barest affection, your most sought for approval.
I am lost without your affirmation, tossed to the lions
of my own persecutions of doubt and undesirability.
my words, my weapons of incarnate light, are nothing
if they cannot pierce the veil and conquer the whim
that keeps us from the transfiguration, for as much
as I crave you for my wife, I desire to be husband
to you, and you alone, to atone for every false idol
I knelt before in times before the revelation of you.

ebon flow

In the light of an argent moon, the blood is black.
Semen of the dark soul, sacrificial passion
pouring over the stone, the bone revealed we stack
our frail prejudices and wait judgement to run
and drip in slippery vow solemnization.
You infected my flesh, then my raw blood, burning
my veins and possessing me like bitter ration
of the sourdough of life, hunger made yearning
and the yearning made into desperation held
with fingertips at the edge of the ice, the cold
enfolding us in the liberation of gelled
blood, nod to an inevitability more bold
than death itself, to give my life in a dark kiss
that dances with the decades in a wicked bliss.

the origin of religion

God is within you
as I would like to be
not just in the spiritual sense
or in your thoughts
but deep inside the flesh
sharing pleasure and power
like a flower blossoming
in season with beauty
and indelible memories
and evidence
that God is within you
and within me

heaven

If granted my most devout wish,
that I might spend the sum of my life
seeking your joy and bliss
and making you happy, know this,
that there is no need of an heaven,
for I have already been there.

until the blood flows

I can hit you harder with a word
(racial epithet)
than you could ever hit me with your fist
(sexual orientation slur)
bruises on flesh heal
(religious sacrilege)
bones knit
(individual mockery)
scars have a certain noble pride
(revelation of childhood trauma)
but
(deeply held fear)
I can make a legacy of your fears
(rampant misogyny)
that will endure long after you are dead
(self-serving slander)
and that, my friend, is power.
(truth)

winds

you will find me there
wind in my hair
praying to the gods of odds
to make even the road I walk

these are not ordinary winds
but the desert blasts from God's nostrils
that carry the mood altering ions
of the Morongo Valley

seventy miles an hour and it whips
and slashes and crashes against me
as I bend to its power and glory
like tumbleweed hanging on for dear life

you are in this wind of fury
and I am caught in it, aware
that it may strips the flesh from my bones
as it gusts to hurricane force

imperceptibly, slowly, and with effort
I make my way up the valley
against the winds that batter me
determined to do more than hold my ground

surrendered

I have not given up my weapons and skills
but sworn them to your defense and whim.
I am yours to command, demand of me sacrifice,
allegiance, and the passion of an high priest,
foreswearing all other faiths that I might
lay upon your altar and follow you into heaven.
I am in awe of you. Your beauty and strength,
your grace disgraces Aphrodite, your words
are like bandywine in my veins, hot and red,
praying for a sign divine to evidence that I
am somehow an acceptable offering in giving
all that I am. all that I have. all just to you.

seducing

every second of every day
you are seducing me
with your thoughts and movements
the sinuous way you walk
when you want me to watch you
as you walk, a cat in heat,
calling out to me to follow
into the next room
and see how feral
we can get, wet with sweat
and the sweet honey
of your desire
every second of every day
I contemplate this
and want you to know

some days

the roadkill
that just moments ago
was a bright eyed forest creature

the table scraps
scraped down the garbage disposal
while the family dog looks on, wistfully

the stray cat
shooed away by flung boot and curse words
because I wandered into your yard

the outsider
forbidden to even leave the fog of his breath
on the windows of your party

dawn

A perfected stillness lays upon the yellow grass lawn.
Dawn arrives, dressed in cool sweat and gossamer, avatar
for a more serene affection than my soul allows, gone
to the arcing corners beyond the pillars, out so far
that you cannot find me, you cannot bind me, I remain
bound, found in orbit like captured debris of a planet
that wandered too close, drawn to the light, caught in tidal chain
holding me as the sphere contemplates my fate, a vanity
that ignores the essence of the universe, potent
potential energy drawing strength from the rising sun
and storing it in the darkened ruins where the provident
prayed to gods they did not understand, victories won
not on the battlefield, but in the soul, fires burning bright
as suns kindled by patience and sentience, overnight.

not dead yet

I am not dying

well

no more swiftly, to my knowledge,
than the guy sitting next to me

and he looks like he got laid last night
so he has that on me

I am not afraid of death
I made my peace with it at eight
standing in my room
contemplating funerals
I would one day be compelled to attend
that still have not been held
but that
actuarily
are pretty damn inevitable and imminent

but I digress

I am not dead

yet

nor have I fallen out of love
or given up on poetry
for either would be worse
than the sudden run down
of the wound up clockwork
that is my internal organs
such as they are

even when you walk away
as you will
for your own reasons
having found the taste of this confection
runs contrary to the fairy tales
you thought I was a part of
I will not die
not physically, at least

sorry
to be part of your disillusionment
but I

am not dead or dying
yet
but would like to get laid tonight

no more second chances

will you mourn me when I am gone
and the clock continues, past the killing blow,
impassive to the mess it and I conspired
to leave behind for others to sort out?

will you mourn me when I am gone
and so many words were left unsaid, the truths
that frightened us both so much that we lied
and said nothing when our souls screamed?

will you mourn me when I am gone
and we failed to get to certain things we felt
needed to be done before the sun set
and now I can never speak again for myself?

will you mourn me when I am gone
and you read between the lines in all my poems
and find who I really was, and what I was,
and what I had hoped would pass before the end?

in exile, deo

one hundred
and
sixty nine
stairs
lead to the door
at tower's top.

a voice from within meanders
like a prophet in the desert
or any homeless wino
down on Charles Street.

"So once again, my electric lady,
You dance into my life and i must choose
to live a love that all who live would envy,
Or in my arrogance your love refuse..."

too much and not enough, it seems.
dreams like porcupine parachutes,
defeating themselves by their nature
in the long race to inevitability.

"the cup contains curdles and vinegar.
the mug, meat desiccated with age.
the mug, brandywine of a field so far
that even to seek it shows courage."

the sound of fist on stone, the bone breaks
and then heals instantly, painfully,
the curse of immortality mocks the clock
and only scars tell the tale and tapestry.

"in a barren orchard.
words on deaf or absent ears
we repent truth."

paper burns, silence reigns and washes away
the desperate holograph in red and rust,
dust becoming a constant companion
until the candles are forgotten.

"lied to in fields of orchids.
faith becomes the currency that folds,
I press away my pie, untouched,
and considered this cage of epithets."

as the night fades into mourning
the steps are retraced and the mortar
lays thick against the bricks as we seal
the reality to allow another legend in the city.

amour courtois

I have taken the task and mask of champion
to a lady who asked my favour and desire,
higher purpose is there none until I have won
her public acknowledgement that I inspire
her as she does me, profoundly, completely,
the religion of love as Lewis did define,
amour courtois, and yet more than this, for mercy
dictates our surrenders encompass the divine
in such a way that we are at unity at heart,
given and taken, master and servant, bound, free,
the grave comfort and light airs that both end and start
within the vows we have, in a sense, made as key
to a quiet place where we may face our demons
and angels, ascending to unity as one.

flesh

words be damned, as I am.

I crave the eloquence of your flesh,
meshing with mine in divine communication.
your message clear and certain.
I would command the veils be ripped apart
as you would my heart if what passes
between us were to be proven a lie.
punctuation of every persuasive opportunity,
wet and hot and taut and tight, a delight
that burns me but leaves me feral
for the next carnal immolation.
you alone speak the language of the lover
that translates into divine revelation,
consecrated in your glossolalia
as you receive my sacraments.
no need for prophets or poets
when we see with eyes
of stained glass and fire.
and feel ourselves burned pure
in carnal reconciliation
in a religion of Stygian baptism.

immolation

take up your arms and amory, your whim
drives hard forces Zeus would envy, skies crack
and the red rains are burnt into dim
incandescent lights of the nights we stack
as a cordwood against fading passion.
time that makes ash of our bright appetites.
I will speak my grave vows as a mission
to the antipodes to grant your rights
as a regent decree in which I shall
carry your crown's banner as evidence
of my given honor and vow morale
of a martyr when the fires make pretense
to burn my raw passions that I might yet
prove you my faith and hold to vows I've set.

surrender

in tender surrender I have set aside my pride,
unilateral collateral for alliance
between fallen forces of unnatural nature,
drawn together in pain and doubt, without promises
beyond the quiet vow to find a way, in the end.
every day I feel the sharp stones and the thistles,
impediments to a more pleasant path I will walk
with the devotion of a blind pilgrim seeking cure,
or at least a place of safety in a most cruel world.
I would and should shed my skin and kin if required
to be your constant companion and proud paramour.
I want the world, the stars, the underworld to accept
that I am content and at peace with your love and will
do nothing to evict you from the place, the palace
you asked within me, with innocent respect, desire
and a faith that we could transcend memory and pain
to lay claim to one another, tender surrender
that asks nothing, but demands and commands our souls.

counterpoint

another fell lover
pretends to my throne,
defending your promise
falls to me, and alone.

a distance persistent
locks me out of the light
mocks and blocks my affections,
sealed away from your sight.

a lover discovers
precious precedent paid
and calls from the shadows
to illume the charade.

the violence of silence
defiles smiles and dreams
cutting deeper and darker
than the innocent's screams.

theme

the lover that hovers
when no other persists.
warm lips and hips christened
in the glistening mists.

virgins

for all our time and trials
we are as virgins.
for this is something new.
perhaps vaguely derivative
of passions we have felt and fed
in other time and bed
but nonetheless
unique
and we enter this
and one anothers' essences
with fear and desire
to cross a threshold
and fit into something
beautiful beyond words.
even mine.

lullaby

rest for now, know that I am keeping watch.
I am sorry it took so long for me to find you,
hidden in the improbably corners of life,
but I never stopped looking and hoping, believing
that there would be someone for me to protect and love.
breathe the light and exhale dreams to intoxicate me,
I will not resist your anxious arms but will not
fail in being your personal dreamcatcher.

submission

above all other flowers
that have bloomed
or even been imagined
you will be honored
and respected, loved
and cherished, even
in crimson moments
when you want to be taken,
dominated and drawn
into the fires of desire.
a perfect petal, your lips,
and the nectar of your hips
would make Dionysius swoon.
above all other flowers
you will be loved
and treated with tenderness
even when we are mad
with the hunger of our bodies
and feed, relentlessly,
seeking absolution
in the surrender.

you, and you alone,
shall be my sustenance,
pleasing me perfectly.

purge

scourge me
purge me
urge me
to release the venom
pounding black in my veins.
grounding the pain
that it may flow through me
and not linger
like the stinger of an angry wasp.
I know I am
unsuitable
unworthy
unwanted
lingering so long
it has become awkward.
perhaps.
or is it just the poison
talking in mocking whispers?
perhaps I shall know
if I open another vain vein
and drain a little more
of what once was my blood.

saints

the long dark night of my soul.
the saints' taint and memory.
oh, to be as a sloth,
double rib cage to resist the crush
of the constrictions
designed to make of me a feast
remembered only as one of many
fading into insignificance.
I learned war in the sphere of Venus
yet was never more than mercenary,
no regent claiming my body
when the battlefields were cleaned
for the next round,
bound and burned
to warm the peasants.
shards of light bite me
like angry insects in a swarm.
warm is an alien comfort
when you are away.
when the Thomases play with my mind
and every shadow is a challenge.
I must not allow myself
the luxury of jealousy.
I must not allow myself
the empathy of memory.
for
like God
you are unique.

where we lay

take me down with you
and let us curl like pinwheels,
metal foil and bright colours,
around each other
fitting the way we seem
to have been built.
I will guard your dreams
and you, you fulfill mine
every time I wake to find you
in my arms.

I want to talk with you
about whatever you think is
important, even just in the moment.
I want to laugh with you
when I do something stupid
or when we just need a good laugh
to keep from taking life
too serious and the stresses
of being apart tear holes
in my heart.

I want to whisper your name
as I fuck you, so that you know
that I know it is you and no other woman
holds my desires like you do,
tight and in a reassuring manner,
your breath a sacred prayer for release,
in the cradle of your hips
drawing me in until I am turned
inside out and leave a part of me
inside you.

I want to be your champion
and never say no when you need me
no matter how willful you've been
because that's what lovers do
that's what lovers
are supposed to do
whether or not they make public vows
in this world gone mad
except for the corners
where we lay.

god

god is not just in you
god is everywhere
however
the best evidence
of god
is in your existence
for god does not hide
in manifesting you
but just as gasoline itself
does not burn
but the vapours do
I am convinced
you cannot see god
as well as we can
for we are not already submerged
in the sublime
as you are
and you are incandescent
even when you keep to the shadows

against the steel

against the steel. against the stone.
I lay here, shattered to the bone.
the violent silence, I am alone,
and yet my choices I'll not atone.

I love you in the world's disdain,
willing to take all shame and pain.
the heart of poets are not sane -
but I am mark'd with your stain.

do not presume me weak or frail,
I could easily peel apart this jail,
but for your hand, I shall not fail.
you are to me an Holy Grail.

so make of me a distant thought,
a bartered heart you had once bought
for pyritc coins you count for naught.
I'll battle back, your ardour sought.

Eurydice

do not dance with the naiads on our wedding day,
as I do not wish to fulfill the myths.
Orpheus was a coward, you know, choosing
to chase a shadow rather than join her.
rest assured, if I follow you into Hell
I will stay with you, blind to time,
laying on my hands to draw out the pain
that is incumbent from your faultless fall.
I will play you a simple melody
and sing for you poems and mysteries
that will distract us both, for a time,
from the pain that surrounds and engulfs us.
and you will kiss me, when the time is right.

spare people

I don't want to be one of the
spare people
who sit in your trunk, in the dark,
hoping something blows out
and I am suddenly needed.
not my style.
not my desire
to be an old tire
with just enough tread
that you can put me to use
if the need arises.
I'm better than that.

gratitude

of all the multitude
of people and experiences
and things that are neither
yet still please or content me,
I am most grateful to God
for your presence in my life
and the possibilities
presented by your existence.

Occupy the Planet

Take up more than air, Mon Frere,
let your voice be heard.
It's we the people against the evil,
the hornet nest is stirred.

Dictatorships sometime subsist
on lies and media buys.
The ruling class will bet its ass.
Let the ninety nine percent rise.

Take up more than air, Mon Frere,
let your voice be heard.
It's we the people against the evil,
the hornet nest is stirred.

just words

your wish was to know
what it would be like
to be loved by a man like me.

so far

you have nothing to go on
but words and those trinkets,
parlour tricks, that pass for caresses.

one day

I shall be unleashed
and you will see that I am
more than just words and sleight of hand.

for now

I wait my opportunity
to be more than a shadow
in a cave within a cave.

your wish

is far from fulfillment
as this genie boils in his bottle
anxious to love you with more than

just words.

manifesto 2011

poetry
for want of a better word

should be the kiss
with just enough tongue
to make you want more

should be the sun
drying your bare skin
as you lay by the pool

should be the pill
you swallow to focus
on sixteen lines, not six thousand

should be the eyes
of a lover, boring into you
at the moment of mutual release

should be the faith
not the job or the hobby
as a band-aid does not make a surgeon

should be the truth
even if speculative about lovers
you will never actually meet or coit

should be the craft
learned then sublimated
to allow inspiration a channel

should be the page
not the caterwaulings
of a performance artist clown

should be the blood
of lovers and heroes and saints
traced upon flesh at the moment of death

poetry
for want of a better word

clarion

sound like a bell,
curved and swerved, the undeserved compliment,
mental exercise for the exorcism of a schism
that is artificial at best, a test of faith.
I could walk away tomorrow, but I wouldn't.
I choose to lose myself in you,
where the sounds are not muffled, a duffel
of reliant, defiant bells, clanging for the hanging,
tintinnabulation for a tribulation
faced with grace and a taste
for the dramatic.
queens moving like knights
as the lights flicker but do not die.
I. singular, first person.
I am of my own devising,
reprising not the roles others held.
I have been shelled by other artillery
and the witness tree has never seen us
together.
Not yet.
The odds are long
but don't you fucking dare bet against us.
I'm not here to take home the leftovers.
But I'll make a feast of the vapours
if that's what it will take to make
the sound, rebounding, into a summons,
a celebration and a commitment.

A night of Sundays

I walk these walls and halls.
Ever to the left side, to make
room, should you choose to come along.
I walk these walls and halls
for the most part in solitude.

I walk these walls and halls.
Watching as you run off to this
or that or e'en sometimes them both.
I walk these walls and halls
in case you might choose to see me.

I walk these walls and halls,
for I made of myself, guardian,
consort to an unfulfilled kiss.
I walk these walls an halls
as a legend, a meme, abstract.

I walk these walls and halls
because I have sworn a patience
that surpasses understanding.
I walk these walls and halls
as the lights in the chapel dim.

I walk these walls and halls
at night when the distant courtyards
ring with your bright laughter, blithe muse.
I walk these walls and halls
in memory and prophesy.

I walk these walls and halls
for now, as flesh and blood, and yet
there may come days when I am gone.
I walk these walls and halls
regardless of my final fate.

I walk these walls and halls.
I walk these walls and halls, lover,
as you have held my vow and smiled.
I walk these walls and halls.
Even when you choose another.

pen

I dreamed the other night
that as we made love
I wrote poetry on your
beautiful, warm back
with fingertips and my tongue
and even the head of my cock,
leaving black ink and white semen

you want to know what I wrote
but you knew
as it seeped into your skin
and you felt the comfort
and heat and wetness
that you pulled out of me
with your beauty and truth

I wish I could write something
worthy of your skin
the words and letters rough
as I would pen them
as I fucked you for love
and release of both our sorrows
into each other, expressing art

step on a crack

step on a crack and break your mother's back.

can't imagine my mother with a broken back.
and I've probably, inadvertently, stepped on
more than a few cracks in the sidewalk,
considering all the places I have laid leather.

my mom had polio when she was little.
she still walks with a limp, her foot
corkscrewing as she walks. she doesn't walk
as much as she used to. at 78, you don't.

step on a crack and break your mother's back.

she's from a generation where corporal punishment
was considered okay. more than one wooden spoon
or yardstick met an end across my backside
or that of my brothers or sister. thwack!

she has a temper. but she has the patience
that comes from having lived long enough to see
those she love live and die, rise and fall,
struggle and fail and dust themselves off.

step on a crack and break your mother's back.

she takes good care of my father, a decade older.
he's in his late eighties now, hearing shot,
half a century and more of type 2 diabetes
hasn't killed him. or putting up with me.

her brother died years ago, her only sibling.
her mother is 100 now, slipping in and out
of a world in dementia that seems a happy place.
but it isn't here, and I miss her sometimes.

step on a crack and break your mother's back.
I'll bet against the sidewalk, first.

malevolence

while my words seem faintly saintly, throwback chivalry,
I am not above the lustful malevolence of my gender.
I can deconstruct your walk, your smile, and while
you think we are having a pleasant conversation
I am imagining how those lips would feel, wrapped
around me as I violate and desecrate you.

I am not above wanting to, in the right time and place,
hear you scream my name and feral blasphemies,
indicative of an intensity of pleasure and pain
as I lose my last veil of civilization with you,
taking you, making you the release for ceaseless energies,
trapped, now tapped as you sap my sanity with your legs.

yes, as we sip our drinks and each one thinks thoughts
that are civilized and proper, my peripheral senses
examine you in ways that would make you blush, flushed
with outrage, perhaps tinged with a slight delight
that right now, despite my cool demeanor, I am ravaging
every curve and corner and depth of you in malevolent hunger.

Drakon Thespiakos

are you my Menestratos, set to pierce me from the inside
for my scales have proven too durable to weapon or pride?
I know your nature. I know your purpose. karnage o'er kronos.
and yet, I am so hungry and you took my vow, heaven knows,
to feed one last time. only upon you. so whether I starve
or am pierced with your bronze spikes, I die, no more to cut and carve
my name into the fearful, tearful hearts of maids and warriors.
for one last time to dare to dream of a world without hungers.

covenant

in the time you grant
my love is unconditional
no dealbreakers

baptism at 32,000 feet

the clouds will stream past me
a River Jordan in the sky
and I will leave behind
for the last time
the first things
I thought I couldn't leave

not the faux carne vale
of a Fat Tuesday
but an earnest quest
for peace through surrender
not a pretender
but looking for a religion

tasting the cold crystals
as the logical liturgy
of so many promises
left behind, like a forgotten hymnal
during the invitation
angels wait for me, one last time

bleed into me

bleed into me
and I will share your pain and stain
and heal you with patience
and a passion you never imagined
for that is my nature when you
bleed into me

inside

I want to look into those eyes
rimmed with red passions
lips wet with my kisses
and feel your exquisite body
roll like the ocean
beneath me.
I want to feel your long hair
brushing my skin
as you lose yourself
in taking me in
until your body burns
and I am drawn out
by this radiant heat.
I want to touch those breasts
and hold them in my hands
as I take you, tender
and yet with the fury of lust.
I want to lay beside you
after being inside you
and know I have left a part of me
with you, forever.

tyrant inside

I am not saint. the taint of man is mine,
the wine of sinister harvests bare held.
inside of me is the tyrant, divine
in no aspect. feral teeth, claws, the weld
of dark metal with the silver tongue, caged
by an ever draining margin of will.
blistering my heart, soul, and so enraged
that it ever upon itself feeds, ill
and yet storming titan, striking the spark
against the stones of memory as call
to the challenge of my better stripes, dark,
evil as any bastard, cruel, fool as all
would not believe of me, and I am here,
bound as Prometheus, to conquer fear.

whispers

you are so kind to let my eyes touch you, even in modesty.
there is life to you, and hope, and dreams. and God.
yes, God, for in you I see the design of miracles,
the purpose of love, the magic of faith, even at night
when not everything is as it should be. but will be.
I wish I had your glass slipper, the words to win you,
not as a stuffed toy, but as an equal.
and every day I walk uphill against doubt, not in you
but in my own worthiness to one day hold your heart
as you whisper to me the dark passions you need fulfilled.
I would die a joyous martyr for your peace and desire.

lost or found

lost and found
the sound of certitude
when the mood is upon me.
but I have my doubts
and fears, nearer
than I care to confess to.
nothing terrifies me more
in the thin skin spaces
between our embraces
when I am cure you reconsidered
all the promises you've made
and the fantasies we've spun
and I am about to find myself
left by the side of the road
like an underperforming prom date.
but I found myself with you
and promises are only real
if they are sometimes inconvenient.
and I do love you, even when
you cut me, by accident.
forgetting that I am here.
forgetting all that I have surrendered
to walk a path that you asked
me to walk with you.
and will not reconsider.
because at the end of the road
I am sure to find you.

precognizant memories

origami hearts
folded until the crane
is all we can observe.

you remind me of a girl
who died in a car crash.
she was from the neighborhood
and had big, dark eyes.
but she is gone, like cookies
left too long to cool,
stolen away in regret.

you remind me of a woman
who had to rebuild herself.
recovering from a brutal rape,
she wrapped herself in artifice
until she was healed enough
to trust again and found
she was stronger for her scars.

you remind me of a woman
so fogged by drugs and drama.
trading her body for the next high.
stealing from her mother.
bartering tomorrow for the moment
until someone sacrificed enough
that she could walk away.

you remind me of a woman
who was turned inside out
by the touch of her father.
never able to get clean again.
wanting to transcend her life.
not caring if she stole another one
as long as she could live.

you remind me of a boy
who just wanted to be loved.
but he was not from this place,
not inside, he was from somewhere
where people keep their promises
and never hide love, and never die,
except when time runs out.

you remind me of a woman

who found sanctuary in a field
of terra cotta butterflies.
flitting from flower to flower
when the winds were their fiercest.
measuring each taste of honey
against the price paid for wings.

you remind me of a woman
who became the person she hated most
and so left herself and those who loved her
to create yet another person,
molded and folded around that
cookie jar heart she thought was hers
but actually belonged to another.

you remind me of a man
who lost the woman he loved.
not to perfidy or fickle hearts
but to screaming steel and diesel.
one moment she was there and the next
he had to extend into decades of regret
that he had not died with her.

you remind me of a girl
who believed in Jesus.
but He didn't come to save her
when the bad man came to visit
and she decided He didn't really love her
and went and sold her body
over and over and over again.

you remind me of a man
who had seen too much.
and wanted to go away and forget
as much as he could, but he fell
in love and was damned to orbit
forever around a single point in space
and watch reality replay.

foreplay and afterwards: five

be still.
be very still.
listen and feel.
your head, pressed against my chest
finds the rhythm of my heart
matched by the pulse
my pulse
throbbing inside you
every surge of blood
pressing tighter
in an already improbably tight fit.
kiss me.
and when you are ready
move.
slowly at first.
then as you wish
rising up to take full measure
as quickly as you wish
or slow enough to match
the pulse we are sharing
until the barriers melt
and our bodies merge waters
like two rivers meeting
in a roaring turbulence
we'll lose ourselves in

foreplay and afterwards: quad

lay back, lay back. you need only receive
the hunger of my flesh. spread wings of pink
and solferino and draw me in, skin and sin
passing thin membranes to fetch your desire
and stretch you to the point of a madness
that is the vanity of sanity unburdened.
wrap those legs about me, lock them tight
that I may not go far, mere inches, to return
with shuddering force in the course
of expressing my passions for you.
lay back. lay back. my attack is begun
and the battle is won in its commencement.
I want to feel your hands on my back,
your nails scrailing bloody rivulets
as evidence of your feral essence awakening
and taking me as plutonic as your core.
more of you I measure, treasured pleasures
taking the time it takes to make immolation
a desired, required, inspired poetry of heat
in expressing my passions for you.

foreplay and afterwards: trey

I explore your body with fingertip precision,
eyes closed so as not to be distracted as I
find my way along the gentle curves to the nerves
that make you move, like that, and sigh, like that,
and relax enough, just enough, to give me access
to more than soft, warm flesh, but your secrets,
your desires, the fires of your heart and mind
that will burn me before the night is through,
but not before I find how deep you'll let me in.
in metaphor and throbbing, curved shaft that slides
into your sheath, as your senses boil and roil
and your body becomes incandescent to my touch
and trespass. you are tight and warm and wet,
and your arms and legs bind me to you, as if
I could ever imagine wanting to not go deeper
into the labyrinth of your passion and lust.

foreplay and afterwards: two

lay back, rest your weary head on pillows
soft and cool. soon enough they will burn
with the pounding blood in your veins.
but for now, lay smooth shoulders back
and slide your fingers into my hair
to guide me, to add another dimension
as my hands part your slender, tender thighs
and my lips kiss scar and pink flesh
going solferino to my attentions
and intentions, as my tongue parts folds
to find entry into you.
my hands, they slide beneath you
pulling you against me as your fingers
twine in my hair, showing me the rhythm
you want me to set as I wet and whet
feasting on your ardent hips and lips.
feel more than hear my moans of delight
as they mingle with your own, your legs
rising to wrap around me as I slide tongue
to tease and please and ultimately
release you to your own need for my touch.
deeper than you know, and yet, not yet,
to ride inside you to the edge of madness.

foreplay and afterwards: one

the shadows in the room are soft and patient.
not at all like me, as I am waiting for you, now.
I watch you cross the room, dancing on bare feet,
a faint smile of apprehension on lips I will kiss
and violate. first tongue. and then while I
explore your fragrant realms with my lips and fingers,
it will be to you to draw me in and find the pleasure points
that will anoint you with my need and seed
as I feel your body writhe to my touch and trespass.
drink deeply, for the night is just begun
and by morning, we shall be wasted and worn, torn
from the security of who we thought we were
as the lines melted and burned and I yearned
to hear you call my name, one more time, impaled
upon my desire. unlike a boy, my hunger is undiminished
by a single meal, and you feel yourself taken in ways
you did not imagine in your most heated fantasies,
penetrated, desecrated, violated, elevated
and let to fall, limp and helpless as I consume
all that I wish to, your body a chalice of heat.
feel my flesh inside you, gliding through
the channels of your release, your peace
earned in nerves electrified by an ardent tutor
who shares what he has learned that you might,
for one night, feel what you should feel
every night for the rest of your life.

dance

dance
to the music of the night
when we will lay together
and find that some things
some things
just fit
no matter whether or not
we harbour certain doubts
about if the world will
in its infinite cynicism
cooperate with our plans
dance
to please yourself
and I will see your smile
and draw pleasure from it
and from what the grace
and the beauty of your dance
awakens in me to take you
and lay claim to you
as you have asked of me
and I have promised to do
as you dance beneath me
and offer up your song of songs
dance

the sabotage of gods

the gods sabotage themselves.
tired of being different
in a world where mediocrity
is prized above all else.
I have seen your radiance
as you shade and jade it,
pretending to be nothing,
pretending to be grey remnants.
it is difficult to be deific.
painful to rise above the muck.
we are our most comfortable
when we are nothing extraordinary.
it is easier that way, that path
of fieldstone and failure.
the allure of artificial urgency.
the gods sabotage themselves.

fill me in

fill me in
I'll return the favour
dreams and thoughts and memories
shared between two sharing space
and saving face in tender madness

fill me in
I have room for you
I hollowed out my heart and soul
when first you asked for sanctuary
recognizing you for what you are

fill me in
and I will treat you with a passion
and a respect you cannot lose
even if you, in time, crawl out and away
and leave me, hollow and dying

paper

paper anniversaries, folded into boats
to ride the runoff of the storms we know
are inevitable. your friends and family,
mine as well, will give us grief when falls the veil.
if ever.

I know you have your dark reservations
and every day I expect you to come to your senses
and make your defenses permanent and hard,
sealing me out, with a word, and rendering my life
tribute to a lost love, unrequited. I don't want
to wake up to that fate, second guessing the moment
when I read your soul and discovered
that I could fit you in without doubt or reservation.

and the paper boats seem inevitable.
caught on currents, blown by the wind
and slowly sinking by their own impregnation,
their very nature to soak and sink.
even as the ink of vows we've made blur
and dissolve in the water that streams away
to vanish around the next curve, pressed by
expediences and the ephemeral nature of mortals.

pearl

you are a chocolate pearl,
dark beauty built around
a flaw now obscured but the genesis.
ornamentation, but profound
and sound enough to start a prophet
on his path towards metaphor.

I love your laugh. it's honest,
like your smile and the way
your eyes play with the light.
nothing semi-precious about you,
even when you are hiding in your shell
from a really fucked-up world.

you are exotic and erotic,
a colossus of dreams for futures
beyond my life, and yours and ours,
when lovers will read of you
and dare to hope they find someone
made of nacre and nurture.

birds

predicated contingencies.
we hesitate to use the words
that others use as filigrees
to masque their hearts like crippled birds
that hide behind the compost heap.
I am no one but myself, and yet,
I carry the mark of ev'ry creep
who ever tried to sell you dreams
in a paper cup then leaking
and soon to crumble like the lies
told for no purpose past seeking
your earnest heart and kiss and thighs
for but a moment's dance and flight,
as crippled birds limp out of sight.

today

if I had my way
if I had my say
I'd be there today
and never go away

Heisenberg's orphan

I am an orphan of my age
you are no longer castaway
but I am
nearly ronin
caught in the moment
between my saying the words
and you saying the words
and living to them
it is a grievous place
this instant expanding
to explode on me
like a balloon full of water
taken from a dubious spigot
out back
not knowing if the moment will come
or what it will contain
(sweet water or sludge)
for Heisenberg damned us
while Schoedinger laughed
and I am watched through
a one way mirror
while all I see is my reflected
passion and affection

photoshop poetry

never been a maker
of photoshop poetry.
give me the moment.
raw and pure
and sure of the truth.
not some patchwork
retcon of what we think
we saw with our hearts.
moving the shadows and figures
to suit well-meaning critiques
until the original image
has been raped of all affection
and truth doesn't matter.
better to lay with my lover
when she has one strand askew
than the cold wombs of distrust
found in the fictions
of someone who wasn't even there.

one more thing

one more thing, you said,
then, with a cock of your head
you were gone.
I always wanted to be
a renaissance man
but you beat me to it
and five hundred years from now
they'll still be speaking your name
with awe and respect
and marveling at the world you created
with a missionary's zeal.
You built no weapons
waged no wars
but changed the society
I and my children
and their children
will live in,
and for the better.
You were the poet-king
of technology and the future.

all the pretty predators

all the pretty predators
stand beside your bed
hoping opportunity
spins a silken thread
that weaves them in your tapestry
if only for a few
for all the pretty predators
feel it is their due
to be a part of everyone
regardless of their will
and for unchastened hastened tastes
would lie or cheat or kill...
or merely show and come and go
and laugh about the night,
pretty predators that prance
and sober with the light.

ritual sex

deep within the valley of the shadow of life
I left my sacrifice of leper's blood,
white wine splashed on solferino walls
to mark my passage
and leave claim to the priesthood
of the rites of your pleasure.
you spoke in tongues
on the Egyptian cotton altar
as the temple trembled
then gave up your secrets
as you drew blood with sacred nails
convulsing in a fit of contorting release
and commanded me
to never sacrifice to another goddess
ever again

centric

the question recurs.
should I be selfish, self-centered.
take more than I give?
how do people live
with themselves like that?
even as a child it made no sense to me.
we are at our best when we give.
when we live
for others.
lessons learned.
best, shared.

til the dawn

the dreamers and the drifters
the grifters and the priest
all will answer to their own needs
until their enviable release
I'm not looking for a door
just a floor to lay upon
for I am here not for myself
but to hold you til the dawn

the prophets and the poets
all know it's not the same
they hearken to the divine spark
keeping darkness with the flame
held back from you while resting
dark memories, long gone,
for I am not here for myself
but to hold you til the dawn

the cynics and the sinners
each well-intentioned friend
all ask of you the reason you
would stay until the end
at any price no sacrifice
if your peace is finally won
for I am not here for myself
but to hold you til the dawn

suns

tenderness
and patience
hallmarks of the lover
who wants more than the brimstone strike
of a match, unconcerned
with what happens after the house
burns down...
I am burning
and of a lambent brisance
but I am sentient
and of an experienced life
such that I will lay my fire
in a controlled burn
hotter than any spark or wick
but more enduring
than any sun
burning ten billion years
against the cold brutality
of the hollow space
of fickle lovers

solitude

in my solitude
I wait for you
out of phase with life
waiting for a wife or lover
to emerge
from her cocoon of doubt
and claim her swain
in deed and word.
I am not all ways
at peace with this.
I strain to stand
at peace, aside,
and wait my bride
without my doubts
consuming me
and dooming me
to solitude
of a differing magnitude.

no more deaths

vengeance is not virtue

there is no recompense
for a lost child
or wife or mother

or friend

some of the most primitive societies
in the world
are not as blood thirsty
as the State of Texas
or Georgia
or any other semi-sovereign unit
of an increasingly ignorant
and hypocritical nation
that allows men and women
and children
to be executed
and does not consider this
cruel and unusual

Jesus wept

and we are all worthy of death
each of us, saints and such...
considering the number of
state-sanctioned martyrs
in the early Christian church
they should probably consider it
an honor
to be killed by the agents
of the new Roman Empire
and join the multitudes
in an inversion of the religion
that is supposed to uphold mercy
even in the face of persecution

Jesus wasn't packing
at Gethsemane

we, the people,
have lost our way

black monday

the ebon and gold bands
that interlock
lay upon my desk
I envision them in space
as separate parts
and as the whole

odd, the way they fit
together
and yet incongruous
like lovers so difficult
to explain that
we take different roads

I decline to name
or describe you
outside of my poetry
and you decline to
acknowledge that there
is even someone here

inelegant solutions
mad resolutions
bringing revolutions
I am disused to subterfuge
and so I feel odd
and sometimes out of sorts

while I play my port and part
so central to your life
but like an hidden gyroscope
balance was never your strong suit
and I, a turtle hatchling,
am against the waves of your tidal forces

I accept the gift I give myself
and to you, without regret,
for courtly love breeds poetry
in the end, that is what the rings
represent, a one-sided vow,
to prove the world is not all...shallows

elder gods

I worship the elder gods.
the gods of love and joy and peace
who are facets of the one
but whose domain has been since time began
looking out across the void
and saying, with hope and vision,
that there needs to be life
and light and love and above everything
faith in way the world unfurls

I worship the elder gods.
the gods of inarticulate happiness,
whose voices are those of children
and the people who never let go
of butterflies and catching moonbeams
on your tongue at midnight
that you might know the truth
and understand the way things
are supposed to be, in this world

I worship the elder gods.
with kiss and touch and poetry
that transcends memory and dances
of a sad-eyed kitten in the corner
as she strives to find the steps
that will bring back innocence
and the perfectibility of two,
cynicism abolished by dreams
that rise like fog from a lake

I worship the elder gods.
every stroke of skypaint and cloud.
every scent of cinnamon and raspberries.
every texture of a woman's body
and every sound she makes
when I touch her with reverence and desire.
there is no blasphemy in knowing
that there is and was and will be
greater things than I and seeking them.

patriarch

whether bound by word or bands of metal,
or just by whim of unrequited hope,
I am committed to this path and all
that I must do to walk in truth and trope.
if you are weary, or broken by fate,
wracked with disease or mad when sullen scars
overwhelm you, I will not hesitate
to stand for and by you and find the stars
in darkness, patiently calling their lume
to comfort you and be your champions,
banishing pain from you as I assume
title as protector of your visions,
filling my role as best I dare and can,
that you may never feel orphaned again.

death

death is a dark and most jealous mistress,
committed to the tenuous relationship
that she does not tend, but waits her dance, dress
of black with red satin trim, her graceful legs long,
strong as she parts the crowd on the dancefloor
and tells you that it is time for a final fling.
there will be those who hate her for too soon
spoiling the evening, but I will thank her
for at least giving me a class exit

aching

I ache to take you, make you mine own flesh.
tracing my firm desire from front to back
and all throughout your claiming form, to mesh
my curve to ev'ry nerve and cul-de-sac
that traffics in the alchemy of need
to transform, to perform deep ritual
to sanctify and violate, to bleed
the white blood of my life in critical
urgency to our very sanity
and survival, knotting the pulsing thread
of tapestries into a vanity
of the honor of desecration, wed
to what we are, the pain slaked in the pierce
of membranes more than flesh, in frenzy fierce.

Promethean

you bring the fire to the edge of Heaven and hold it out for me
to seize and carry to mortals, who live their lives barely aware
that there is such incandescent fury in the world, improbable
but oh so possible in the hypergolic frolic of meeting souls.
I will carry this fire to Earth, but only if you come with it,
only if you come with me so that I can show that I was not just
imagining the light and heat that you sparked in brisant life.
I am little more than messenger for the contraband of your beauty
and will, in the end, find myself bound for infinite torture
for my arrogance in carrying your flames as a wreath about me,
cracking Apollonian skies to undo the lies of the limits of love.
come with me. step light tread to my path and I will carry you,
if need be, if you need me, of you may run with the fleetness
of Atalanta, mocking Mercurial pursuit. but come with me
as I play Prometheus to the faces turned to taste the rain
the thunder throws as tears of joy that I have found you.

stillife 1

dark brown plastic
tape dispenser
facing away
sticky side down
the opalescent
adhesive impregnated
strip that rolls out
to be bit off
by a single metal row of teeth

stillife 2

slightly skew
words meaningless
row upon row of yesterday's thoughts
soon to be folded
or crumpled
or tossed full sheet
into the wastebasket
as a casket
to a lumber by-product

apparitions

I will wait for you in the precognizant memory
that lays between illusions and apparitions that slip
through fingers that reach to touch and comfort them, energy
passing to matter and back, a wisp of smoke that will trip
the cascade of brain chemicals surpassing all reason
to infect and addict us to shadows for a season.

like Abraham

like Abraham, our children shall number
in the tens of thousands, nations that rise
and fall because of our blood and faith. sure
we are of a legacy, sure that skies
hold not as many stars do as our lines,
children of word and dream and the courage
to be creators not only in vines
of our loins, but in our hearts' parentage.
you are mother and midwife to a birth
as natural and vital as any,
the small gods dancing together, the Earth
rejoicing in a voice that brings many
to the altar of that which is both right
and true to lovers' religion, tonight.

standing

on the edge
on the ledge
take the pledge
that the sedge withering from the lake
will not be the path that you take.
Blake or Byron, not defeat with Keats.
seize the sky
never die
dare to cry
'gainst the lie that the past makes tomorrow
as sorrow burns away and you borrow
coeur rage from the sages in stages.
rain will fall
pain will call
gain it all
caterwaul the passions and survival
in a revival of a religion carnival
in the manner of the Romans, Bacchus broken
for a token more than the bartering of everything.

slipped away

would you notice. would you care
if I slipped away, for just a day
and played in the gardens
where the roses bloom to my words
and the snapdragons are hungry
for even a mention of their beauty
by someone who doesn't think
"hot" is the highest compliment,
burbled out with beer breath.

would you notice. would you care
if I turned my head away in a bed
where you don't even lay in.
would the fading sound of my breathing
set you grieving, even though
I was already alone. waiting
hours into days into months into years
that I watch slip in sand through hands
I will never touch you with.

would you notice. would you care
if my pessimism showed for just a moment
and my time in a self-imposed exile,
longer than the average murder sentence,
came to an end and I lay with a friend
to recall what it is like to have someone
beside you, kissing you as you sleep
and sharing the day without IOUs.
you might not notice or care. but I would.

loud in the shadows

the keening wail of an indistinct presence
echoing in the unmitigating silence, sharp
as razor wires on bare fingers, lingering
wounds against my face, the disgrace
of not having a really good explanation
for being proud and loud in the shadows.
speaking in riddles, in code and ciphers
that you alone know, a glossolalia apropos
that strangles the angles and curves
and leaves what do we deserve as question
to be answered in debate and irrelevancies.
I will die with your name on my lips,
even if I must muffle the sound to hide
your face, your grace, your trace because
to define you is to unmask you, ironic angel
of the music of a night still too far away.

arbol hru

You draw the light with your presence, my blood
turns to the ore of the heavens, pure gold
malleable to your wishes, a flood
to my passions, sweeping away the old
and trite forget-me-nows, the vows that wilt
by apathy in each shallow lover
who broke with the heavens I had once built
in altars sacrosanct to discover
that to feel love is not to conceal love
but to let slip the traces and to fly
into an eclectic tempest, above
all illusion of peace beyond the eye.
I weep the blood of suns for your faint bliss
and would foreswear all others for your kiss.

the limits.

steel and alloys of vanadium and rare metals unnamed for national security reasons.
a shell of ruby-blue perfection, ferrying the living to the deadest corners of thought.
I would have been on that starship, I would have built it with my own hands,
but, as Ani once said, I got distracted. no regrets. none whatsoever,
as the limits of known horizons, to my reckoning, are not in the grey clay
of alien seas or the mad screams of atmosphere at penetration, ions to irony,
but in the moments when you open your eyes and I see corners of you
that no man or woman has ever dared to tread upon. spheres of madness
and of that uniquely five dimensional mind of yours, erotic and beautiful.
I know no greater fear than that I shall lay too heavy a step on your soils,
virgin earth that will mark my print for as long as mortals dare to dream.
I know no thrill greater than the sunrise of your eyes over canyons of hope.
I know no greater rush than to explore this horizon and to claim it,
as you have instructed me to, from as far away the nebulae of Andromeda.

at peace

my Grandmother
has found the peace of forgetting
all the pain of life.
her mind, slipping away
as the days to her birthday
creep up like a tender fog.

one day, perhaps,
I will join her in the mist.
but, for now, there is no peace.
and I feel the scars
everyday. I have earned them
and burned them into my flesh.

I am proud of them, and those
who have shared their moments
and memories with me.
I watch my Grandmother
as she fades and I kiss her forehead
and whisper names she will never know.

Nazarite

guide me to the pillars
that I might
in one last act of sanity
pull down the artifice
of the idol worshippers
and pass, with some dignity,
into the questionable histories.

when all is said and done
and shed and won, the truth
is that I will die alone
in the presence of my enemies
and be eulogized by those
who deserted me in life
as an inconvenient passion.

a season for lions

it is a season for lions.
the necessity of a loud couer rage,
that intimidates by presence
and mythology, but is backed up
with power, and grace, and command.

orchard winds

the blossoms have long since retreated
to form the bud of the fruit, red and green,
crisp to the bite. tart to the tongue.
any day now. I will fulfill my duty
and take a knee at the edge of the orchard,
while the subtle fragrance is carried out
to us by the winds in the branches, a scent
of hope and innocence, rediscovered.
do not think I am here for anything less
than everything you are and will be,
to share beyond this insidious box I am in.
for now. ten months silence bought to prove
that I was and am faithful and true
to words last summer and, if declined,
will ask again in the next apple harvest.
Eden is an overarching metaphor for this,
hidden behind the trellis of an hasty haiku.

lover's awareness

pain is proof of our passions
that we can feel at least something
in this world, where lovers are martyrs
and we are locked in vermillion.
reaching for something we need.
afraid we will catch it, indeed.
pain is proof of our passions.
you are precognizant kisses
that I would not miss for the world.

rebirth upon orbital insertion

we are born in the morning
and
we are borne until mourning
and
we are worn from our warmings
and
we are warm from our forming.

the hollow spaces

we are most alone when we most need to be,
walking through the hollow spaces, listening
for the echoes of a faded laughter. silence.
such is pain, not when the arrow pierces,
but when we pull it out, the damages done.
fallen from a height, fractured on the floor
of our most terrifying avatars of Icarus,
watching the waters rush up to embrace us,
helpless to do more than cry out
as we are swallowed by the waters of isolation.

cryptos

the code is not cold
but dynamic
like the spider with the
overlarge legs
that stumbles on the desktop,
used to the grace
of a silken trapeze act.

so many falls and the catcalls
are resonant.
no critic of my own actions
greater than myself.
squandered treasures
no doubt.
two nickels rub together
and the trick is more than
sleight of hand
or heart.

the colossus stands
but bronze grows green
then buckles
under the very mass
of the gravitas of a man
trying so hard to be epic.
and the spider metaphor
sustains itself.

stay in the web.
stay in the web.

words kissed and missed and pissed away
like random drug tests
for the integrity of our hearts.
mettle forged then forgotten.
prisoners of dark strangers
who sweep aside the cobwebs
to occasionally make mock
of the ticking clock, pocked
with the scars of our own best,
tested, forays into environments
where we are bartered and slaughtered.

stay in the web.
stay on the web.

hook and hold, the cold strands
a place where I can be at home, alone,
atoning for the sins of others.
and my own, many as they are,
but I've never put a scar on you.
and never want to.
my web without adhesive.
unlike yours.
where I must remain
until drained.

teacups of pale venom
having no effect on me,
for I am trapped of my own will,
holding tight to the headboard
metaphor you offered one night.
when you had a hunger
and I was
I am
patient without condition
for another metaphor.
and perhaps
nothing else.

stay in the web.
stay in the web.

an rational heat

there is an rational heat between us.
needs fulfilled. scars covered. nightmares banished.
more than needs, the seeds of something
extraordinary.
the stuff of rumours. of legends.
new wine in an ancient vessel, etching
unexpected revelations in base metal,
traces of gold and cinnabar. coming
to life, to lives, to cast shadows
and throw light like strange candles.
the heat is best when sources merge
that we might purge ourselves of the urge
to self-immolate, to self-desecrate.
I will worship you in soul, mind and flesh
for as long as I live and will proudly
play whatever role you allow, yet ever,
like the wick'd, wicked flame,
seek to light and heat and involve
the fragrant oils of your very existence.

consumed

what am I but flame and wax?
burning for a season, then released
to the memory of those for whom
the heat was pleasant and the light, kind.

you let me burn at the higher degrees
and please you with my aspects.
for this, I will be grateful, as grateful
as any ephemeral taper can be.

secrets

within the corners
affixed to the walls of your soul
like a spiderling cocoon
behind the rosebushes
you keep your secrets
from me

in part out of practice
at keeping people at bay, away,
and in part to protect yourself
(a worthy purpose, I believe)
yet those filaments keep out
my love

I believe in you
and all the crazy kaleidoscope colours
you wear on the outside and in.
I believe that the eggs will hatch
one day, and let all the secrets out
to play

I don't care, really,
what they are, as I am beyond artifice,
beyond caring what is hidden,
so I will consider the websac
as I sit in the rosebushes
a test

maybe you are afraid.
afraid is bitch of a world has one more lash
to lay across your skin and grin at your pain
and I am to be the harbinger of it all
because I dare to want to protect, to
love you

but I am not a spider
nor a grand-daddy-longlegs, here to consume
the soft scented secrets in your web
as you wither with the contemplation.
I am here because you, secrets and all,
called me

ebb and flow

More than a year of Sundays, high and low,
the complexities vex us, hex us hot
and cold, primal emotions that run slow
in the flow of our day to day masques, caught
between pain and possibility, bright
with wonder. The epic epigram hides
unfulfilled kisses, near misses at night
when we play proxyfingers for our prides
that damn us and dam us, holding back deep
and thundering releases we deserve,
for we serve gods of passion and of sleep.
In dreams we find shadows of ev'ry nerve,
living our lives together in REM state,
but for the wet sustenance we yet wait.

tenacity

even when the surfaces are so cool to the touch
that I cannot find the sustaining heat to warm myself
and keep blood flowing through outer limbs,
I will find a way to cling, to hold, to endure,
for I am sure of your intentions, I trust that dust
is not regent in a world where you are alive.
alive and aware of all that you have before you
while I watch the sands recede from my days,
waiting, not wasting, unabated breath until death,
whispering only your name. and those sweet,
veiled obscenities you like to hear me whisper at night.

defiance

This is not a Jeremiad,
I have tears enough to shed, red
with the blood of friends and kin, sin
for me to think I have earned, burned
self immolative into true
flesh, drawn and quartered by mnemonic trick
that makes it all dynamic, sad...

come round

sundays come round
every seven days or so
just long enough for God
to remake the world
to start over and this time
make sure to get it right

we are by nature
rebirthers, craving second chances,
convinced that this time
we'll get it right. or at least
better than last time, faith
in ourselves compelling dreams.

every seven days
my calendar mocks me, when life
seems as far or further from me
than it was the day before.
I don't want to wait for next sunday.
but will, because I believe.

she comes..

she comes with the night
(dark corners playing metaphor
for those parts of her life she still shades
from my deepest scryings)
(walking on bare feet
unaccustomed to the rough stone
but treading so lightly)
(naked but for her dreams
that I would be a part of if she
would only come in the light)
(lover. friend. peer. I pretend
not to notice she hides the wreathes
behind her back, uncertain of me)
she comes with the night
(still weighing the virtues
that I present and represent,
the good man chasing the evil done)
(her hands are soft and warm.
her kisses are like raspberries in the sun.
her legs, toned and bold, gold to my base metal)
(her eyes burn me, turn me to stone
the better to enter her, what she allows,
more than skin, despite her words and wishes)
she comes with the night
(the chalice of my questing,
the legend I have spent a lifetime seeking,
just beyond my reach and beseeching words)
(invited savagery, she begs me
to consume her that I might exhume her
battered, bartered heart and desires)
(I am hers and in time, I hope,
she will be mine, claimed and proclaimed
by her lips and hips and the tips of her fingers)
she comes with the night

fang

I want to sink my fang deep inside you...
not to draw your blood, but to feed your appetites
as I fight to slake my thirst in tight trespass.
your lips, your flesh, your most perfect portals
for my mortal hunger, granted immortality
by your surrender and my words. I will use you
to your own pleasure and measure my delight
in your screams, matching my release
to the exact moment when you give up
you last barriers and let me bury myself
in a body that is mine to ravage, savage and possess.
drain me, pain me with unrelenting lust
for you and you alone. princess and ragdoll.
I will fill you with my essence and presence,
leaving artifacts of my existence inside you,
and in sticky white remembrances on body
and hands, to be tasted between courses
when you are impaled and breathless.
finding all the curious corners unfilled
and unfulfilled until you embrace the madness
of finally knowing what it is to let a poet love you.

the vacated shell

we have all lost, even the most callous.
sudden silence, the sound of nothingness
echoing in corners where we perceived life.
from celebration to the tearing down
of dreams and the trappings of joy.
you will smile again, but for now
permit yourself the fundamental luxury
of grief and the hollowing of dreams.
if you need anything, I am here for you,
willing to walk the miles and share
whatever is required, desired, to ease
a pain that I, as man, can only imagine.

stones...

the thirst for the rubies of your desire consumes me
in a fire like blood gone hypergolic with the sweat
of lovers' touch, such fire, such fire, my skin crisps
even hearing you in the hallways, not knowing
if this time you will open the door and come in
and lay with me until mourning finds my ashes.

if I am radiant, it is in the spessartite tiger eyes
that Byron lent me when I was spent with pain
and would have stood apart from my heart.
but for you. for you. the taste of a mandarin
on lips given to morsels and mould.

precious topaz. a clear light, a night
remembered wrong as it never happened.
but beautiful and perfect nonetheless.
I would gift you with a necklace of such stones,
each for a year of your love, falling between
your breasts to rest against me when we
explore the hidden aspects of our union.

as emerald as your soul. kisses beyond the dawn.
the smell of a forest after the rain, moss
and a trace of cinnamon, left behind to remind us
that we are not the only creatures who have dared
to walk these paths, even if displaced by decades.

I have sat on a throne in a hall of sapphires.
waiting for you. for it is your throne, not mine.
I have just been the placeholder, stealing seconds
from the inexorable clock that will defile and destroy me
long before you decide on what you want.

a nameless midnight stone. not ebon, but indigo,
holding secrets in its facets and flaws that I cannot pierce.
fierce protector of the nights you would have left,
but could not find the reason or the season to stand.
I will carry you from the night, if you but ask me to,
and I will fear no evil that may be locked within.

amethyst thirst, cursed and pursed like lips for a kiss.
we are here now, by your will alone, for I am not
capable of resisting your gravity. the royal essence of the sky
catches my eye and I will die, with or without you.
but I have my preference.

Gordius

King Gordius made knots
with ropes and madness,
challenging those who thought
they were smart enough to untie them
to earn his kingdom.
but some knots are not made to be
untied.
and thus Alexander himself
cut through the hemp with steel.
somedays I feel I am
Alexander.
other days,
Gordius.
and other days
just a man,
unworthy of mystery or legend.
or a kingdom.
but knots
persist.

in the end

in the end

I know the odds are impossibly long
that you and I shall ever kiss or touch.
impossibly long. but only the hopeless
find hope and only the most impossible
of all dreams are worth dreaming.

in the end

I hope to know the moment of my death
that I might speak your name one last time
and let the historians untangle the knot
that got and garroted me from within,
whimsy and sin and a tenderness recalled.

in the end

you may not even know I am gone, having long
ago set sail to other horizons, remembering me
only as a chapter in a book, a line in a poem.
not a life, a home, an existence you could ever
have bought into, have fought for, have held.

in the end

I won't surrender, this time. I have just enough
of the stiffer stuff left within me for one launch
from the highest of the towering precipices. my home
is not at rest, but in the climb and the fall
and perhaps those rare moments of Bernoulli's blessing.

in the end

my legacy will speak of you so loudly and proudly
that all the other emotions, as relevant as the seemed
when I dreamed of something perfect and passionate,
will be viewed in shades of grey and eggshell paint,
background noise lost in the lyrics of heaven.

in the end

clown feet

whose turn is it to walk with eyes
downcast
pretending we don't know each other
because there are those who would
mock us
even ourselves
for having the temerity to feel
whatever it is
we define it as
today

the lies pick at my eyes and blind me
bind me
to an irrational fairy-tale that I alone
must inhabit, as that much truth is mine
to claim
as I walk, faceless,
into an October wind, tripping
over pumpkin rinds
cast in my path
for sport

cauterize

I want to cauterize your heart,
burning the scars away with the Holy Water
of my loins, drawn in sacrament
through your perfect lips and hips.

exquisition

slow and meticulous. every pore cries out for more
and I am not one to deny a command from my lover
or her body or her soul that I should pour out
my flesh, my tears, my words, my dreams to weave
a tapestry of two fabrics, now intertwined such that
future generations will look upon it as an apogee
of two people standing beyond labels and fables.
I will kiss your scars and purify myself in your sweat.

thunderstorm

your fire, your fire, it fills the heavens
with light, with light, reported in the thunder.
you are the morning rain
you are the sky without a cloud.

you are, you are, a force of nature.
I dream, I dream, of no one more or equal.
and decades from now
I will harbour no regrets.

silent Sundays

struck enough, the crystal cracks and we are so fascinated
by the light that sparkles off the man-made flaws. we forget
and stand too close. the brisant report of the facets' fail
and we are showered with the razor splinters of our folly.
jolly good fun to the observers. but there is still a pulse,
deep within the core of this frame and I am not one given
to more than an acknowledgement of difficulties. blood and pain
are not reason or season to turn tail and run to the horizon.
battered, yes. bruised, yes. but even when the tethers slip
my grip on the headboard where you bound me with a promise...
remains. hurry home.

Again

I have found that I bleed
everyday. everytime. for the crime
of loving you. I confess my guilt
in this and grip the wooden handles
and taste the leather between my teeth
and mutter

"Again!"

And even the fates are beginning
to take notice of my persistence
as the lash comes down
in steady strokes
against my flesh, disused
to such torture.

"Again!"

I will die. Or you will dry my every tear
and bandage my wounds, one day.
But I will not recant what I know is true.
I will not worship false goddesses
with my soul and my flesh and my heart,
roaring in the flames

"Again!"

opus

the lens bends light, sometimes making colours from white,
sometimes making shadows a photic sibilance that dances
with the subtle eddies of air and ether.

the artist. the poet. the sculptor. the composer. all driven
by the light. not the light within them, but that which washes
over them, and through them, and out.

nothing is discerned without the light, the inspiration, the flash
of light and distant (often) thunder that shakes the world
and shapes the works of the creators.

the creators fight a war to liberate the soul that Sisyphus
would be happy to neglect and let the stone roll over him.
but we, you and I, are made of the lens.

or at least, I am, needing your fusion and fury to shine through,
barely feeling the heat that is the core of your existence,
but feeling nothing without it.

feather

pretty plumage. from the carnage rises the phoenix.
cool to the touch, an aspect such that I am near blinded
by the glory, the history of mystery made quick,
the flicker of snickering doubt for lesser witnesses.

a feather kept. and I have slept to dream dreams that heal me,
that will seal me and conceal me in my sarcophagus;
the lessons learned, the flesh unburned by self-definition.
a friendly womb that becomes tomb if no room left to fly.

this path

the presence of your flesh is commanded, demanded,
as evidence of your heart, broken but spoken for,
more token than you may care to barter for my offerings.

I have, at times, no faith in the future, and maintain hope
like a rope over an impossible drop, not daring to look
in fear the fear itself will rob me of my will and I fall.

in other times I am given to hope that even within my box,
locked and stocked beneath the daily masques I am denied,
that inside things are well, and I am not a condemned man.

I chose this path and keep my choice to voice my will,
but this world and you are not malleable to my wishes,
and I will, most probably, find this a trail of tears.

a prisoner, even by his own request, in time finds his bars
a part of his self-definition and would not flee if he could,
for he sees good in that which others pity and mock.

this improbable emerald

this improbable emerald, a stone
that is alive with the essence of dreams.
plucked from the sky by reflex to atone
for past hesitancies, it almost seems
as if all other precious gems were but
place-markers, just holding open my soul
that there would be an assured place, cut
into my spirit, a patient, pure hole
requiring only a crystal of light,
worthy and warm, beautiful and fitting
as though my life was made for the night
when all things would transcend time, suffering
to calm my sad heart and wake elation
as the touch of divine consecration.

fingertips

I have stared at the unfeeling ceiling,
lost in the possibility of you.
Your voice, hovering like the morning mist,
cool and dense upon my skin, fingertips
tracing every thought I have caught here,
asking for your love when you are many
miles away. A seventeen hour drive.
Nine hundred and eighty miles if I grew
wings from my hope and desire and rode winds
to where you sit, even now, with a smile
upon your perfect lips that you cannot
explain to those with you, for I am not
yet a part of your presence, a future
that may or may not come to be, we'll see.
Craving the possibility of you.

perihelion

the sunlight comes at an aberrant angle
through the tangled limbs of the tree
I keep promising to trim back a bit
when it scrapes against the side of the house
at night
when the wind blows

you are curled up, phone in hand,
talking to a friend of indeterminate identity
but whose presence in your life
obviously brings you joy
and someone to talk to besides this old
sour sobersides who sometimes
sometimes
is playing Casca to your Titania
but loves you, nevertheless

your eyes, half-lidded, except when you laugh
when they spring open like traps
to draw in the evening light
and my soul, punctuated with a sudden
and earnest sigh, lost in your beauty
and the life you share with me
that makes me content, for the moment,
to just stand and look with awe.
captured in your orbit
like the sun.

bleeding

you're bleeding into me
even when far away and the day...
well, the day
is not cooperating very well.

we've both seen Hell.
you, perhaps, more vividly,
but that doesn't mean Orpheus
isn't ready to shake the status quo
when you say "go"
and the decades of experience
find their relevancies in you
and all that you want from me.

you're going to get mad at me
and turn away, at times,
when you just want to be alone,
far from my complex chaos and kisses.
and that will be okay
because there will be days
when I too am too human
and Apollo wants a cloudy day.

but, above it all, please stay,
perhaps in time settling your orbit
as a bit less elliptical
so I know what my heart already knows:
that you are going to be a presence
for the rest of my life.
friend, partner, lover, wife (if I am lucky)
but you will be there when my eyes close

every night. and even into the long night.
and that's the way I want it to be.
I've demanded little, asked not much more,
but given you everything I can.
this is the measure of love, the pleasure
of surrender, even to a dominant role
if that is what is called for by your mood,
by necessity, for you are that mother.

you're bleeding into me.
I see your image in memories you could not
have had a part in, but there you are,
a ghost of beautiful possibilities

correspond

I say you are beautiful, and I mean in ways I have seen.
the eyes of a lover, the smile of an angel, the grace of a dancer.
but also in ways I have not seen in form or soul of others,
you are unique to my heart. unique and beautiful.

I say you are brilliant and I mean your intellect radiates
both heat and light, enough that, were I never born,
you would still be capable of outshining the lesser suns
that dot the night and make us wonder at their nature.

I say that you are a miracle, and there is proof enough
in your beauty and brilliance and passion and smile
that I have found a strange tranquility in my dreams
and hope sand prayers and purposes, as they are of you.

erotic

my hands touch
the small of your back
and feel the way
your spine moves
a secondary core
to my impaling join
where we merge
our expressive bodies
seeking comfort
and pleasure
and an annunciation
of something passing
more than mere fluids
shared as a statement
of desire
meaning more
than either of us
would ever dare to say
aloud
although sometimes
sometimes
when you say my name
at the moment you feel me
release inside you
as you surrender sanity
to the mad thunder
of your own delight
it comes close
and we come together

cleaving to the past

I remember the summers when the sky was alive
and fire was magic, the spring peepers sang
just for me, reassuring me that nothing malign
was coming across the water as I slept.

The miracle of innocence, water and ice
transubstantiating in my cupped hands, breath
turning to rabbit fleece clouds in the dawn.
The cool bedroom over the converted garage.

I am still there, bound in the wood and tile.
I still sit at the massive dining room table
and argue my point in politics or theology
with family I remain close to, that will love you.

For they have been with me through the years
and cannot help themselves but love someone
who loves me and makes me happy as you do.
And they will share summer skies, alive with dreams.

nourish

without flourish
you nourish me
with your beauty.
you don't have to try
to be my greatest muse.

you just are.

I accepted that fact
and every act
loses the purpose
of the pose
that once was so important.

you just are

the radiant point of light
that summons the metaphors
and the eloquence
that time will not quench.
for your nourish me.

you just are

more than the sum of your parts,
your pouting lips
soft hips and dark eyes
that burrow into me.
you are the well of my dreams.

arcitexture

you said it.
I heard it.
and I believe.

not in the moment,
but the four dimensional
construct of my soul.

lives merged:
a house on the edge of a great vista
where you can see the sun
rise in the East
and set in the West.
memories filling the canyons
slowly, inexorably.

topsoil memories that cover
each past pain and lover
we'd rather forget
while letting the seeds of joy
find root and flower.

the rain comes at night and washes
the gullies clean of darkness
so that in the morning
when I bring you your chai
and sit at your feet
after brushing aside your bedroom hair
just long enough for a quick kiss
the world is new and all things
seem possible
because they are.

we are proof of the beauty of improbable things.

you let slip your heart
just long enough for me to see it
and like some unique miracle
in a fountain in an old villa
that melts the scales from the eyes
of old beggars and pilgrims.
you illuminated my soul.

and yes, I love you, too.

raw

the pain is pure and it merges with the surging rain.
I live within the shadows seeking for your stain.
I watch the world fall away and yet I remain,
raw, but resolute.

there's a freedom in the way we come together,
feathers in the hurricane, buffeted forever
before the fury of our natures, surrendering never,
raw, and absolute.

waiting for the harvest, the chance to make my case,
the dance, the chance, a stance to leave more than a trace
when the morning comes, a claim made everyplace,
raw, all doubts made mute.

sand

unfathomable, midnight blue skies
peering with a billion flickering eyes
at us, curious of our trespasses tender
on the sand, hands champion and defender
of hearts surrendered to a truth higher
and purer than mere hunger and desire.

Miss Vickers

to the purpose, the wick burned down
and Miss Vickers' flame faded
in a night so long that no one
knew when the wind blew it out

just cold wax and scattered memories
of a greater arc, a common spark
that was fanned, then in bland and bleak
shadows accepted the inevitable

will my eulogy read as well
that no one knew for as much as a year
that I lay, surrounded by memories
that are inelegant effigies of love?

Miss Vickers got one last headline.
maybe not the best of words, but mine

will probably fare little better.
after one last flickering wick.

Aphrodite reigns

Aphrodite reigns
despite what war gods wish were true
love transcends the sword
passions bind us more than chain

Aphrodite reigns
the scent of jasmine, warming flesh
stealing will away
taking champions to her side

Aphrodite rules
fools deny this to their regret
soft lips and callipygian hips
conquer me to my delight

chalice

our desires will coincide, our passions intersect.
my need to feed will not be denied, you'll slide me in you,
to measure fantasies that are suddenly pale, correct
only in the dancers who weave the grievous healings through
touch and whispers of dark necessities, perfection bound
in the texture of me inside you, taking and giving
flesh and fluids, sweet and intimate, memories resound.
the death of solitude, rude and raptured, captured living
to be made our sanctified and consummated promise
to each other, lovers in word and deed, indeed, my seed
is more than just in thrusted flesh and pulsing, heated kiss
where you take deep draught of me, as your suckling flesh now bleeds
me as a covenant of my devotion, your name a curse and prayer
as I pulse into you, chalice for all that we dare share.

the cards are dealt

the cards are dealt and the verdant felt
lays grass beneath our blossoming fortunes.
spades turning earth, uncovering diamonds,
gnarled club-like roots and our own hearts,
parted from us by the disease that is pain.

one more hand, I ask you. just one more chance
to see if I have learned enough to tough it out
and wager my will against the whims of liars
for whom virtue is an effigy and we are fair game.
turn the cards, I am not afraid of damnation.

the scandal of our touch

your hands invoke the scandal of our touch,
measuring and pleasuring me to your desire.
fire, higher than any herb or turbulent adrenaline
could invoke, provoke, concentration unbroken
by soft lips that taunt and haunt and tease,
blinding me with your rituals of binding,
finding me properly prepared for your hunger,
strung taut to enter taut sweetness, deep to sweep
away, to dispel, doubt and darkness. impalement
to a capture of a rapture beyond spiritual,
riding this horseman of our apokalypsis
as I am made hoarse calling your name
and my body slides ever deeper, like my heart.

I kiss your scars

I kiss
your scars

to heal
myself

and you.
the taste

of you
is sweet.

dancing
on lips

that are
for you.

as I
take you

and kiss
your scars

I vow
that I

will ne'er
cut you

out of
malice

but out
of love.

I kiss
your scars.

fleur de lis

the tender petals draw me in to drink deep the nectar,
honey unconcentrated, raw from the natural source,
a wine divine, shared in a most sensuous surrender.
the cup is passed to me and I drink my fill, this sweet course
an aphrodisiac to my mortal restraint, so kind
you are to bind me to you, like Persephone, a taste
holding me in thrall to the beauty you bid me to find
in gentle fantasy and words that spread wide, undisgraced,
to draw into narrow corridors of sacrifices
we both would make in time and temptation, embracing each
petal touched and pistil-whipped in past shadows, the prices
of our curious centers, our passionate cores that teach
us what we need to know to be reborn in innocence.
beauty in all things, made of the fleur de lis' scent and sense.

eschatology

seeking kairos. apokalypsis slips through lips,
spilling into the wind, thinned thoughts brought forth to curl
like prayers of smoke in the cold night winds. the veil rips
and revelations become ambient and random, the stones that hurl
against the battlements of our esteem, pounding
like a fist of the vulcan gods long forgotten.
I have sworn devotion, emotion and sounding
of the syllables of odd, ancient religion
that denies us our lies, spoken in fear as we kneel
before idols forced on us, coerced against us
by the evil of others that smothers the real
in a fog, demagoguery, lying onus
for the sins we can seal, heal and mend, not pretend
this is not a cruel world. but ally to transcend.

Hispaniola

when the sun touches the sky with ardent fingers
the blue of sea smiles and laps the sand with designs
no less than mine for you. I wish I was with you,
making sand angels in the middle of the night.
but I send the sun as my proxy, to kiss your thighs
and remind you that I am always, even at midnight,
a memory worth remembering, leaving tan lines
only if you want them, for I would rather touch
everything and all that makes up the incredible you.
a discovery more profound than any by Columbus.

virgins

all true frontiers are for the tears.
fear and trepidation. new sensation
and an awareness of a purpose in words
you'd heard before. more than skin.

finding the colours in the blinding light,
the knight rides to the horizon and melts,
content in the convent of your affections,
where God is more than ritual release.

peace is in you. that, and the winds of change,
strange times that rearrange your skirt
in pillow billows. slip me in, entranced
by the dance you and I have just begun.

virgins, sacrificed and priced beyond emeralds.
heralds of a dawn we thought gone in shallow
pools of light and delight that were a semblance
of the remembrance we will take from this night.

Sunday is more than the day of rest for deities.
it frees me to please you, however long in coming.
you are poetry. and you flow through me like blood
to form sigils in squiggles at fingertips pressed.

let us untangle the knots that others wove
to bind us to the Earth, to find us lesser roads
than we were meant to walk so that they may own
a nugget of the sun, burnt too pure for mortal touch.

illuminati

you rise in the sky and I,
I am surrendered to your radiance.
the arrogance of lovers that hover
at the edge of the precipice,
missing nothing but the kissing.
pieces of a puzzle in space,
facing only that which we perceive,
we relieve as we relive the fall
that calls us all in hallowed crack!
the shattering of our light to make
stained glass of what has passed,
the illumination exercises.

you climb to the zenith and I,
I am burned and spurned and turned
from flesh to phantom and back again.
you come to me in love and I wait,
fated to stay in orbit about your heart.
part of me a skyrocket socket
into which we put our dreams, promises
we will keep, if only in our sleep
as we weep tears over fears that shadow
proud and pretty trust, the crust is crushed
and prayers are hushed by the heretics
with their word tricks and cowardices.

you glide to the horizon and I,
I am content that I will dream of you.
true to my word. cured of the absurd
that cannot be put into simple songs
that are the hymnals of the pale pilgrims.
slim chances and dances of the arabesque,
I must confess my sins to you and ask grace,
that I may face the quiet hours empowered
to consider you as you lay your head
on my chest and ask my allegiance and love.
yes. for tomorrow you will rise. climb. fall.
from my sight, but there is an illumination beyond light.

blood in my veins

while there is blood in my veins, it is for you.
whether to keep alive my heart and mind
to bind the universe to your wants and needs,
or to feed you when you are frail and fail
and the morning sun burns you deeply
and you require sustenance given in course,
without remorse, and in love. yes, love.
unconditional, married to hope, carried
in the crimson, rich, sweet flow you know
I will never refuse you, never choose to
place for my own sanity or life, in vanity,
above your safety and comfort and peace.
the release of my life, liquid white or red
on which you fed in bed or stead, stains
your lips and slips me more inside you.
while there is blood in my veins, it is for you.

the sunday girl is all right

sunday has both day and night
and that's all right
as that is how the world turns
one face to the sun
the other into the cold contemplations
but the dawn follows the night
and that's all right
for the Sunday Girl lives
in both fire and shadow
the dark and the light
and that's all right
as that is part
of what makes her worthy of love.

purpose

I'm supposed to be there
when the clouds are dark
and the heaven's spark
is full of chaos and thunder.
I'm supposed to be there
holding you to your need
helping you to succeed
in all that you care or dare.
I'm supposed to be there
to be your champion
your banner of the sun
over every bastard nightmare.

base metals

we are made of the base metals, denied,
in the ancient defeat the heat captures the light
and makes malleable our real purpose and pride.
our faith in our self and our passions shields the knight
from the rabble of pain. but we are slow sometimes,
brutality has made it inside our shelled steel
and traps it in, rending in us the crimes
against soft eyes and trusting hearts, until we feel
ourselves as imprisoned by a deep pain
we have no hope ever to purge, courage
alone not cinnabar to draw from us the stain
of a silver less than living. we wage
the wars of the pained past on the bleak battlefield,
leaving our alchemies irrelevant, unhealed.

elemental

you are the very air I breathe
(your breath)
the holy water that purifies me
(your sweat)
the philosopher's stone that transforms me
(your body)
the tongue of fire that immolates
(your kiss)

all in a single alchemy of hope

the madness of devotion

better I should weather this storm, the warm
and the raging rains stain me colourless.
if I keep my silence, none will inform
what I have seen and been in my loveless,
lifeless internment, dead and set, at last
as a monument to those who believed the words
the argent sergeant spoke and broke when cast
at undesired, uninspired birds
that flew around the sky, restless, nestless,
seeking a place to land. tired, the wings
that bring me to this roost, nevertheless
it is not my place to remain, and sings
the subtle sirens that could never drown
Odysseus, but their songs draw me down.

broken souls in the shadows

you take offense
but none was given

looking for hatred in kindness

the world has you beat like a dog
and you snap your yellow jaws
at any unfortunate who offers you a bone

fleas and disease, you do as you please,
a broken record token of other cruelties
the futility of the damaged and the damned,
slammed hard and left for dead
and only your body got back up

cast aside

if ever you should

cast   me   aside

don't feel guilty or mourn.
for I died
the minute I became aware
that you were in the universe
and were aware of me.

for as Moses was blasted
by the merest glimpse of Yahweh
and Dionysius' mother was

i m m o l a t e d

by the countenance of Zeus
so was I blasted apart
when I felt your heart
beating in my hallowed, hollowed chest.

mortal men
should avoid the divine

the art

masquerade charades that have played their part,
the memories indelible and dark.
you lay against me, listening for my heart.
knowing while it beats, efforts hit their mark
and all the arrogance of the fates fades.
we can connect and strike the Leyden spark,
storing our light and heat to illume shades
that are not empowered now that we arc.
our energies magnify our passions,
touch and words and hearts that open their eyes
to light bright the darkness like merg'd suns,
take for ourselves what cowardice denies:
stronger bound together than held apart
we find our hopes revealed in lovers' art.

peace

let go the jagged, ragged strain
that batters you in day and night.
trust me to shield you from the pain
with tender prayers and warm delight.

fusion

I'm waiting.

maybe for nothing. a pascal's wager
that was just too long and the song

ends

with friends who forgot something
they had said to one another
in another time, the rhyme and meter
petering out like a stream in the desert.

I'm waiting.

a jolly folly. passing on sure things
without the strings that tangle me

up

in my brain chemistry made alchemy
by the right word on the right lips
calling me to follow a hollow path
into the shadows, where my light is mocked.

I'm waiting.

second choice, even my voice is in the gulag.
try everything, you said. but I won't usurp your

will

as that kills my soul and then you are back
at square one with the merchants of flesh
and fantasy and it would be up to me
to play the noble and crucify myself for a lie.

I'm waiting.

the hours into days and nights into weeks
and months, perhaps years and then you one day

wake

and say it is time to crack open the casket basket
where my bones are all that is left, drained
of life but scrimshaw with the runes of memory
to sell to those who never knew my grief and relief.

I'm waiting.

infrared

get in bed and spread I said
the lights are fading fast
skillfully make quick of the dead
a conqueror wyrm against the past

you are so tight and the heat is sweet
that draws me deeper yet
baptize me, for your fantasy complete
when you feel my sudden sweat

every thrust an offered charity
of what no one could ever earn
a sacrifice of boiling ice, free
to sublimate in a radiant burn

pillow talk is not the walk, yet,
when you speak of your need to feed
I am sealed like a bridegroom set
to the wedding bed, pledging his seed

waiting

I should not be standing here on my own.
For the efforts I have not dared to spare
I have earned at least some mercy be shown
from rude solitudes to which I seem heir.
I have no memory of your soft touch.
No perfumed card to mark for me your smile.
I am made new, in Pascal's wager such
that I cannot my passions reconcile.
Yet I remain here in these vacant halls,
prophet to a passion I won't deny.
Dancers come, cast their veils in hungry calls,
to lay with them would be heretic's lie.
So let the dancers entertain the priest
as he burns incense, awaiting the feast.

attrition

fire. ice. stone. steel.
and all the killing tools we conceal.

it's not a game to those with skin in it,
attrition only to the eroding soul.
no buttresses or champions guard as each bit
gets carried away, carrion taken from the whole
so that, should the reanimation occur,
it is a patchwork abomination that remains,
tottering on unsure legs, unsure
of anything but the energies of the pains
of the wounds of the lash of a shaded vow,
kept in vain, the rein of rain, saline
and sinister. living for a future, but now
is where the pieces populate the board, seen
as an abstraction but by those who bleed,
those who need, and those who concede the seed.

liberati

eros over chronos. kairos be damned.
jammed. slammed. the jammed doorways
playing with my mind, I find my way
on the low ways, beneath the roses.
private conversations, confessions and such.
kisses in the silence, malevolence and yet
the wet communicates well between amomancers.
yes, there is another, unconsecrated,
but not the lesser of the dreamers.
when my seed bleeds white inside you
will you take the last of my power and flower
like a sacred blossom, risen from earth
to stalk the walkways between the states
of legend and desire. fires that never tire
of our inhaling the smoke of broken chains,
stains we wash away in naked glory, transcending
the rote rot and cardboard boxes of complacency.
I priest is released for the feast and refuses
to be locked away again. freed, indeed, in need.

merged

sweet and tender. mender of my heart.
player of her part you are the dance
and the dancer, the angel as your warm wings
wrap about me and lift me into heaven.
the steady beat of them as we blend
into a single merged entity.
the perfect strain and pain
of what connects us, flesh for faith.
the wraith takes form and warm wine
fills you in every way you ask.
the task is a blessing, confessing
how much I need to bleed inside you.
hold me aloft as I find my way into you
as you already did into me.
call my name in stunned revelation
when the circuit is closed
and we see the purpose in the pattern
as we rest in furious and curious acceptance.
and I feel your breath and heart
as you part and take all I have.

dreamcatcher

what a blessing to, at last,
end my day in the way that feels
like a transition from stress to rest.
to play dreamcatcher to you.
curling you in my arms
and feeling your last waking breaths
as a warm, subtle breeze
on my skin.
as you surrender to the night,
knowing the darkness
holds only the comfort
of knowing I am there
for you. and only you.
to hear you sigh
as you snuggle against me
and close your eyes,
mischief perhaps on your mind
and in your grind against me,
but nonetheless a loving thing
as I bat away sorrows
and cradle you in my life.

vernal

your presence, even in the virtual, in my life
is like the sun in spring, awakening the seeds
that had spent wasted time in dormant torment,
aching to reach with live tendrils towards you,
to entwine their designs into your existence
and satisfy their need to please you with tender
growth, persistent and resistant to doubt.
you are the light of my existence. the reason I wake.
believe in me and I will bring the seasons back.

I have found a way

to stop my heart

to steal and seal pain
and all pleasure

bricked up, sealed away
so that when you

want it, it will be
as it should be

yours, without a doubt
without the taint

of stranger's handprints
on my soft gift

and all other things
the come with it.

wet

string again your cithara, the wet frets
making sweet music against my fingers,
proxy for the penetration, glissando.
wrap legs and arms about me, whisper or shout,
draw me in, the sin of skin is in denial:
wasted hours, days, years, when I should have
pressed the suit to stare into your eyes
as I enter you, center us on a communion
of flesh and fluids, the druids of a new religion,
built on sacraments of shared urgency.
a claim of a promised life, built on fire
that rises within you as I lose myself
in your tight, sweet, wet core and release
a sacrifice of my own flesh, to fill
you to the lips of wordless wonder, thunder
of your lightning. kissing in chaos
where our bodies are merged avatars of love.
I will hear you call my name without shame
as you shudder and surrender the final gates,
waiting no more for a moment that would not come
if you did not need me so much in this moment
that I feel the rhythm of your heart
in every curve and corner, sworn to me,
born to be mine, as I am deep and yours.

Abaddon

in dark and sparked glimpse we fight our fears.
moments now turn to days and decades raged,
the passions that pass into legends, tears
of the first kiss, we miss the bliss we caged
that time still holds hostage, uncertain prayers
we speak, sotto voce, we hide until
we kill the essence of dreams and nightmares
that once we shared, a birth made still and chill
in the pale pick and flaw, hearts elastic
to pull and pinch of barriers rising.
the guard is hard and stands erect to stick
fist in the air and defiantly sing
anthems of anathema and the fold
fabrics we wrap ourselves in against cold.

into a neon sun

when I am
falling
fading away
into a neon sun
the apple blossom yellows
go to gold and then to crimson
their fragrance on me lost
until the next time I breathe...
the world is cold
but for those moments
when we stop reacting to the shadows
and step to the light
I am not used to living in the darkness
and my blood drips so slowly
it just can't be right...
so I will sleep in silent memory
of things that may never come to pass
and I will dream of sanity
that feeds the vanity of the victims
and the cruelty of the past

embrace

tonight I held you. long past the chimes that separate the days.
and nothing separated us. not fate or faith or fear. it was clear
that we fit, like a short stack of runcible spoons, edges and bowls
nested to take up the most practical space, to not offend the gods,
who looks for unfitted mittens as a sign of mischief to be made.
you stirred, more than once. asking for a drink of water, a kiss,
to tell me you had a bad dream and I needed to make you smile.
I told you a joke, badly, but you laughed, anyway, at my intentions.
you were warm, and your curves felt good against me, too good.
but you needed comfort and rest and not the charge of passion.
time enough for that later, when you are stronger and surer
and I would not feel like a thief for claiming you.
tonight I held you. and I haven't let you go. and won't.
you made me promise that, once, and vows do not fade like dreams.

the fissures form in the night

risen from a prison, the prism tilts and splits the light.
soul cage raging, the phage in phases putrefies the dream
and we. no. not we. me. I stand, the precipice my place.
defiant to the last as I cast myself the martyr.

morsels and mould

on these rocks I lay myself down.
bones shattered.
grey matter spattered
like fingerpaint in a nursery-school fight.
the night
is no longer my friend.
it is my lover.
covering me with kisses
that miss the mark
but spark
at least some awareness
that I am
by some definitions
still alive.

sacrifices

twigs and leaves
thrown on the fire.
small sacrifices of things
already dead.
lifeless.
given to make light
and heat
even in the middle
of the longest night.
you wonder at my sacrifices.
how much have others done
for love?

yes, love.

I am autumn into winter.
you are spring.
I have seen the cost
of an ill-prepared season.
reason and rationale.
I have seen things.
done things.
been things.
I have won and lost.
paid the costs
you can only imagine
until the sacrifices
make the smoke
that breaks the boundaries
and you accept me
as I am.

as I have, you.

transcend

rise above the timestream.
dream in eclectic arcs,
sparks that we are made of,
afraid of in our own passion.

fashion me an idle idol of clay,
play the princess to my touch.
much will pass between us tonight
to the light we are drawn now.

on flowers we are each petal,
mettle forged in true fires,
desires we hold at arm's reach,
teaching us the essential touch.

such is the conundrum of love.
gloved spinster spiders weaving,
leaving traps, prophylaxis
to tax us of our own restraints.

the taints of memories, chains
and stains that drain our joy,
croix at the crossroads. I wait,
hating the waiting. but here for you.

fitting

it is a fit feast, the golem released to find
the binding unwinding inside, with pride. I tried
to discover what was to come, and it was you.
you blew through and found your place, within me, fitting
like a glove of softest lambskin on roughened hands.
the hermit quitting his isolation without
hesitation, to answer a request for peace.
a victory still just over the horizon,
but so real we taste it in moments we've stolen
like Jean Valjean with a crust of bread, a step
on a path to a place we will face together,
whether we rise or fall on satin or on stone,
I've years to atone in the gardens of idols
that were not you, perfect and precious, I open
the windows and the sun rises on cue, and you
are Helios, Ra and inspiration to law
greater than the politic of fools. Passion rules
and we bow to authority we surrender,
my tender and patient friend, bend me to your needs
and the seeds of my heart and flesh are yours.
I am saving all my misbehaving for you.

in the hour

I alone shall mourn my passing.
I alone shall know the hour
when the flower fades to wasting
and the fragrance, sweet to sour.

when the petals fall

will you wait for me
when the petals fall
and the earth becomes
a triumphant wall
that seals away
our heart's desire
consuming love
in a funeral pyre

will you wait for me
when the rivers die
and there is no grass
there is not sky
when the memories fade
and tongues are dried
and we all have crossed
the bright divide

I will wait for you
though the aeons fade
and there is no voice
for a serenade
and the flesh that touched
seems a masquerade
every earnest thought
now a fool's parade

I will wait for you
and you'll see me there
I will bring an halo
for your hair
understanding
kairos, after all,
Gotterdammerung
and the quantum fall

but I wait for you
in a modest scale
with a lover's smile
and a martyr's tale
never asking much
but I promise true
I will wait for you
I will wait for you

I will live in this world

the flowers did not fall this year
but held on for dear life in the autumn winds.
I have no explanation for this
but would not for the world tempt fate
by plucking them off by my own hands
out of a sense of restoring the proper order.

I will live in the world that is around me.
I will kiss only the lips presented to me.
I will look away at the folly of cowards and fools.
I will live in this world.

Valentine

I am sitting here, beside you,
even though yet miles away.
I have such a need to touch you
and so many words to say
that I can't get them all out.
I can't be certain what you hear
is what I am trying to tell you
and is getting through, and clear.

I've got to say that
every day is a just for you,
in the words that I am speaking,
in all the things I do
be they prayers of intercession
for your safety or your peace
or be they laboring to make for you
a life of fond release.

I have little I can offer
beyond passion and my pain
and a knack for casting magicks,
with the words that rise, refrain
of some strange celestial choir
that projects the light you give
to this pilgrim of your passion,
wishing in your sphere to live.

converging

your smile. no, the merest thought of your smile,
fills me with a sense of joy and delight.
you are light and warmth and genius, no guile
but that which is essential, ebon bright
is your presence, slow, inevitable.
the nature of a seduction in space.
converging lines in the distance, stable
chaos as a quantum shift, in my place,
a vector to merge at velocities
relativistic, natural to us
to move so swift gravitons cannot seize
and tear us apart, light passes through us.
we are free to plot our own horizon.
seeking a far point from a colding sun.

exiles

in life
we are all exiles
from what we want and need.
we bleed
our prayers on knees
torn and scraped, striving
to stand
against the shadows
and the inconvenient gods
that fight
us at every turn.
let them come, I am ready for them.
for you.
when you are ready.
as I have seen redemption in your arms.
and I
will make the seven years
worth every moment and near miss.

I live among the rocks

chaotic landscape.
sulphureous and stony.
I chose this ring of Hell.
constant ache and thirst
such that even my own thickening sweat
feels like a Spring shower
in the desert of dreams and dramas.

I live among the rocks.
sacred cinnabar and pitchblende.
fingers raw and skin scored and scorched.
not even recognizable as a man
to any but those who watched
the transfiguration, who demanded it
as proof of fealty and passion.

lesser beings play in the grass,
passing time, unmindful of me,
an abomination of twisted guilt and sorrows.
the rugged limestone is my bed.
the sound of an ancient wind
if my lullaby, defying silence.
it makes me wonder.

I am curious how long a man twists
himself into a contorted mockery of himself
before the change is permanent
or the pain makes him stand, screaming
as the bones and muscles and flesh
realign themselves, tearing and cracking.
the price of failed commitments.

I live among the rocks.
it is not beautiful here. I am not,
for I am alone and hungry and cold.
the night sweeps in like a plague of sand,
ripping my flesh and leaving me
malformed. how ironic that by choice
my voice becomes a death rattle.

you smile in candlelight

I want to hold your hand
and watch the sun rise and set,
though not necessarily in that order.
See you smile in candlelight
and the final vision of the night
being the purse of your lips
as you blow the flame away
with the essence of your life.
I want to feel the cool sheets
as they cloak us, invoke in us
the comfort of an embrace,
face to face, no trace of disgrace.
For you are my life and death.
My love, my light, my night.
You are the scent of ocean winds,
and the hope of the morning light.

Mythology, theology

You wake me, make me touch the sky
with your lambent, cinnamon soul.
Dreams and nightmares I can't deny
you have sown deep, and made my goal
to see you rise, that all this light
will ignite the world in your name.
I have seen, in your gentle night
the worthy purpose for my flame.
Incandescent, a fantasy,
perfect, erotic and sublime.
Mythology, theology,
a passion past all space and time.
I know this much, for sure, as true:
I want to build a life with you.

consort

I am not here just for seasons, reasons
christened in glistening remembrances.
You called, I came, a tame consort, treasons
against better judgment, the dark dances
left in their grey, the light, delight to find
such a sweet mind, shining in the divine
transfiguration of soft lips and kind
surrenders of pink and the warm, white wine
you asked, you tasked me to only to you.
I assented, prevented pretenders
to a throne you took to all too well, true
to your nature, the regent remembers.
I am consort to the passion you share,
ready to receive all that you would dare.

rage and defiance

God or gods, what are the odds? Long, it is certain,
but I will play my role well before the curtain
falls to sever my soul from the bittersweet sky
that roars and scores sores into my flesh as I try
one final time to bring the thunder, arrogant bones
into an objectionable object lesson
for the last of the poets, the pyres miss one,
death becomes a chess game on a celluloid beach
the tender surrender just out of dreamers' reach.
the cold sands are argent goads of the broken faith.
I am warm to the touch, but still the ghoul, the wraith,
left to shuffle and paw through all the lonely bones
of lovers that lost their catechism to stones
of the infinite mobs of the thick heretics
who still want so little beyond the word that light
is anathema as they swallow the cold night.

Cairo

January brings
the thoughts of revolution
back to the cradle.

deep, deep

make to me your confessions
that I may take my fill
of all the trespasses
when your hunger is such the grille
of this box is frail veil
and will fail against your heat,
sweet and the defeat of doubts
as you speak your true name
and I claim wicked corners
deep, deep inside you
even when you sleep.
deep, deep inside you
where my flesh shall weep
fluid and flesh
leaving behind the ancient mind
that you may think upon it
as you drink with lips and hips
that slip away to consider
whether I am worthy of your sacrifice
and the indulgences
of your redemption,
unbinding me from purgatory
to ravish, ravage and savage you
in the name of love.
deep, deep inside you
gliding to the precipice.
deep, deep inside you...
the altar of my sacred worship.

Pavillons

passing horizons
piercing the dark
stripped to the essence
of the beauty so stark
finding the colours
condemned to the light
bleeding to ashes
when left to the night

you will wake in the morning
to find I am still there
smiling with the mysteries
as I touch your dark hair
lost to the finding
bound with a kiss
claiming surrender
with a perfecting bliss

hold me for giving
forgiveness for doubt
keep me within
from being without
your brilliance and beauty
your fire and ice
the value of my angel
beyond virtue or vice

flowers for your hair

Crocuses peak out
and ask me my intentions!
A life, together.

commitment cell

I examine my cell.

the walls are smooth, hastily constructed
of beeswax and rare barks peeled from baobab trees.

fragrant like
honeysuckle,
magnolia and,
of course,
night-blooming jasmine.

they give slightly to the touch,
soft like your breasts.
there is an eroticism to them.

I press against them,
the palpable texture
communicating echoes of voices,
like at a distance.

I do not press hard enough
to break through,
for that might be arrogant
and seen as a broken promise
I made, more than once,
to stay where I am put
until told I am either free
or you come for me
or I am executed for my impertinence
in loving you.

yes, I am hungry.
hungry in so many ways
that were I speak of them
you would burn with an alien heat.

thirsty, as well,
for the wet sustenance
that seems forever in a lost grail,
spoken of in occasional scriptures.

and the solitude.
ever, the solitude.
there are moments when the grief
you speak of is a material thing
like wet, clogging mud,
drowning me and filling my eyes,
my ears, my mouth.
I have wept from it, and found strength
in waking up so many mornings
when I had prayed for death.
I have never known anything so crushing,
so suffocating.

so purifying.

the doors are unlocked, I know.
but I promised I would stay here.
I am told you would suffer
if I were to turn my face to the light
and walk out into the courtyard,
even though you have told me
that you would understand.

that is not my way.
I am not some happy hour suitor.
I am the prisoner of my heart
and of yours.
patiently waiting the denouement.
for whether this ends
tragedy
or
comedy,
coronation
or
martyrdom
this is more true
than anything
anyplace
anywhere
anyone
I have ever been.

and I will lay, my face pressed
to the walls you have given me
and smile softly as I weep
and listen for your voice
a thousand miles away.

permafrost

sometimes all hearts sleep,
deep beneath the permafrost,
pain denied is held,
shelled in crusts of frozen mud,
but as kairos comes
the warmth, it liquifies our souls.
though lies deny our faith
we rise to crack the bitter earth.
rebirth is inevitable.
sometimes rest is all we need,
embracing penetrative cold
that pains, but never kills the seed.

dancing with the coconuts

that was not a promise made lightly
for a binding, just nightly,
or an awareness, so slightly,
of my heart in your hands.

enfolded

that dreams may come and, at length, have their chance
I will wait until long after the dance
and hope you saw me, standing to one side,
eyes averted, that you can't see the pride
I have in you, still fighting for rebirth,
against the pain of this immutable earth.
I will not press my suit except for here,
where words weave tapestries, but will be clear
that I am keeping word and vow to you.
my presence is consistent, my heart, true,
and I will find my way, even in grey
moods, lost conversations. not fade away.

TITANS

more than mortals
we can manipulate
the very ether.
pulling light and thought
into hot liquid glass.
wards and swords, the cords
of the umbilicus of God.
hammering with fists
that Hephaestus would've envied
as we fashion our passions
into the immortal tools
of warriors and lovers.
the covers that hover
against the friezes.
the diseases of our hesitancies,
the dependencies of the triptychs.
the power that picks and sticks
like primordial matter, tar pits
where the memories are held
for future generations.
we are the colour summoners.
we are the light weavers.
we are the thought warriors.
we are the titans who retake Olympus.

miracle

tears of a saint ain't nothing but pale brine,
the divine is in your heart, that part of you
touched so often you grow calloused to survive,
driving you to the brink and until you think
there is nothing left but flash paper promises.

watch this. closely. or you will miss the miracle.

I am Valdemar

at the point of death you seized me,
binding me with your mesmeric passes.
and now I am trapped between this world
and the next, bound to a grey decay.
waiting for your mercy to end it all,
this terrifying abomination of the order
that should not be tampered by the hand
of man or woman. the goddamn bush,
self-immolating, as a sign of the divine.
or the imposition of will against nature.
you will never need face this arabesque.
I will never know the taste of Jamaican salt
to halt this bondage, couer rage corrupted
for an idle curiosity. pity the cataleptic.
I could rise of my own will, but it would kill
too many innocents, and the one I love,
becoming again a phoenix until the next
dilettante parlour game of "what if?"

surrendering

I want to be passionate.
take your heart, fashion it
a safe place to play and stay.
to love you in whatever way
will give you joy and peace
and as great a release
as your gentle soul and form
requires, desires, to warm
each corner and recess
you surrender to me to bless.

malevolence 69

none may long recall
the moment of the fall
but Eden leaves a scar
on all our hearts
a kiss that never came
is never quite the same
but passion will devour
us for our parts
the lies, they will not mask
the penance of our task,
the perfumed loom of doom
where we were made
the nakedness we share
will follow, everywhere,
and in the end consume
our masquerade

perfecting

no one stands alone
when the day is done.
we think we are finished when we have just begun.
passion is the purpose.
fire in the winds of fate.
love unwinds the bandages laid over the wounds of hate.

measuring treasures
by inexplicable scales,
the conditions of our perditions is why so much love fails.
and we are cynical,
doubting the our very essence,
born, then torn, worn down in our own presence.

that I love you is evident.
that I will love you is my path.
I will gather all you give to me, in happiness and wrath.
I will whisper your name, mourning,
no matter which of us will pass,
and will always see your image through this perfecting glass.

mettle

this is a test
for the next indeterminate moments

or aeons

my faith will be tested

dropped from heights that look dangerous
run over and trampled by doubt and diversion
set ablaze to see what colour of flame it makes

and I am expected
required
to take this all with a British grace

I have Katherine Hepburn's attitude towards screen tests
but just enough humour to make jokes of the pain

and faith, in the face of silence and seeming indifference,
that this is the illusion, pale veil laid across the truth:

my theology of your worthiness
to be celebrated above all women

and I refuse to be the tin soldier who fails and falls in the furnace

Le Pavillon

a little light legerdemain
feigning a laugh, feint and taint
not a saint by any measure
just wanting to dance
kick off those pretty shoes
and turn the blues electric red
like your lips.

your hips move with the bass
I like the look on your face
when I touch you as we turn
earn another go round
to the sound, dance
and tell me without words
what happens next.

and forever

of an aspect both naked and unforgiving.
the skin and sin we share in precognizant memory.
I am here, waiting, stating my allegiance
in patience that is uncharacteristic of my gender.
but this sender is no pretender to the tenderness
he offers. the sacrifice is nothing. nothing and forever.
I know the arcane stain of time and sentience.
you know my heart. it troubles you,
for you are not certain what will come of it
and of the disturbing desires, the fires unsubtle
that immolate me daily and lick your flesh,
summoning someone to stand point
against the nightmares you dare, the void
you stare into and the new nudity in your soul.
I am clothed in your faith, forgiven by your grace
and will face whatever I must to win your trust.
and all that is yours to surrender, and forever.
and if I die tonight, know I died in my faith,
in your grace, and at peace with my love.

Sunday Song

I love the way you look at me
with eyes that let your heart to see
that I mean for you nothing but my best.
The years will wear this suitor down.
One day, in tears, I may yet drown
but I am bound to this quintessential quest.
I see you in the brisant spark
that comes to me in brightest dark
and calls me to the purpose of my path.
For all the trials and trails I've found
were meant to guide me to the sound
of Sunday Song you whispered against wrath.
So to your choir I add my voice
and pray, in time, for mercy's choice
that lets me build a life within your sphere.
But nothing will ever make me doubt
that I am less when I am without
your presence in my soul, of that I'm clear.

small things

I remember with the clarity of December winds
the diving beetle we found
stumbling
through our side yard one summer morning.
No one knew
how he or she got there
but we put them in a big glass jar
and let him/her/it
swim around, banging carapaced head
over and
over and
over
again until we could make the walk
down to Duke's Lake
and set the alien intruder loose.
a lion back on the Serengeti.
----
the wolf spider that ran
across
my
foot
as I sat on the bare concrete floor
of our basement

startled
me

but was gone before I could react more
than a strangled yelp

I waited to tell you
until we got home
(as you were driving)
that there was a spider in your hair,
testing clumps of blonde madness
for the necessary strength
to support an anchor web
to build a home
because I knew
as soon as I told you
(once we had parked and the engine was off)
you'd flail like a drowning man
and I was right
----
as I wrote you a love letter

to include with a carefully selected collection
of "nothing, really" trinkets
and a book that was my last earthly possession
worth more than many people's homes
my attention was seized by a spider
trying to be graceful
while walking on the light chain
and failing
magnificently
and I pondered the omen
and carefully pinched off the web
and took her outside
and gave her your name
before sending her
on her way
and finishing the love letter

I sat
impassively
as the mosquito drew long
Slurpee gulps
from the back of my hand
needing my blood
to lay her eggs

she deserved that much
for the patience she had shown
in waiting for me to sit still
long enough
to provide a meal
and a future
for her children
----

when the cruel little kids
threw the fuzzy caterpillars
into the dying coals
of the barbecue
I fished them out
with singed fingertips
much to the derision
of the kids
who would grow up
to be people I didn't want to know
because
you can measure anyone
by how they treat
fuzzy caterpillars
----
you remind me of the curious flying things
that, at a distance, look like tufts
of cotton.
but on closer inspection
you see the wings and body
and legs.
faerie flies, I called them,
as I never knew where they came from
or what their purpose was.
but knew they were beautiful
and mysterious
and always welcome.

an untamed manticore

strings wail an angry tone
I seize the microphone
and all the audience fades to sound and light
I'll sing of you tonight
of sorrow and delight
a spectrum shattering the monochrome

for I am left with just
the setting and the rust
the evidence and memories but nothing more
you left me on the floor
an untamed manticore
an empty belly bartered for the dust of trust

TALISMAN

My heart is not a talisman
to be worn casually, as a defense
against whatever it is you are afraid of.
My heart is more dangerous
than any imagined goblin of hob
hiding in your closet, to frighten you.
Worn without respect, it burns
and leaves a mark deeper than any blow
struck by fist or forgotten evils' vagaries.
That I am kind and charitable
is not of question, for I have allowed
many to shield themselves with my power,
but the season and reason comes
when I have use of it myself
and it is not greed or vindictiveness
that I would want my heart mighty,
to be able to do what I must, at length,
and not just be a plaything or a talisman,
a good luck charm to those who want it
to make the road a little easier
at the expense of everything else.

manifest

the power of a thought is not brought from notion to full flower
until written or spoken as token for the reality.
the words. just words. words that splinter hearts and damn souls dropped from the sky
to see if they can fly on wings only expressed in abstraction.

I remember my first kiss.
it was soft and sudden and
was just a polite expression
by a girl who wanted to see
if I was interested in her.
I can be slow, you know,
moments to months to note
a flirtation, time for a woman
to move on with her life
and I catch up with a frame
that is no longer open to me.

we are not the first, or the last, generation to put ourselves
higher on the food chain than the society we live within.
greedy little monsters, we would, for a sip of germ piss or puff
of harsh smoke, watch people die and deny our culpability.

I taught someone that dance once,
the words gliding on slippery tongue
to untangle and tangle the heart.
I regret teaching it, as they used it
to their own ends and murdered the world.
and now it is on my head to make right
what people can't even perceive,
as they believe that whatever they want
is what God wants, what a horrible job
to have, to be deity to this selfish race.
spoiled children in soiled garments.

an hero is a martyr. if the rich man with the flashy smile
doesn't die to purpose in throwing or catching or kicking
a ball or making music that cynical accountants dictate
to the top of random metric charts, they are, at best, meaningless.

romantics meander

there are those times
when I feel alone
words on the page
not even the phone
memories held
with no artifacts
to signify faith
in our spirits' pacts

for dreams are not just given
they are taken as well
and a road of best intentions
often leads into Hell
I have kept to my vows
and have held on so tight
I will find if my wisdom
was borne on the light
I will wait through the night

there have been sparks
and fires in the sky
but will I know your sweet heat
in my soul, ere I die?
it is you whom the riddles
are answerable to.
in this contest of dreamers
I will find out what's true.

for dreams are not just given
they are taken as well
and free will has its place
in the face of the spell
I have traveled so long
and my rest is yet far
I will keep to the course
of the once promised star
worth every stumble and scar

emeralds

precious mettle, bright as ten thousand emeralds.
the air burns with the premonitions of what comes.
love approaches, beyond the dreams of cold heralds.
it walks with steady tread where others have but crawled,
footfalls alone pounding like a great legions' drums.
precious mettle, bright as ten thousand emeralds.
the unanticipated champion, once walled
and left for dead, I sustained myself, dreams and crumbs.
love approaches, beyond the dreams of cold heralds.
when all doubt was stripped away by scourge and by scalds,
ripped away scars and stars, becoming what becomes.
precious mettle, bright as ten thousand emeralds.
I wait, hesitate, I watched the gate unappalled
for the sign of the lover, the cithara's strums:
love approaches, beyond the dreams of cold heralds.
no fear, no pain, sanctified by a union called
by your lips, your eyes, and the succubus succumbs.
precious mettle, bright as ten thousand emeralds.
love approaches, beyond the dreams of cold heralds.

the road to lethe

aletheia fails. passion pales.
and the vow to seek the road to Lethe
is found, burnt into my flesh
in a moment of precognizance.

I must follow. the hollow hells
hold nothing but the butter brickle
riddles that lead to the Rube Goldberg
chaosium, invoking a dream of the damned.

this valour is an malefic mélange,
the rune and ruin of the lake's knight,
courtly love in a graceless trace.
the cinders of sin, cold for ages.

we read cunning in the naivete,
and stay away to watch the grey go black.
the stones are my friend, the lead me
to where I am less necessary than wanted.

bleed

burn me, turn me into what you most need, I bleed.
the seed, the need, the greed to be the deed you own
as part and consummation, no hesitation, freed
of the doubts of self-preservation, the seed sown
to grow in row upon perfect row, glass roses
shattered for what has mattered more than only skin.
measure me as the pleasure treasure that dozes
in fitful catalepsy until we begin
and cease marking time until the horizon fades
and we are enraptured, captured in the pure act
of satisfying earnest hungers, promenades
of twinned consummations, consumed, doomed in the fact
that we are all mortal and we scream our release,
defiance of shared, paired breath that will one day cease.

wordbound

patience earned and learned, until fleshes run rampant.
I am bound by word, cured of the pretty poisons,
inoculated by the fated touch and cant.
the chant of your paramour, withholding seasons
of the passions that will echo, hearts defiant
in the sweet heat burnt into us at the first kiss,
where we shared, passed more than tongue and taste, transcendent
to the definitions we once thought before this
total penetration, beyond pleasure and pain,
the beginning of a merged, purged pattern reborn
in torn fabrics of time and tapestries, the vain
injected with the sublime, the sacrifice shorn
of all pretense. wrap yourself around me and take
me, the subtle rebuttal of what we can make.

claims

I may claim you but never tame you, I am yours.
yours to use as you choose, to refuse what you will
and even to kill with an unkind word, the course
of fragile hearts, tempered adamantine but still
under sway of the kiss of the alchemist who
poured the cinnabar and jet, fashioning man
out of inorganic matter, the blood you drew
with the red heart of a fallen star that once ran
across the sky with the omens of love and death.
awake me to break me, to take me into you
as friend and lover and servant with ancient breath
and patient touch of guiding hands, feral and true
as you speak incantations you wrote upon me,
binding me, finding in me your epiphany.

occult

sharing breath and the petty death until we live,
free from the spiral shell cages we extruded
in desperate need to hold tight on, to forgive
our words and deeds in fear of being excluded
from a promised land found in inconvenient day.
kairos over chronos, my love, patient passions
shatter stone that seeks to crush flowers sown in clay
and when the snows are too deep, I sleep, emissions
held and forests felled with single stroke of the pen
that is dipped in bright blood you infected me with,
carrier of words, fantasies fantastic when
unleashed by word and vote you elected me with.
I dream of you in every night's surrender
and will fulfill your charge in lusts earnest and tender.

dire, carnal

tenderness and the dire and carnal need to feed
upon your willing form, warm with desire and sweet,
sweet as nectar and honey with jasmine, you bleed
me of my white wine with lip and hip that slip, heat
transfiguring friend to lover that hovers high
and hard, balanced on your passion and grace, craving
all and more as sacrament of my spirit's cry
to seek the unpierced corners of you, not saving
anything for anyone else, all given free
and deep and even when you sleep I must ravage
you in tender savagery. the fervent needs we
have found, earnest to a purified state, savage
madness and sensation of skin on skin, within
and, without each other, we are lost to soft sin.

ebb and flow

there is an ebb and flow to passions that would grow,
memories yet unborn but as real as our Gods.
lines of Pascal's wager are calculated so
that we comprehend the risks and accepted odds
that may at first seem mad and sad betting against
the evidences, solely on the shadow word
that has pierced our rusted, crusted heart, well defensed
yet not enough to betray love summoned absurd
against all logic and practice. cithara strings
and a wisp of barriers implacable, stacked
against the pulse of a touch whose soft promise brings
an awakening in the tidal fates we lacked,
tossed as starfish on a raging beach, accepting
ebb and flow while awaiting the promised lifespring.

heptahedron

there is an ebb and flow to passions that would grow.
tenderness and the dire and carnal need to feed.
sharing breath and the petty death until we live.
I may claim you but never tame you, I am yours.
patience earned and learned, until fleshes run rampant.
burn me, turn me into what you most need, I bleed.
precious mettle, bright as ten thousand emeralds.

the sacred

I knew a man who went to church
every Sunday
for eighty years
because he believed in God
and knew,
he knew,
that God was real
and no amount of time or travail
was too much
to stand in the presence
of the divine
and feel the purification
and redemption
and joy
of stepping into Heaven
and knowing the sacred.

That's how I feel about you.

airs

the softness of your skin is like music,
warm and inspiring, desiring to be experienced
how and why it was created. I like to think
that it was made for me, just me.
that is selfish, I know, and unrealistic,
but you intoxicate me with the surreal beauty
that resides in the curve of your back,
the slope of your thighs, the bend of your neck.
and for long, irresistible moment, I want to play
the music of my desires upon you and within you,
a soft duet of tension plucked and released.
until we rest at the end of the measure.

spring

although I love the Winter, I believe in Spring.
if I did not, I would have withered long ago,
younger than you, when I dreamed beauty
and grace and a true heart I would not see
for so many seasons. but now I can smell
the crocuses and the grasses as they escape
the cold and necessary blanket of snow.
and it makes me think of you, pure and kind,
beautiful and in your own way an innocent,
discovering Spring, as if for the first time.

to a beautiful soul

the soul is white
like snow in a perfect world.
touched and tossed by hands
and the forces of nature
that in time mold and sully it.
but the essence remains
and we are called to see,
see behind the powder of dust
and the arrogant bootprints.
we are called to love what is
the nature of what is,
and to smooth over
the critical and sometimes
crippling marks
made by the business of life.

the gorge

the gorge, it rises
to forge surprises
for the passive and the weak.
a sky on fire
prophesies desire
as the shadows pale and peak.
I am in shallows,
fleeing the hallows
where the fates keep their counsel,
trembling memories
that feed the stories
we tell ourselves to justify the false and fel.
nothing burns as true
as truth itself, blue
and perfect as a lover's recall of a kiss
that, in truth observed,
never had occurred.
and we weave our lives of a manufactured bliss.

death

I am not afraid to die, it is unproven
if death itself would be enough to hold me back
from being yours forever, a constellation
of a sky already pocked by stars that must stack
deeper than imagination's well for I am
still here, laying unrestrained where you had left me
with words of love and promise of just a damned dram
of your touch and sanctification, liberty
a curse, an illusion of those lacking mettle
hard and shaped to fit the curve of your troubled soul.
but still within you boils an alchemist's kettle
of passions restrained by scar and tar, and control
is but a draught away. I will pray for your couer rage
and live my vigil, waiting in my promised cage.

Pax Vobiscum

Peace be with you. It is that time, that season,
when we turn to the better angels of our reason
and wish well on friend and stranger alike, love
becomes more than lace and lube and lies, above
all else we seek to feel the sense of family
with even those we barely know and rarely see.

I wish you all the best of times at this time.
Where there is war, let there be peace, crime
give way to forgiveness and reconciliation, pain
fade and the troubles of the past fade to stain
and then to nothingness. I wish you poetry, art
and the magic of self-awareness on your part.

Do not be alone, even if you are, gather everyone
you love and have community with and shun
the crushing solitude of those who cannot hope
for more than an empty belly and a way to cope
with the despair we wear like brittle crowns
too often, soften your will and force back your frowns.

This is a time of triumph, when even God kept word
and offered up a sacrifice for our reconciliation, absurd
it may seem, a dream of a whim. But in the lights and trees
we celebrate more than one faith, more than what frees
us from our daily toil. We celebrate hope and rebirth.
And peace. Peace and joy to all who live here, with us, on Earth.

Brave Bragi

Brave Bragi tried and lied to hide
his heart in bright orthography.
But a woman's heart stands apart,
finding truth intuitively.

fragment: invocato

all you have to do is wish and believe
the rest is my command
to grant you all you can conceive
by sweat or thought or hand.

all that there is you dare to ask
I will find the way
to manifest, a quest, a task,
I will change darkest night to day.

the walk away

for you to live then I must die.
not a martyr, just a friend
knowing what is necessary.
death not in the suicide watch
but in a more spiritual sense.
a rewiring of a soul, already
held together with duct tape
and a pilgrim's will to love.
I wish I could explain it better,
but for all your hyperbole
you are still so young to this world,
and I am grey with experience
I cannot explain. weathering
fresh facades does not make them
ancient, just weathered and worn
more than they should be.
forgive me, if you can,
this last indulgence. this immolation
that will illume even distant worlds
one day. after you and I are gone.

pink petals

The pink petals of your sweet lips
transcend my touch and penetrate
deep. Deep within my heart where slips
the edge of your beauty, serrate
in its cutting. Taking all doubt
and each question I have harboured
in my fear of losing all out
within your whim and will, a bird,
if you will, caught in sticky bind,
finding itself fearful, tearful
and an echo of past unkind
treatment in hands as beautiful
as yours. But the petals taste true
and I surrender dreams to you.

bending

I continue bending the sky that I
may please you with efforts earnest and true.
From Heracles I learned to not deny
any noble effort for the queen you
serve, deserving of your fealty, sweat
and the legends that will be recorded
in the labours to win her heart to set
the skies alight, a lover's night once said
to evidence the birth of new titans,
springing full grown from the lips of lovers
when they comprehend and dare to frighten
even the fates, Pallas discovers
a new wisdom in the amomancies
that rise from the very stones to flood seas.

then you...

there are those who will say that you should have
left me where you found me, dead in the sand.
no pulse, no breath, merely the artifice
of words and the visions of the poet.
like candleflame, a flickering taper,
doomed to exhaust tallow and wick and light
and pass into the memory of those who might
for a moment remember the purpose.

but, you did not. you called me up, a wish
I had no choice but to grant you. a kiss,
like out of some fairy story, that wakes
sleeping victims from their endless slumber.
and now I am golem, phoenix, poet
once and again. straining against constraints.
asking only that the sweet kiss remain,
lips pressed to lips to feed the seed of need.

I was ronin, content, alone, legend
to those who cared to dare to share visions
of love and a perfecting peace, released
to the bright winds and whims of hearts
that could cradle the hope that life was sweet.
untouched by the amomancy, I slept
until the dry desert zephyrs stripped me
of the desire to rise again, then you...

guitar

I would have taken the time to learn to play guitar
if I had any talent for it and I thought it would impress you.
But I have never been very musical and the words
are so much more natural for me to bring as offerings
and I just have to hope that three words and the truth
will be enough to make you feel the harmony of my heart
as it reaches out to you. Words like a really good major D,
waking up the parts of you that wander towards the grey,
making your feet dance without knowing it, a smile
of recognition for something new and unfamiliar.
All I have to offer is everything. Immortality and the envy
of all those who read my words and, for the moment, believe
in love bigger than a drunken bang with someone they met
in a bar, something sweeter than a childhood dream
where the prince doesn't stop just because the dragon
breathes fire and the castle wall is awful high to climb.
I've got words. But even God can be summed up in a word,
the right word, from the beginning, so forgive me
that I didn't bring my guitar. Because I don't have one.

eclipsing

shadows ride on the night tonight.
silence buries its own.
there's no proof that you ever were,
not even a voice on the phone.
disconnected from the fragile veils
I meander, lost in the grey.
trying to build something without form,
making bricks without clay.

whispers at midnight in photons and glass
make up for not one missing kiss.
I can drink envy until it ferments
knowing just one thing amiss.
I dream of you with eyes that you gave to me
and asked me be brave and be true.
when the moon drinks the light I'll still be here,
answering a summons from you.

wind chime

in the morning, soft,
the wind rises, makes music,
not unlike your soul.

kryptos night

et semper nocte ac die in monumentis
et in montibus
erat clamans et concidens se lapidibus

where I walk, you cannot follow.
but I will leave adequate crumbs
for any and all who draw out the dimensions
and fit time against space to face
a riddle and a giggling countenance.
dance to the middle and count the bricks.
months to build. a lifetime to decode.
make that two lifetimes, lived in parallel.
such lines should not meet, but you and I
know better. the metrical foot of a friend,
less girl than the sound of a cithara,
not what was said but when and where.
not where we lay, but when and what
will it matter if it is raspberry beer?
the trinity finds the minority report
and makes sport of the shackles.
hackles and dander and invisible boots.
the truth disputes itself and, on his shelf,
Buddha hides his face so you cannot know
when he is laughing and when he is crying
and when he is just trying to get through the day
without thinking of white lace and an old book.
we are what we value. ergo, I am you.
more than I am a poet, for I would,
were this the ultimatum of Psyche,
choose a different path and risk wrath
of all but Aphrodite. but you know that,
intrinsically, even as I know when you bluff,
and find it charming. I shouldn't,
as that is so indulgent of me, but I do.
and you still haven't decoded my sense
of humour. or even the Latin in this poem.
Irene would, even before her train reached
Bohemia and you will too, one day.
until then, do what you must and I will find you.
because you asked me, tasked me, to.
and now Hephaestus becomes Heracles

and chases the golden apples in a blended myth.
more ice for the pearl of wisdom,
a claim ticket refunded but not forgotten.
every day, rehearsals for the grand entrance.

et semper nocte ac die in monumentis
et in montibus
erat clamans et concidens se lapidibus

equality

I am convinced of Your sincerity
by the soft veils and the permanence
of Your impertinent passions,
whispered in thin corridors to shield
both Our hearts as We find the signed
doors into the deeper places
where We may conquer the ruinous runes
that would control Us if We allow them.
I want no other lover, no other kiss,
no other flesh to claim Me its own.
You are the universe to Me, sweet
and certain even in the uncertainties.
I believe in You and would grieve
the rest of My days were You to pass first,
bricked up to pen My elegies of Your beauty,
the duty of any earnest lover.
I am, I admit, impatient for the rest
of Our life together, but will wait
until I may rest in Your arms, alone.

sense

there's a price for innocence
after the first time around,
the sound of boneyard, hard stones
against the dry earth, denial
and the vile pressure of lies.
we find ourselves in consequence,
our own ethos is profound
but found is the unlost key, metal
that unlocks the pocked heart,
liberating that which too often dies.
the first word was eloquence,
and now the clatter shatters silence
and the violence is in our ears,
fears and the pounding blood floods
and stifles the word we should prize.
most lies are cowardice, not arrogance,
the couer rage phage that weakens
like a Nietzschean predator, waiting
for the folly of the attack that does not kill
but weakens us when the blood dries.
I never understood why, to some, ignorance
is an attractive state of being,
seeing only in one colour, regardless
of the current trends in fashion or culture,
open pit minds instead of infinite skies.

the red surrender

we are caught up in the red surrender.
I'm tripped and trapped between the night and day.
whether you are just the dark pretender
I'm still going to have to pay to play.
faded, jaded and misguided, we pray,
the earnest in the furnace and the weak.
they stumble along a pilgrim's pathway
knowing never exactly what they seek.
heat and hollows, the meshing, threshing gears
and the bitter dreams of the damned divine,
celebrations of the pain and the fears
we spill innocent blood and drink the wine.
nothing but the illusion and the wait.
excruciating, but not random fate.

snowflakes

your lips are like rose petals
but snows will still come
to wilt the pink preciousness
to leave your kiss numb

I have no illusions
but I have seen many Springs
and will wait through the Winter
to see what faith brings

the snowflakes are part of
this life, I find,
and I must endure the cold
being patient, and kind

tremors of an unsteady hand

Time is but a measure of what we can or cannot do,
bottling lightning in the dark to show we're not afraid,
to prove we're powerful, to prove we prayed
to the right gods, at the right odds, our aim is true.
And you told me once a secret, and I kept it sealed
behind the wax of my faith in you, malleable,
but evidence of my beliefs, a steady, stable
tongue of fire in the violence of silence, concealed
from our lesser inventions and intentions.
I play in the light, I walk in the dark, and shadows
don't scare me anymore, I've grown and shown
that I know who I am and can give what I own,
I can stand in the wind, tougher than the bluff, prose
in a world of poets means nothing but smoke and dust.
I will not surrender grace for an illusion of trust.

The Alchemy of Flesh

Faint scent of you remains, stamped in my soul.
The chemistry becomes magic and I
am but another crucible to roll
over the flames and melt base metal, my
contribution to arcane ritual
you make of me, take from me to merge
the frail shadows of souls we are, eventual
victims of desires, boiling to verge
on the moment of incandescent heat
into the alchemy of human hearts,
gold, platinum and silver slivers sweet
as arsenic, swallowed to follow parts
we vivisect ourselves for, mysteries
of futures hung upon our histories.

inversion, version 3

to strike sparks without touching fire
    to touch the fire without being burned
to be burned and not be consumed
    to be consumed and not be gone
to be gone and yet find the light
    to find the light without striking sparks

anthill

the anthill
not a metaphor for man
or the struggle of nations
in the face of a bemused

god

holding out a miniature marshmallow
to force war

just a diversion
life in all its randomness
and chaos

with an intelligence
at the end of the tunnel
and a queen
worth dying for

sex

yes, it is sacred to me, the act and the fact
that you are here, with me, curious and yet,
furious with an hot desire. fire of chemistry
possessing the biology and forcing the alchemy
that demands, command me to please you,
not to the satiety of the flesh alone, but my heart,
expressing arch and ardent desires in my taste
of you. the sweet musk of your ambrosia,
feeding my fires, my desires, as my flesh conspires
with yours to override our best intentions.
moments to minutes to what seems like hours
I draw nectar from the flower to sustain me,
though it pains me to not yet drive summoned steel
to sheathe and wreath myself in your fragrance.
feeling the tightened tensions of your surrender,
taking me in and holding me in a grip that slips
mere inches at a time, a trespass of conspiracy
to find myself within your grinding hips. lips hot
and impatient. the pulses synchronizing as you.
as you. as you writhe like lightning through my soul
and take control of me in your release, drawing
me out and into you, deeper than you dare to care
to admit you'd ever tear my seed and wear it,
inside, bride to my consummation, your hands
still clenched around the sheets. sweet, your honey,
dripping from me as a baptism of your body
for the deep draught of the white wine you take
and make a part of you, our mingled sweats
set to whet our appetites for the next joining.

life is short

life is short, ephemeral.
it could be gone tomorrow
or before I finish this sentence.
that is why I try
to make sure my words
and actions are worthy of remembrance.
that I tell those that I love
that I love them.
that I speak the truth
with softened grace.
that I write of those
worthy of immortality,
in the literary sense,
for at least I have some say in that.

I will be gone, one day.
maybe tomorrow.
I ask no sorrow,
but celebration.
for I have lived a valiant life,
earnest and faithful
to my heart and my craft,
and laughed, and loved,
and fought, and prayed,
and been what I should have been
when I could have been
far less.

I have few regrets.
not for things I have said or done
but of things I have not said
or left undone
like the last button on a lover's blouse.
or that kiss that will remain
unsanctified, as the sands ran out.

to rule

you make me want to rule the world
if only to protect you from the edges
that have cut and rut themselves
into your flesh. you deserve better
than I will ever be able to give you,
but I will give you my all. my soul
will be the widow's two mites, everything
as alms and balm to the pain and time
before the fates relented and sent me
to beg your service, to surrender myself
in perfect fealty to the reality of you.
you make me want to rule the world
if only to make it a token of my love.
and when I am witnessed on Olympus
know that my thoughts will be of you, alone.

sonnet: perfecting

at length, what need will there be for poets
when the themes are complete? the sweet savour
clinging to tongue and memory, sow its
seeds in the human heart, the behaviour
of the mortal inheritors altered
by an earnest realization of truth.
we play for our extinction, untethered
to the graceless wars and whores, the uncouth
yammering of decay and decadence
bartered as coin and joined to the fetid.
amomancies bright and bitter, we sense
our own infirmities and pray morbid
hopes for our release, the peace of the grave,
where worms know not the fallen dreams we gave.

patience

there's no clock ticking. the thorns that are pricking
are on rose stems alone, so put down that phone
and recognize that there's no hurry, don't you worry,
I'm not going past, I'll go as fast as you can last.
I know you can't run in those shoes, so I choose
to take a more leisurely pace, not a race with time,
it would be a crime to make you walk alone,
especially in this neighborhood. I'll do what I should
to make good on all my promises. you do what you must,
the dust is still far away and if you want to play
I won't get in your way. I like it when you laugh
like the girl you haven't left far behind, yourself.
so trust in my patience, I'm here for a while,
at least long enough to make sure you smile.

dreams in the lonely night

in the lonely night.
you, the missing element,
make darkness profound.

soft

you have never heard me raise my voice in rage.
what value would there be in such a madness?
you have heard enough hard words in this sphere
and I would never want to be the architect of a tear
from your perfect eyes, that deserve to see peace,
happiness and a world that bends to her will.

arcane

you are so beautiful, so young,
but I do not hesitate as my tongue
traces the essential runes upon you,
laying claim to the warm form promised
in a moment of heightened arousal.

I will take the communion of your body,
and return you my own wine, heated
by the desire you create in me to transcend
the arrogance of mere flesh, only skin,
the pain and passion of commitment.

deep I will trace my place within you,
deep and beyond the shadows.
I will make of the moment an epiphany,
the sanctity of your lips, saying my name
when you are beyond sound and thought.

I will chant my prayers and purposes,
laying hands upon your warm form
to communicate the subtle madness
that grips me as we slip into unity,
granting us immunity from doubt.

this moment is a sanctification of love,
of passion, more than only skin, sin
purified in an alien heat, sweat and certain,
as we merge into a new existence.
I will surrender my all to my goddess.

thirst

you beg me quench my thirst
and bare your tender flesh
but I say ladies first
in all things where we might mesh.
the bitter and the sweet
shall mingle in our veins
the tyrants of defeat
shall lose their reigns.
for what is this but sharing
our most perfect needs?
and we are so daring
we fight until death concedes?

the inner eye

the inner eye turns outwards and sees

desolation

the shadowdance of the damned
flecked with sparks
that might be diamonds
or emeralds
or even sacred rubies
set in the mouth of new idols

still powerless
but fresh and therefore
novelty of a literary sense
fresh meat for the slaughterhouse
where I hang myself on hooks
awaiting the disembowelment

the clarity of charity
is only in the heart of the donor
the receiver and the deceiver
are not always one in the same

but often
and that softens the blow
to know
that there is no illusion
just a delusion
of ascendancy
born in dilletante dreams
the faerie glamour

midgaard is a madhouse

in time all three riders will agree
but for now
I write alone
but will not reveal myself
until the others learn of their own accord
because patience is the only virtue
worth practicing

leather and the night

the soft snow hardens in the thaw and freeze.
a dance floor for the bravest, the winter breeze
blows blond hair against the perfect skies,
where breath mists like dragon breath and dies
in minute curls. the sound of voices in the still,
echoing on forever. you laugh like you will
always laugh, with passion and delight.
music was made for leather and the night.

endure

endure every sure and impure thought
you've caught as they slip away, out my eyes
from the dark and elegant corners, fraught
with pleasure and desire, seeking the prize
that is more than between your thighs, flawless
though they be in fantasy and in fact.
unshackling, awakening the lawless
elements within me, who have made pact
with darker entities, the wicked girl
you hide behind the veneer of control,
her heart tell-tale to her presence, the curl
of brimstone and jasmine, a buried soul
of Dionysian fury, denied
far too long by an irrelevant pride.

surprise

would it surprise you know
that I love the snow
and have been known to walk
barefoot
in knee-high drifts of it?

would it surprise you to find
it's been said I am too kind,
so much so I have been known
to burn my fingers rescuing
caterpillars that cruel children
throw into the campfire?

would it surprise you to see
the scars left on me
by every lover who promised
what they couldn't deliver
but that I kept faith with their
secrets and gave them
free passage, carrying them
to where they wanted to be?

would it surprise you in the end
to know that I was your friend
and took upon my back
more than I should carry
but never let you see me break,
for friends do not to that?

would it surprise you to hear
that I was more laughter than tear?
that I celebrated even bad times
with an indomitable will
and was known to walk out of Hell
untouched and unburnt?

would it surprise you in main
to know I knew of your pain
but you had to make the choice,
ignorant of my wisdom and wishes,
free of my electioneering,
for I know the fate of persuaders?

would it surprise you to track
that I never changed back
my last will and testament
and that you will, perhaps,
one day inherit my legacy?

trance state

pain cuts a million ways
and when it stays, it plays
many roles in the many souls
it infests, it digests, it wrests
the foundations of joy.

tempestuous

you asked.
I made purpose
out of your tender quest.
I found
bread and circus,
needs fulfilled as your guest.
but soon
I found that I
Prometheus would play.
bound to
a rocky fate
for bringing fire to fae.
I wish
you were certain
of where your heart shall lead.
but I,
bound by valour,
will keep my vows, indeed.

back to the shadow walls

embracing.
fully embracing
the gifts granted with recompense
undemanded
is like turning around
in Plato's Cave.
you will see things.
you will know things.
you will say things
that those still playing shadow puppets
cannot comprehend.
it will cost you lover.
friend.
family.
but it will be a greater truth
that you will be a part of.

with fortune, you may see other faces
also looking into the fire.
the other brave souls
your true family.
your true friends.
you true lovers.
you will be part of an order
older than time.
but it will cost you
your humanity
and you will mourn this

lyric: present tense

I cannot touch the future
and I cannot change the past
all I have is in this moment
it is now the crucial die is cast

you can't warm yourself on ashes
you can't feed yourself on dreams
you can only seize this moment
in the swift temporal streams

the oracles are blinded
by what they want and what they need
and you can be so open minded
the wind blows away every seed

power checked is power harnessed,
thunder held in titan's rein
for the moments that may never come
we are born to more than pain

you can't warm yourself on ashes
you can't feed yourself on dreams
you can only seize this moment
in the swift temporal streams

it is my will to stand here, resolute,
until ends both space and time
but in truth I master neither
just my purpose in this rhyme

reality

the dream shifts. the dreamer persists.
and all our free will illusions
bind us to what we find resists
our fatal, natal natures, sons
and daughters of the slaughter done
in the name of life, mockery
and memory, songs to a sun
too distant and luminous. we
speak dark matter, undetected.
we dream variations, measured
in our allegiances respected
by the hypocrisy we cured
by curving the hyperbole
and finding what we bind is free.

black rose in the hall

a black rose stands in a vase in the hall
petals like satin, and soft,
the colours ran out, crimson, I recall,
as red as your dreams, held aloft.

but beauty it is, and beauty persists
even though we wish it would fade.
fears disappear, but the passion persists,
if we linger to the last serenade.

next year, the desert

the ocean calls. my lover, Thetis, reaches out,
offers me an embrace of earnest surrender.
I trust in her as I have, without fear or doubt,
trusted all women, the priestess and pretender
both walk my mnemonic corridors of power,
raping my vision and shaping my legacy.
venom and nectar, served in a jasmine flower
that calls to me with a fragrance that offers me
a chance at peace and shelter from the coming storm.
I am cyclopean at heart, one eye, aware
that fate is set. I know too much and as such form
a sorrowful figure on the parapet, fair
only at a distance, in silhouette, vision
narrowed by the dark barrow, my final mission.

claim

you have claimed me, tamed me.
I am yours. bound and delivered,
my life is to your will and whim, free
am I given, with no coin bartered
for that which is yours, by right, true.
I would lay such claim to you, in time,
as you have asked and tasked me to
make of you mine own, not just in rhyme
and meter, but in soul and only skin
to fill the corners of our hollow shells,
shared and dared and bared to sacred sin
in ways never before, heavens and hells
fallen to our passion and affection,
my commitment to you approaching perfection.

temple

soft you are.
soft and warm.
your form an extension of your heart.
your heart an extension of your soul.
and I, I am lost and found
within the sacred ground
of this temple of your affections.
trespass, perhaps, but I will
observe the rituals as you define them.
I will keep to the path of rose petals
you have ordered the acolytes
to line the correct path with,
that I might not place flesh to cold stone.
for I come to you, naked and alone,
my weapons discarded, my tongue silenced
that I may speak with an humbler eloquence.
the poet rides in.
and asks your grace
to stay and make his case,
or at least to rest
within the walls of the city
until such time as
you have no more need of his services.
then I will walk out,
followed by the children
who have heard my voice
and choose to make choice
of an ennobling dream.
barefoot and arrogant.
like a poet.
I will stand, facing the challenging sun
of my brother of a forgotten religion
and give up nothing to the wind
but your name
as a new allegory
for beauty and love.
that when civilizations have risen and fallen
it will still be carved
in the essential stone
of lovers' hearts
as proof that there is
something purposeful
beyond hate and fear.
there is love.

put your hands on me

put your hands on me
and show me what you mean
when you promise me pleasure
beyond any I have known before,
surrendering my fantasies
to a reality more intense
more perfect
deeper
purer (in a manner)
than anything I imagined
when I saw your smile
and imagined those lips
tasting me
when I saw you walk
and imagined those legs
around me
when I heard you talk
and imagined your voice
screaming my name
as your hands directed me
setting the rhythm
like a well-trained equestrian
guiding her mount
(and the allegory isn't lost on me)
and riding me hard

put your hands on me

beautiful truths

the sand is
always there
sliding by
and we don't care

until

they are gone

it has been my fate
to lock into uncertain   orbits
where the waiting room
takes longer
than the honeymoon

that is a tragedy
but a necessity
as most doubt their worthiness for joy

many are so beaten down
that they believe every curse
spoken by someone kicking them
and cry in the mirror
because it is a lie
because it says nice things

it is hard to believe the beautiful truths

hard to believe the poetry
when we can still count the scars
still feel the doubts
and have anesthetized ourselves
to the point that we feel nothing   real

just whatever draconian illusions
we tell ourselves we deserve
for the sins of others
who made us their messiahs
having us carry their crosses
because they were too weak
to carry their own
and in their chalice of malice
they slipped us a stale whine

and we
human as we are
bought it

and became their victims
so they could point and laugh
and tell us that we are broken

malevolence - walk away

coming out of the corners
faster than a random thought
caught between blood and thunder
what you made and what you bought

pain and fire
the desire
takes its form
it is warm
and lingers
by your will
or it will
walk away
walk away

eyes are now screaming
the light so bright it blinds
your skin is dancing
moved as your soul resigns

walk away
walk away
taking the light
and the night
pain and fire
the desire
needle sharp
angel's harp
by your will
or it will
come to stay
come to stay

irrevocable
this summoning made
unforgettable
the price in passion paid

come to stay
come to stay
walk away
walk away
run away
run away

the smaller the vessel
the greater the pressure
the tighter the measure
the daemons we wrestle
awake to the warming
of discontent forming
the chains are quite daunting
but...

acceptance

you are no diaphanous ingenue,
but of substance, purpose and purity
that can transcend time and bid to replace
God in the prayers to heaven, sanctity
of your love offered and accepted, soft
as morning sun on dried tears. furious
and curious futures await, aloft,
the brave and the patient, not spurious
vows that allow us wiggle room, but wise
acceptance that love is not a box, bound,
but an allowance for weirding times, lies
are not a fit veil for your beauty, found
as it is place in my adamant heart,
my religion, my science and my art.

lyric: vanishment

if you don't strap in.
if you don't hang on.
I'll peel out of my skin
and be gone by the dawn.

I'll pass you on the right
so fast you won't see me.
burn a hole in the night.
relativistic velocity.

if you don't strap in.
if you don't hang on.
I'll peel out of my skin
and be gone by the dawn.

acceleration delta
that will leave you in the red.
calculations cold and raw
that will leave you in your bed.

if you don't strap in.
if you don't hang on.
I'll peel out of my skin
and be gone by the dawn.

a chiropteran Orpheus
doppler shifting back
what once had passed between us
as my light fades fast to black

if you don't strap in
if you don't hang on
I'll peel out of my skin
and be gone by the dawn.

obscurity

it was as the Greek girl said
late at night, relieved at my forgiveness.
popcorn left on the stove
to be the midnight banquet
when truth showed me her ass.
and I gave her a cigar.
she said she smoked it
but I think it was for the
Freudian symbolism
to see if she could get me
to feel like she was a woman,
not a flushed-face leopard
trading spots for stripes
in a field near Tucson
looking for reassurances
that I found her attractive enough
to sweep Tampa off the map
and send an impolite farewell
to the redhead who stole
those outlaw stories.
I can work around the underwear.
proved that more than once.
never did go for a swim
like I really meant it,
waiting for the words
that never came, unlike
the graceful poetess,
hiding lovers like stolen candy.
I died, more than once,
waiting for the rainbow
to touch down and give it up.
the short lady sang.
the telephone rang
and it was 10:15 and she knew.
she knew. my address already.
but we only kissed before
she invoked A Pope and fled.
I'm not some training-wheels
drunken bar pick up that doesn't count
if you can't remember his name.
she left early, paying the penalty
and leaving me to drive alone

to Palm Springs, windows open
and the 105 degree desert heat
burning away my indignation.
picked clean after all the pretty words.
pretty words. a coward's dance.
I have no use for the kindness
of people stranger than myself.
I have no memory of you.
None, whatsoever.
And so, from obscure to impure,
to unsure and suddenly, the void.

the darker angels

a unity of luminescence, the presence of an ethereal,
incandescent thought,
caught in the quintessential webs of our predestinate,
obstinate denial of what
is not less than the truth. reality, flinty and dark,
like obsidian geodes, hard
cards in the tarot deck on the infinite universes' possibilities.
a guard
pardoned for their diligence
by their sleeping masters' whim and will.
killing time with a clockwork knife,
a blade unsheathed to silence,
violence foresworn for the incumbent
threat of guilt and penance,
from whence flows our memories,
cold and callous and calculating.
and God sleeps with one eye open, tonight.

bearing gifts

Cicero, you know.
He spoke in Greek and it seemed so
elegant and relevant.
Well, not to the Romans, the cant,
the canto of the orator
and the bleak conscience of a lover
are not my gifts. I am but a poet.
A trouvere, a good man set
on a final quest by your whim.
It was your words that made me trim
my sails that were set for the edge.
And now I sit, adrift on a ledge
of stone and solitude, rude fate
for the pilgrim you said to wait
by the wall at the pillars of Heracles
and you would be there, eventualities
inobscured. But the ground grows hard
and without word or kiss or card
to fulfill promises made perhaps in haste
I am left, alone to ponder if I waste
my last moments on an illusion.
A game. A transitory confusion
where you joined the chorus of those
who wondered what, If I chose
to follow your lead and bleed,
I would taste like as you filled your need.

dimittis

it isn't really giving
if you've anything left to give
and it isn't really love
if without it you can live
it isn't what I bartered for
but what I gain at last
in the solitude of memory
and the die which I must cast

I seek a new horizon
battered but unbowed
across the city streets I walk
and across the prairies, plowed,
for I have seen what I have seen
and done what fate would allow
and for every dream I'm promised
there's a hollow in me, now

I am out of place, I guess,
in such a graceless age
and the question always has been put
in the temples, on the page,
where shelter is never given
and peace is but a dream
I cling to my religion
like a driftwood in the stream

serenity

I will lay down beside you, no other,
for there is no one who can claim my heart
but you, the pure angel of my release.
my surrender is but to you, I start
each day with an earnest, deep prayer to you,
of you, for all the true magic is found,
bound in your soul and flesh and heart, I knew
nothing before you descended, profound
in evidence that I was lost to life
and that you were mysteries incarnate,
come to reveal the frail beauty so rife
with the sweet perfection in the duet
of prayers that have, for me, been granted grace
in your sweet spirit and seraphic face.

spiderweb cracks

how deep is too deep?
when will I hear the spidering cracks
as my shell implodes
and I am crushed, the blood flushed
from my veins to mingle with the medium
within which I am violenced
beyond recognition.
beyond life.
then I will know.
even now the pain persists
and I resist it only
to close accounts.
I knew the risks
in this descent
and am bent inward,
the pain excruciating.
I can hear the subtle pings
of the pangs
as I splinter.
holding on.
holding out.
holding hope
in hands going cold.
growing cold.
with the inevitability.
not enough time
to organize
an escape
and I sealed those passages
against cowardice.
the spidering cracks
fill my field of view
and I write
these words
as journal of
whatever comes next
in these awkward times.

aubergine, my passion

deeper than solferino,
flushed with the rushed, deep royal
taint of my fiery desires,
aubergine is my lust.
dark and tumescent.
omnipresent
as you are in my thoughts
and most mortal of dreams.

the nosferatu's quandary II

would I
feed on you
if I were near to death
and you
offered me
a share of your breath
if I
promised you
I would not take all
and you
did not ask
what brought me so to fall
that I
am needful
of your tendered life force
that you
might save me
from a painful end, cold and coarse.

theogonia

not in chaos but in the nothingness.
the void. entropy before the Big Bang.
the egg, cosmic. without fire to bless
the dark with an illumination to hang
in skies, begging for light in the deep night
to split the fears and solitude that weeps
once the fury of the solar rage, bright
and warm, slips through the horizon and sweeps
our best awakenings into irrelevance.
we are the gods not yet in ascendance,
but we are real and here and born to chance
the edge of worlds long forgotten, romance
and the poets', their imagination
marking silent whispers and salvation.

Pallas

Well, my goddess, you've done it again.
Kicked my ass from here to the horizon.
I am bemused and delighted that you
are willing to contend with me, for so many
step down and back, the skies of Olympus
too intimidating for their grounded sensibilities.

You are wise to put me down from time to time
for I am, in my own way, dangerously chaotic
and without the occasional cuff and chuff
would probably drive you crazy in ways
not as much to your delight as my better aspects.
Do you think anyone will notice if we slipped away?

There are a thousand reasons for deities
to stand apart, never touching, hoping or dreaming
of the possibilities in an embrace that faces fate
with a synergistic sensuousness and energy.
Let's break the sky and never die, my love.
I will wait for you by the oracles, hungry and resolute.

blithe

blithe and lithe, the choice that voices make
but never take in forsaken remembrances.
beauty defined, refined and in time, a prime
and perfect fabric of dreams and memory.
I hope, I pray, to walk with you yet a ways,
to see you evolve and the world revolve
around you, by your own remarkable essence.
your presence fills me with wonder and I am drunk
of the possibilities of a life I had given up,
convinced there was no one or nothing left
to blind my pain, to find my waning will
and fill me with honey and ambrosia and nectar
the likes of which Aphrodite would envy.

Hail Mary

Opportune hearts, parted by circumstance,
wending their ways through days devoid of touch.
Senses sheltered like skin against the chance
that the rays of the sun will burn and such
we guard against even the benefits
that the light of creation would grant us.
Not a miracle, but our faith admits
that love is a fragment of God and thus
our passions are a flicker of divine
and immortal energies, granted rare
in the hands and hearts of mere mortals, wine
from water, practical miracles, where
we can be so bold to ask redemption
in a Hail Mary not to be undone.

amomancy one

(adagio)

call back the worms. they are inelegant in this setting,
whetting only my sense of the absurd, word transcends
rock, paper or scissors, lasting longer than any artifice
of the hand of man. I can lay scars that will never heal
but seal you in, cold cataleptic to your own presumptions.
puddles are not ponds are not oceans are not worlds.

(vivace)

worlds. hurled from suns long black and stacked
to the heavens still do not reach even the sky where I,
and I alone, watch with unflagging amusement.
the others have wandered away, bored by the triviality
of what you would barter with and for, a crop of desolation.

(andante)

desolation is but the tabula rasa of the natural order.
a clean slate, grated down to the dust by forces
that course even still, in a distant land, to return
when the call for them is given. a resurrection
in the cycle of death, taken in positivity if benchmark
if made at the high tide of hope and love and dreams.

(allegro, con fuoco)

dreams? we are all of the flesh. souls soar, sail, fall and fail
but we are all inheritors of the frailty and powers.
flowers rise to our will, and are trampled by our vices,
lovers learn new lessons and definitions that tomorrow
will make the yesterdays a troubling embarrassment.
but we must not step back from the edge, the ledge
where our hearts call us to emulate God Himself
in unconditional passions and forgiveness, judging
as we would be judged, dreaming as we would be dreamt,
and written of in a way that in millennia yet to come
there will be those who read our epitaphs and smile.

bottom of the bottle

at the bottom of the bottle lay the final wishes.
irrecoverable, painfully arcane, buried in
regret and the ruby blue faceted glass, a prison
for what was once a man. now vivisected for whimsy
and whatever sustenance he surrendered too gladly,
madly shedding skin and sin for brittle reality
that was always just in the next pair of eyes that perceived
him, trapped in this lifeless state, waiting for the redemption
from his own regrets. forgiven of God, but not by man,
or woman, damned to be bound in a metaphoric maze
where love is a bandyword posturing children abuse
in their mad rush to be grown into a society
where grace is perfidy, power is abuse, and pretty
butterfly lies are best forgotten before the mourning.

november

cold wind ends the dream
the sweat of the penitent
a failed sacrifice

letters

I wrote her a letter full of grace and truths, fair,
words that cascaded like kisses on shoulders, bare,
expressing my passions and affections for her.
Words that wreck on stones split and rough, emotions stir
into a maelstrom for the daemons that demur.
I wrote her a letter full of grace and truths, fair.
I am lost without her, lost and shattered, aware
of my own frailty and unworthiness, cursed ere
expressing my passions and affections for her.
Is she my angel? Oh, that snowflakes were as pure
and perfect. Like God is in heaven, I am sure.
I wrote her a letter full of grace and truths, fair.
She has poured out her heart to me such that I dare
to believe she loves me, and I wrote, then and there,
expressing my passions and affections for her.
Of her love? I am certain, and my own? I swear!
But to be together, her circumstances are unsure
I wrote her a letter full of grace and truths, fair,
and wait now, her response, my soul to kill or cure.

sticks and stones

sticks and stone may shatter bones
as well as fists and various household items,
but words strike deeper than any physicality
and we are abusers in the darkest sense
when we lash out with tongue and temper,
leaving scars on the souls and spirits
where we should be lovers and bold champions.
hold high those around you, make not a lie
of short, simple declarative sentences
by the way you twist and persist with words
and attitude to savage the self-esteem
and dreams of those we cannot accept as peer.
this I take from those who treat others such:
they have no regard for others, no respect
and should be left to the crust of dust
that covers all lifeless things left behind.
even Jesus said shake the dust off...

ronin apokalypsis

there are worse things than being ronin.
exile from the smile and pleasure of the regent
whose very presence defines you, empowers you
such that the brittle kata of the lost warrior
remains only as a shadow, your heart beating
only out of habit. the pain draining you
until the leeches themselves choke on the dust
of a crushed, hushed heart. how long can it beat
when the disembowelment is fait accompli?
I only trust that God will judge with a kinder
disposition my sins, or I am so fucked.

but, I digress, I would express my emotions
with clarity and the charity of one who never lies
or walks away from an accident, even an enemy
deserves the quick kill or a pardon, but I am torn,
worn, scorned and borne, bound and soundless,
into the presence of my own demons, who delight
in the feast release in a single hapless incantation.
better the pen should have fallen from lifeless fingers
than I should face the mockery of my chains.
better I should find penance in all manner of sacrifice
than be cast into exile for the rest of my existence.

crowns

we wear our crowns, glass, brass, gold and metals
base that hold diamonds and flecks of paint, taint
of our self-definitions. rose petals
strewn in our path to mark our passing, faint
echoes of our egos. I wear mine proudly,
the artist's name filed blank to guard her face
from the sorrows I never meant to see
placed on her shoulders, the disgrace and trace
of regret she has for inviting in
my heart and hopes, the ropes of the gallows
bound to my neck, the inelegant sin
of a bifurcated heart, the sorrows
measured in the kiss of the noble lips,
the crown to fall from sated fingertips.

BC1434

the hollow eyes.
lies
and the taste of vinegar.
blades that have slayed
and laid
tracks to the addict's veins.
the remains of city walls
thrown down with the temple.
pain becoming a drug
to dull the doubt
shouting words
unheard
in the chambers
of a nautilus
deep beneath the cold
black waters
of the Pacific
where I sleep
until mourning
my flesh unfit
for the worms.

filigree

your warm flesh lays as a pink filigree about the entryway
to the mysteries of your desire
why me
why now
for how long

but your body is a temple
and I am a acolyte, seeking answers
and the favour of my goddess of dreams
of desire
of hope

I touch with tender aspect
and a heart filled with awe and delight
barely restraining
the plunderer's fury
the need to bleed
white blood
into your tight pink core
and bring you to life
sympathetic with my flesh

I taste you
tentative
and uncertain as to the feast
and the willingness
to let me set my pace
my face basking
in a sublime and perfect heat
radiant and captivating
your tender flesh
meshing with my fantasies

your hands guiding me
to drink deeply
to probe and kiss and
take my fill
and yours
making ready the paths
of later violations
that shall reach into
the deepest courtyards and corners
from which I will not return
intact and untouched
for I will leave a sacrifice

as a prayer
to the goddess of my desire

and you will measure me
worthy or unworthy
to return
for future mysteries
parting the pink filigree
with eager intent
as we build the histories
of a passionate future

benediction

I would take to a knee for the moment,
asking with red rimmed eyes closed tight to fight
my soul from escaping, stirring lament
to the lachrymose and beyond, the light
blinding me that once bound me in idle
idolatry, laying sacrifice
beyond imagining, a recital
of vows unanticipated, the price
of artifice, the pose is clear and dear
from the steady hand of the craftswoman
as she expresses a variant sphere
where she can be what this life does not ban
with the bandywords of the distractive,
the carny barker's legacy to give.

shed my skin

like some arcane spider
I shed my skin that I might grow
and in the moments after
I have discarded the chitin
I am as vulnerable as possible
my flesh is soft to the touch
my soul is visible
my heart could be plucked
and cast away with little effort
I shed my skin that I might grow
every second of every day

beyond the orchards

beyond the orchards
there are mighty trees
that do not pander to our senses
with fragrant blossoms
and sticky-sweet fruit.

they rise to heaven
unapologetic.
their roots rip through
the very rocks of the Earth
to hold them strong and bold.

barely bending in the wind.
not acknowledging the pinpricks
of the occasional bird or beetle.
gods of the forest. mountains of life.
beyond the orchards.

Brutus: Act One

This diseased horizon. No smooth line to define
the necessity of good and evil, merely expediency
and the illusion of honor. The eyes of the prophet,
taken like Cicero's tongue, in outrage and revenge.

I walk this bloody parapet, stains visible to me, alone.
Asking gods and goddesses that are now trivia
to those who have not yet the bark of many winters
to allow them to measure the relevance of sin.

The coals flicker, but never die, sustained by will
and made merry in a sideshow feast of jeremiads,
everyone weeping until the clowns and jugglers return
in the next act, to sweep clean the inconvenient emotions.

Every stone speaks a story that I am deaf to hear.
Every story was important when it was a moment
in a day on a life that fell to those who lived it,
making the same half-aware sentiences of the world.

The honorable are played by the ignorant, who think
the upper hand is something of an higher order
of evolution. But it is the last poet standing
who determines the legacy, as words stick wicked.

I have no use for the bartered truths that get us
through the day and on our way to our next abomination.
I have given up my ambitions to serve an ambiguity
with the faith best held for the temple mysteries.

voyeur

you cannot see me, here, hidden behind my wall of electrons.
carefully examining your expressions of thought and light.
you are beautiful, and were I not caught in Bandersnatch shackles
I would perhaps speak my mind beyond the occasional
witticism and faint praise, the marks of a smitten man
who does not know where his next meal of the heart
will come from, or if it will come, but is nevertheless
unwilling to feed merely for the glutton's curse.
I see the curve of your hip, the softness of your lip
and feel the heat rise from your thought and expression.
I envy those who touch you. as much for my solitude
as for their pleasure. I hope they are treating you well,
but I do not, when I close my eyes, imagine them
laying beside you, peeling away the final layers
of the chrysalis that folds your ultimate beauty.

mirrors

your eyes are mirrors, not windows,
for I see my love in them.
red and regent flashes of light
burning back at me when I look
to see if you see me as I am.

and you do. there is a beauty
in seeing with mirrors for eyes,
letting the world see themselves
as you see them, magnifying
the beauty you embrace as true.

I will wait until you sleep.
and kiss your precious face.
content in the visions I have seen,
your eyes showing the world
and me, the argent honesty of you.

disconnect

the line is always open
the airwaves crackle with fire
and words and emotion
that maybe you just can't

connect with

because
    your battery is low
    you're on the wrong frequency
    you forgot to pay your bill
    you're not listening
    you left the mute on
    you don't speak the language
    you can't be bothered
    it's a bad time
    it will roll over to voice mail
    you have a sore throat
    its late

yes it is

cool stones

the right path is seemingly infinite.
cool stones and the solitude of patience.
I am at peace with my decision, it
sustains me with pride and a penitence
for the insubstantial theologies
I fell to, ignorant and arrogant.
not understanding the nature of seas
that were there before this peasant, pleasant
pilgrimage fell to me and I embraced
as a worthy task for my purposes.
the legacies and my own demons faced
to make present of my future, roses
raised to awaken, petals unfolding
to the touch and kiss that I will yet bring.

flechette

bet the wet
and set the fires
I will give you spires
to climb, divine desecrations.

line of sight
the tight core of desire
wound about the axis
of unrealized Sunday afternoons.

questing thoughts
caught on the hot realizations
that you are radiating in the infrared
to my ultraviolet, solferino and ruby blue.

you know what to do
you know what to do
and will get around to it in time
of this I am sure, I won't demur.

light of life
even without parson's playacting
the exacting cuts run parallel
and wash away the day in earnest play.

golem's shade
the phoenix parade heads West
at the crossroads of truth and doubt
that's not what I am about, I shout!

treason against heaven

the flight of the alone to the Alone.
wings of tempered glass, butterfly wings,
borrowed from sorrows yet unrelinquished.
I am Daedalus and Icarus, the sky is mine.

and yet I choose to remain, huddled
against the intemperate nature of mortal thought,
caught in love as if stuck to resin, turning to amber
the glamour wears off and is reinstated

for the natural order is beauty. existing
and perceived. exhausting me but renewing
like the jacked in ionization in the high desert.
a place you have never seen me, on fire.

if God is in all things, then you are part
of the divine. I have no issue with that,
I perceive that in spectra beyond imaginings
for I have flown to the Alone and seen such things.

you are my butterfly, my sacred effigy of life
and love and the recreation of my soul
from the wasted ruins of a fallen city.
pity me not, I have what kings have killed for.

I present my sacrifices, raiment and words,
the blood of my mind, spilled in sacred runes.
you will either find your way to the epiphany
or not, that is your path for now, I am content.

for love is a bandy-word, something to say
in the middle of a fuck when you can't remember
the name of the person you are with or why.
I am not that person. I am beyond the memory.

so I shall call the mysteries and wait their rites,
empty nights with hollow arms and heart.
better the truth of the alone than the illusions
so many feed on in their defilement of the sacraments.

I gather the wind and sculpt your name in clouds
not allowed to be seen from Midgard, but God
sees with earnest eyes and smiles. the test
is ongoing, but the beauty is proven, consecrated.

I fly, tonight, on the wings you granted me,
vague copes of your beautiful membranes,
burned into my soul and one day, my flesh,
testament beyond a will, alone, loving you.

twain

lay beside me
twain of my soul

teach me the lessons
you would have me know
or at least, have me practice
for your satisfaction

I am but a sliver of glass
and your light passes
through me in colours
manifold and beautiful

like your moods and whims
that I want nothing more
than to grant, to make you smile,
to give you release and peace

lay beside me
twain of my soul

classicycle

I. Aphrodite

Goddess of the Chaotic Erotic!
queen of fantasies and flagrant fragrant passions.
beauty personified, like you, irresistible.
I surrender my essence, blessed Hephaestus,
a mere craftsman in presence of the divine,
beauty personified, like you, irresistible.

II. Athena

choices made, wisdom incarnate. understanding.
the power of knowledge and the knowledge of power.
what next is necessary and what are the wagers
and the likely outcomes. not omniscient,
but close enough to drive her forces to victory.
the excellence of superiority, found in reason.

III. Hera

Jealous wife. keeper of the hearth and home.
peer plotter to the most clever, to balance the scales
of fate that matched her with an incorrigible man-child,
who thinks that rage is power and plays his game
in seductions, reducing his presence to an archetype,
unworthy of the crown, stolen from his father.

IIII. Artemis

Mistress of the Hunt, bearer and healer of disease.
the cruel reality of nature personified, implacable.
doing what she, by nature, feels will please
her hungry heart and nature. fate's most able
agent of cruelty, but not of malice or intent,
for she is not judging those on whom her wrath is spent.

V. Demeter

Weep for your daughter, gentle Demeter.
Weep that she is stolen away, to dwell in darkness.
Rejoice in her return, but burn the fields in mourning
when she spends her seasons in the halls
of her most plutonic husband. Weep while nature sleeps.
How the very seasons are affected by your heart!

VI. Dionysia

I think the god of wine and wild revels should not be a man
for what can a man know of the release through transcendence
that women do not already know and show us in seductions.
from the gardens to the Anthesterian mysteries. histories
of the race show us that women lead the parade and charade
when pleasure is measured off the scale through the night.

VII. The Muses

Not the bastardized nine, but the true trinity of the Muses.
Aeode, the muse of song, whose voice and words flowed
like honey from the tight core of the world's divinity.
Melete, practice, to perfect the role and recitations,
to find nuance in the perfecting of passions expressed.
Mneme, from whom memory is personified,
the voice and repetitions granting immortality.
You are personified in these three, my love,
drawing out from me, and their goddess cousins
what of me is nothing less than my last, true religion,
in finding my theology in your arms and heart.

emotions

like the waves on my shore
your emotions crash into me
as reminder that, sooner or later,
I will give in to your erosion
as that is the nature of things
as it is in my nature to love you.

you are like sunshine
and the smell of cinnamon
the wind in unruly hair
and the cry of bird taking flight
you are the meadow and the night
the touch of snowflakes
the scent of cut grass
and the warmth of skin
laid against skin to communicate
desire and belonging
only skin but eloquent
and perfect, like you are,
in my eyes and my heart

I feel your tides ebb and flow
and know that I must stand
and take them, their gentle ebb
and their thunder of a full moon
when the world seems damned
to split asunder to the thunder
of your rage and wrath.
I am of a gentler breed, the earth
knows what the sea wants
and surrenders to it, in time.
as I did. and do. and will.

you are my conception of heaven.
you are my memory of life and love
that I will take with me beyond this place
and give as the password into Elysium.

path

you are bright and dark,
haunting dreams and fantasies.
mine to hold, a wraith,
a blessed curse, a sweet disease.

I am bound to you.
even when it mocks my heart.
holding fast to the epiphany
of all you were, even from the start.

echoes choose the skies.
lovers fade, love never dies.
red sand and stones erode.
but I am fixed on this harsh road.

and "Why?" the readers ask
as to my purpose in this quest.
I did not choose this task.
I chose to seek what was the best.
and thus I came to find
you dancing, in the outer spheres,
casting shadows of the blind.
child of loves and rage and fears.

I will endure the night.
I will endure through every test.
even when you fade
I will follow on the quest.
for it is in your will
that you find me, down the way,
bound to you, then still,
on a course on which I'll stay.

for that is what I want.
and you have asked me here
to endure every taunt
with faith above every toil and tear.

masks and casks

you can't see behind my mask
for I sealed it, wax and lead,
like a precious, oaken cask
filled with essences I've bled
as apothecarium
and amomancer, blending
the fires burning to numb
the agony of bending
our souls into shapes we cast
against the sky to catch clouds,
drag them down to earth, the blast
of air of God's nostrils, crowds
gathering for the esprit.
forgetting their destiny.

moebius

hexameter shimmers, glimmers of the genius,
the eclectic circuit clear cutting the ions
that rise to form the sustaining arch that makes us
heirs and ancestors to loyal, royal lions,
the bestiary of our nightmares, the visions
seen between sweet sheets and completed themes and dreams
bathed in the night sweats in a practiced precision
cast away, let the moment flow like silken seams
torn away and forgotten, like a virgin's prayer
to the impassive Gods who select and perfect
all we will weave into the triptych of our lair,
idle idols we pray to when we resurrect
self-respect and understand the nature of peace,
found in your true arms, in a moment of release.

intricate

you are a

very
    intricate
        woman

complicated
in the way that makes for

interesting
    dinner
        conversation

and a certain level of grey
discussing certain things.

I would like,

with
    your
        permission,

to study the labyrinth
that is your soul, mind and body

until
    you
        give up

your secrets, or I give up
my life, searching for them, in wonderment.

the punishing stone

have you ever watched the skin
melt away on your fingertips?
the discomfort becoming pain.
the pain becoming regent
as flesh burns and peels.
the acid of acknowledged sorrows
undiminished by forgiveness
if it ever comes, for the pain
exists in dark and infinite waves
that crash against me, bitter
is the taste of the brine
that carries the acid that burns
the flesh that feeds the pain
that disorients the soul such
that all other senses crackle
and spit, eyes useless and taken
it the point of an hot needle
driven to blind and bind all focus
to a single sin. I am consumed
from within, fed upon by doubt
and fear exquisite only in its
totality. an eclipse of dreams.
feeling the blood bursting
in capillaries as the acid goes deep
and finds the channels into me.
second after second after second,
into minutes and hours and days
and even death wants no part of this
and turns away, his cruel smile
fading with something akin to
sympathy for the Ouranian pain.
and through it all I must wrap myself
in false skin and enduring good humour
and mock my very sentience
by playing at being a living thing.
for I am dying. dying by every
measure of pain and sorrows.

oblivion would be mercy.
but there are those who need
me to rise on feet scourged of flesh
and walk in darkness amidst
the howling of hungry demons
feeling my way with hands
mangled and burnt until even maggots
would not consume the scraps.
I lay against cold metal headboards
and know there is no one coming
to unchain me, Prometheus and Loki,
the venom is my punishment.
this is my fault, my flaw, my pain
and you will never know it as I do.
and I would not want you to.
for that would make mock of my love.

unbowed

I am my own soul.
you cannot unmake me
or reshape me
but by my acquiescence.

If I seem to passively accept
what you say or do
it is not passivity
but that goddamn wisdom.

You will learn in time.
Either I or others
will reach you, teach you,
the universal lessons of love.

Until then, be the storm.
I will be the solitary figure
standing on the cliffs, naked,
reveling in your beauty.

for that is my nature.

white lotus

transcending pain, the grain forms of nature.
strength and length and the force of the freedom
to choose the right path, the night path, unsure
of the outcome, but certain of wisdom
in the walking without the bartered hearts
that are battered and split, but yet endure.
pure is the consecration that which parts
the sea of blood and sweat to raise and cure
us of our forgotten paths. purposed love
is not weakness, and tears are a baptism
of pain, released like a toxin, above
it all we stand, the pale cataclysm
stretched out like a bad dream fading in light
as we enlighten and lighten out loads, this night.

seasons

have you ever seen the snowflakes that fly
in their haste to descend down to the ground
on the zephyrs of the summer's warm sky?
even though they know that they'll be unbound,
melting into water to run away,
their bright crystals wasted in their release
to feed the trees, grasses and to give sway
to the soft flow, natural and at peace
with the order of things not yet revealed
to the tender, old truths ancient and fair.
in time this love will no more be concealed,
but for the now, let them dance on the air.
I will wait for you to find me, seasons
pass, but in my own time, my own reasons.

eggs

the cruelty of the duality.
we want and need, for both we bleed,
fractured shells, swelling to

CRACK

and then we run away

no

really run away
like an egg from a shattered shell

we learn from
experience
and
observation
and
communication

and I wish you'd believe me
when I tell you the lessons
you seem determined to learn

        the hard way

CRACK

ah well. hell. another mess to clean up.

street...

the heels strike sparks
on the bobbled cobblestone streets;
sweet, the beat, the beat, the beat
keeps time with the rhyme and I'm
still who I was.
curious as to the catalyst's blast
the fast broken and the quick? dead.

it's like I said, words are only words
in the hands of the acolyte. but light
bends and befriends you if you surrender
to it, pretender (to wit), and the tapestries
blossom like magnolias and dogwood.
time enough for rainbows
if there is any time left at all
and the mockery of the clocks
laugh. tick. tock. tick tock. tick tock.
stick the slick and sickened fist
into the air and feel which way
the wind is blowing for the moment.

I will be there, where the wind goes.
the rose has risen, black and emerald.
and in the end nothing really mattered
as the pages are scattered
for trivial travails, beginning with the word
and ending in words
wrapped in burlap and filled
with rusty nails and egregious sins.
street corner magicks are no less real.

spark

what strikes the spark
illuminates
and scatters - shatters
fears and hates
yet all those nagging doubts?
they yet remain.

for we are creatures of our scars
we stand in muck and pray to stars
for a sign to shine like eyes
that brim with tears.

my love for you is no less bright
it comforts me in silent night
when God himself sits patiently
obscure.
my passions are bent to your need
and on my life I hope you'll feed
when yours needs sustenance
I won't complain.

my way of love is mine, you see
and to your path a mystery
you have not seen with open eyes
before.
I am not some buckish swain
who sings some trouvere's old refrain
I speak my heart and nothing else
compares.

so I will burn with passions, hot,
and see if you will learn to spot
the spectrum I emit in infrared.

I'm not infernal or eternal
and one day I will burn to the kernel
but this love will be my legacy and bed.

I promised you, and I remain,
the patient, transcendental rain
that washes you to purify our lusts.

I am your servant and your king,
your lover-friend, most everything
that you will accept into your life.

martyrdom, part 11

I don't want to be
the
    top
of the pyramid.

I can't be.

I know the darkness
that I   carry
like a disease.

Incurable.

The doubts and the
irreversible scars
of every   mistake
I ever made.

Every
    stubbed toe
        twisted ankle
            falling down the stairs
                faux pax ad libs
that confirm the worst
to those who
don't want to believe
in anything more
than what they can
    touch
taste
    smell
feel
    hear.

Faith is an illusion
to them.
An illusion to dispel.
And I don't want
to be believed in
as anything more
than what
        I am.

I've had my Gethsemane.
It isn't pleasant

especially
when no one sits with you
to ask you to reconsider
your doubts.
The burning flesh
the tears after
you are dry
and nothing emerges
but shuddering sobs.

I don't want the job.
But somewhere,
someone,
probably not overly fond of me,
stuck me with it.

And I keep leaving it by
the   side
of the road
hoping someone else
picks. it. up.

And I never have to see it again.

The hallowed hollows
within   me
bleed until they are full
then drain
     away
in precognizant memory
of when the place of skulls
is underfoot.

I am not any thing special.
Just a man in love.
And would trade all fates
for an earnest touch.

One day.

And to some that makes me
    a martyr
to others that makes me
    a hero
but to me it just makes me
    lonely.

serenade

I have never seen you fade to the music of my serenade,
my words exploding on your tongue like apricots harvested young;
tart and sweet but incomplete, the passions are not consummate,
but tell us of a time yet here when if we are true, our hearts sincere
shall find a way to sanctify what our natures must, for now, deny.

transcend

we were not put here to fall into the fey and fel grey.
luminous hearts, despite our scars and scratches, must endure.
for the lamps of many die a slow, flickering death, pray
for the dawn. pain overtakes the night, but we yet are sure
that our dreams are like the day-lily, sworn to the sun soon
rising on dependable thighs to skies that welcome light
as reassurance that sorrow cracks with the trusted moon
reflecting just enough light to mark our path in the night.
my words are like the cold moon, merely a mirror of you,
as you take your place in the center of all things sacred.
I am only seen as you illuminate me and through
reflected light I am perceived as friend and it is said
I am more than I am: Yet, cold and dead but for your touch.
I seem alive because your pure light alone makes me such.

everything

you said
try
everything.

I can only say
that you are my everything.
my words are frail and failed
hypocrisies
of a false religion
if this is not true.
for you
make the sun rise and set
within me.
my creativity is inexorably
eternally
bound to your will and whim
and mood.
you can turn your back on me
in displeasure
but I will not ignore
the truth
that I love you,
unconditionally.
I am capable of hurting,
of despair,
when you abandon me,
but like Job,
I know where my deity is
and that
denying you would be
wrong
a sin
of a magnitude
most cannot comprehend.
so, simply put,
I love you.
and I will.
even to the end of all things.
and not just a book.

envy

There are times I

envy

        you.

Your place in the shadows of my world,
able to

        slip
away

and lick your wounds
when the world gets

        as stupid

as I can be.

I stand here
in the   ionized gases
of an alien sun

unable to even
        speak your name

for fear the gods or mobs

would not understand
even as poorly as we do
what is happening to us.

But I am not trapped.
I choose to stand here
feeling the rise of Atlantis
beneath my feet

the fire of the Southern sky
burning my flesh
my heart
my soul.

And celebrating.
Yes, celebrating.
Celebrating that there is someone:

        you,
specifically,

worth the deep acid etched
rivulets forming on my soul.

And if I cry out in pain
or shame when I stumble
it is not anger or fear.

It is pain.

But pain that purifies.
    Sanctifies.
        Deifies.

And gives me, for all my mumbled
meanderings,

peace
and great joy.
That there is a presence
in the fire
of this alien sun.

the roar

I adore the roar of the ocean.
it reminds me you when you are
at your fiercest, outraged and engaged
in something of real value.
no time for the sequins on sackcloth
others often wear, shadows.

I have invoked, provoked and witnessed
the fury of the waves, crashing down
to grind great stones to gravel
and to sand. the hand of Poseidon
makes a convincing fist.
you would have made a great Greek goddess.

I would build your temple of stone,
but far from the sea, so as not to tempt
Poseidon, or even Aphrodite
(who would lose many followers to you)
to knock it down, for I would keep the fires
bright into the night as I await your presence.

fragment 07143

I want to taste your blood
that hasted, wasted flood
that you summon in the darkness
to stop the tears
the fears
the years
of looking for something in the shadows
black as blood in the moonlight
dance for me with clenched hands
fists that kissed the bitter bricks
as you staged your rage
you are always bleeding...

the curse of the Genji

when the magic fades
there will be no parades
just the sad blue man
sitting in the corner
begging for coins for his cataracts
while the children in the street
whisper
and point
and laugh.

the other half of the story:
free will is the red pill.
you can't not take it.
the loop is flawless.
all creatures of sufficient will
fill themselves with knowledge
until they burst,
cursed to die
while those who
can't see the wall?
they stop in time.

power is the pattern.
coruscating ions in emerald green
ripping synapses like a disease.
stripping down the flesh
to an irrelevancy
except as totem of respect
and affection.
misdirection
in the hand of an assassin.

weaving whims and words.
granting wishes
of love and immortality.
but never
getting close enough
to taste it.
the ladle mocks.
left to begging in the street
for scraps and waving
to the rare acolyte
on their way to
the temple of Aphrodite
to take up the lamp.

malevolences, part one

malevolence is different to different spirits.
sins of commission, omission, emission,
a new clear fusion, a dirty fission
and the frisson of guilt spilt in wilted regret.
wet the frets and reset the petals,
that no one will know what happened.
but you. silence is a savaging, ravaging seed,
the need bleeds deep and your sleep weeps
silent violences. self-immolation, desecration,
that the ashes may be purified, sanctified, denied
as evidence of a sense of sentience inexplicable.

cocoon

I want to see, when you emerge,
your wings unfold in morning light.
to touch you is my sacred urge,
to enter you in dovetail tight.
your chrysalis transcends the past,
you burst awake to claim my soul.
I am yours, cures for black die cast,
Pascal's wagers, a poet's roll.
bind with me and I am fit feast
for your passions and fashions' thirst,
ripped and stripped to a truth released
from blessing born of madness cursed,
fallen away, like the proud shroud
shed in this bed, my vows aloud.

waking state

I woke this morning.

and, for an instant,
you were there,
curled into my massive arms,
sleeping beside me.

I did not want to
wake up
fully,
because I knew it was a dream,
a conjourment of my desire.
an echo of an amomancy,
forbidden in life.

I held you as long as I could.

and wept for the waking.

response

flushing pink and red and burning black and ashen.
knowing the sensation of my kiss even at a distance,
the persistence of my expressive violations of you,
driving you to moan my name to empty ears
and fill you with fears that someone will know
that all these words are of you, and you alone.
you have pulled me from orbit to wait, and I do,
for I see in you the spark that was promised
as evidence of god and divinity and an eternity
I had surrendered to sorrows, reawakened.
words like balls of blistering magma
hurled into the sky to return as stones set
in rings you dare not wear for fear
you will meet the fate of Hypatia.
by my words I make love to you from afar.
and they are but pale token of the inferno
that burns within me, consuming me daily,
but making pretty lights on the horizon
for the skeptics, the mystics and the mad.

abdication

Forgive me my soft sins, a man may fail.
But in malice, I am innocent, grave
may be my demeanor, but passions pale
when measured against my purposed and brave
affections for you. Respect and passion,
immeasurable and of a treasure
unearthed only by your beauty, I've won
nothing in this life if not the pleasure
of your sweet presence in my day and night
until the end of all things. You are birth
and death, the breath of angels in their flight
as they consider a man's word and worth.
I have given mine, and am content I
will lay with you alone, until I die.

as dust

if I must be alone to prove
that my love, it shall not move

from a fire to mere ash,
I shall wear the hermit's sash

and the sackcloth, with the pride
that I carry, deep inside.

a love immutable as grace
that transfigures my sad face

into a masque of awe and bliss
suspended by your perfect kiss.

at a distance, but yet a prayer
in the catacombs, where we swear

to the greater gods of peace
for our eventual release.

until and then, you will find,
by my faith in you, I bind

my flesh and heart and soul
to achieve your every goal

and to place in you all trust
until my bones are swept, as dust.

afterlife

The end of my reign.
The memories remain
But not the glory.
Stories told in red and gold
Are pretty but pity
Is a poor unguent, pungent
And bitter.

the poets

with the pieces assembled, the board is now set.
the players are seated to consider the test.
playing for more than position, the wager set
by Aphrodite, Athena, power to wrest
from the words of Bragi, Apollo, Erato
and overthrow the Word, absurd children of grief
seeking power in the flower of shepherds, no
riddle of Dionysius to make a thief
of the bringers of dreams. word dancers, speaking true
the new religion of the hearts' awakening,
the promise of consummate consecration new
only to children of the latecomers, breaking
bread, echo of a religion of a new age.
we are the poets. we are the priests of couer rage.

the fourth nightmare

carved of stone
to atone for the heat of flesh
meshing in memory
lacking voice to identify
the truth, the lie,
the transfiguration

the light reflects
ruby-blue off the curved surfaces
unnerving, unswerving
the superego id kid
driven into the desert
that passes for the soul of society

sobriety of passions
tears of quicksilver alone
mark that there was
ever a soul
in the heart of the beast
torn out and swallowed

this world

recognize the world for what it is
a witches' brew of both joy and pain.
serenity so rare a commodity
that to walk with the stride of the vampyr
is to invite the derision of the masses.

you are elegance and beauty.
the missing pieces of me are filled
precisely when you touch me and say
what is in your heart, even in the silence
for I hear you in it now, and I listen.

nothing less than nothingness frightens me.
the void where you would not be
beside me, every night without a test
of my sanity and vanity and endurance.
for I have seen the face of sorrows.

a weeping Buddha is my guard for you.
my garden in a patch of words you've heard
so many times you sometimes doubt whether
anyone can say them with sincerity.
but walk a while in my shoes and know my heart.

I am patient. and persistent, and you asked
that I walk this path for you wait for me,
a smile of shy victory on your face, no trace
of doubt as to my passion and affection for you.
so I will keep to this road, this world, my love.

summer grass

I believe in you the way the grass
believes in the summer rain,
even if you're not here right now
you'll be coming back again.
I've nothing left to prove in this life
except you're as perfect as the sky,
and I'm going to stand here, singing,
until you come walking back by.
I've seen many pretty faces, many hearts,
full of angry angels, devils and the fell.
I have walked my path with some regrets
but I'll follow you in this life, to Heaven or Hell.
I believe in every thing you are. Everything you crave.
Your dreams are now my dreams, my soul is yours to save.

never

never leave
never die
never cry
but to grieve in purpose I may soothe.
never fade
never bleed
never need
what is made anywhere I cannot reach.
never drown
never pout
never doubt
that a frown is but a spur to me to hold you.

the quiet crucibles

I come from out of the East

the rising sun the photic mantra
of my rebirth
the earth
acknowledging me
as I tread towards the horizon

I have passed through
the pillars
and stood at the edge
of the cliffs
and laughed as I leapt
as I wept
as I flew downward
32 feet per
second squared but not afraid
of anything
but leaving you alone
if I don't
be as strong as possible
and then some

for I was content
to fade into the grey
until you said
follow me
like some new messiah
and I followed
out of curiosity
and desire
and an affection
I had been carrying
like a rock
now smooth with grinding
smooth enough
to play cannon shot
when needed

so I followed you
and gave my soul
that you might know
I am not one of your
schoolchildren suitors
needing tutors themselves
on the lessons of love
no matter how good it feels
and how malleable
they may seem
to the plastic heat
of your naked intellect

it is odd
that my god(ess)
has more of a crisis of faith
than I do.
troubling and exhausting.
like finding out
that Colonel Sanders
was never really in the army.
or that some
go to heaven
without benefit of the King James Version.

but it is in these quiet crucibles
that we find our faith
tested and molested.
our souls burdened.
our purpose questioned
as other deities smell blood
and show up, full lipped
and slipped into the tightest
of gowns they stole from Aphrodite.
and the test never ends.
and I am so afraid.
and so alone.
but that is where we are proved.
that is the essence of truth.

rest

I shall cast my ashes over the waters
to find my way into the silence I have sought.
the peace of the cool depths, seductive
as the kiss of an illusion. I am caught
in the satellite whims of remembrance,
where I do not command my fate unless
I am willing to take violent hand against me
and grant the rest. the test. to wrest
from those for whom I am a crutch,
resented at times, even when most needed.
alone in the world, a gnarled driftwood shaft,
left to wormfood in the shallows.
I so want the cool silence of the depths.
even as I rise on stout legs of will
and the valor I cannot lay down, ever.

no pit in Hell

I have said it before.
I repeat myself to be clear.
there is no pit in Hell
deep
enough
        hot enough
for a man who strikes women
be it with hand or word.
no justification
no virtue in cruelty
in jealousy
that marks the skin and souls
of the most precious
of our species.

heaven

God is up in Heaven and yet is all around.
so why does everyone think that I am lost
when you are not to be readily found?
Madness, it is, I would say, for the cost
of my patience is pennies to the riches you bear
as my deity and my dame, an avatar
in soft pink lips, dark eyes and raven hair,
drawing me in with coy passions and far
navigations to a pleasant land of peace
where I journey, indefatigable, alone
but for the fact I am coming to release
the sacred doves and to at last atone
for the years I have wasted, waiting for
a sign. alone for a season, but no more.

defiance

Patience is a virtue, passion, a need.
We will find it all within us one day,
moments meeting moments, an earnest seed
planted, love granted all for what we pray.
I am nearby, near enough to touch, hold
and mold into what is most needful. Dream
and dare the dreams to flesh. Consuming cold
defeat with fierce, searing heat and will scream
defiance as my dance in the fates' face.
We are the authors of our destinies
and we will do so much more than just trace
our names in silent wishes, travesties
in the name of defied, deified pain
that we will wash away, like fading stain.

alien eyes

I'm in love
with the girl
with the

ALIEN EYES

those eyes that seem
to have
x-ray vision

and the ability
to cut me to pieces
with lasers and masers
she brought from the stars
or from Mars

the rules don't apply
to her
so I have to be careful
pick my words
kiss her when her guard
is
down

and never let those
ALIEN EYES
see me looking
for anything but a place
to practice xenobiology

she's stuck here
on Earth
and learning
(sometimes the hard way)
that, as a species,
we aren't as harmless
as the advance scouts said

but I'll stick
close by
and guard my girl
with the
ALIEN EYES
from mad scientists
and unruly mobs
and the occasional
curiosity seeker
who gets too close

for their own protection
as much as hers
and earn her trust
so she will kiss
with her
ALIEN EYES
closed

although,
truth be told
I like them
wide open
to the wonder
of the world
and so I can see
her beautiful soul

family

it hurts to think that you may never meet my Grandmother.
that hard working, sharp tongued guardian of the world.
she pulled the metal thorn from my paw and bandaged
my head when rusty nails tore my scalp open.
she raised her children in a one room shack when her husband
took the side door and left her to work for pocket change
riding the Osage Express every day for decades.
she loves me and loved me, and I do her,
she would love you and smile that cracked country girl
smile, unfettered by a life that would have crushed
you or I to corn meal beneath the big wheel of lost dreams.

it hurts to think that you may never meet my Father.
a man of grace and class, more than five decades married,
the man who would read us the Odyssey to put us down
for naps that always seemed more for his benefit than ours.
smart, funny, he could make a friend anywhere you'd put him.
the youngest of six, raised by a coal miner, his eldest brother
died in the Second World War. He is the last of his generation,
now the paterfamilias of a clan that spreads from coast to coast.
he taught me to fly a kite and throw a baseball (badly),
I recall him racing me on foot against my bicycle when I was nine.
I recall every whispered word of wisdom he gave me.

it hurts to think that you may never meet my Mother.
an archetype, June Cleaver meets Donna Reed, raising
five children through life and love and loss. burying
her only brother, and raising us up with the ability to think,
decisively and incisively. a woman of great faith and,
to be honest, occasionally a bit stubborn. a seamstress
and homemaker, a cook, she was the one who rushed me
to the hospital when my own body turned against me
and I almost died, my body aflame with pain and toxins.
she taught me how to cook and gave up on me,
when it came to ever making hospital corners.

it hurts me to think that any of these people that I love
may never get to meet you, and know the spectrum of dreams,
of memories yet to be born as deep and perfect as all
they gave to me. you will be, I pray, the companion
they are at peace leaving me in the hands of as my journey
continues, seemingly forever. I would, I should like
one day to see you with them, showing them the light
that burns within you, a clean and keen joy and intellect,
something I could not have predicted or even perhaps hoped for.
I want to be as special to you as you are to me, and to see
you as a part of the tapestry of my life, as they have been.

vigil

I will hold vigil over your soul,
guarding against all that is under my control
to protect you, respect you more, and yes,
I will love you with a fierce tenderness.

I will be gentle in all of my ways
except for when in the darkest of days
you need a champion to stand the line
which I will do for you, angel divine.

I'm not promising I won't someday fall
or that I will succeed in my all
but for you I will hold to the last
and give you a future, not a past.

an alchemistic chant

the jester fades

the serenades

begin again

silver balls and crystal spheres
the shadows shake the light
the curtains part, illusion clears,
transient to the night.

the jester fades

the serenades

begin again

cithara songs and lyric twists
are echo and repent
emerald and amethyst
refract the light's relent

the jester fades

the serenades

begin again

madness mixed with trace of grace
an alchemistic chant
to mend the heart once ripped apart
confused, refused, recant

the jester fades

the serenades

begin again

erotics

we are prisoners of
an existential love
desires melting in the afterglow.
passions flashing red
an immolating bed
I dream of you, impaled, on satin snow.

I want to touch the heat
that makes you feel complete
I want to enter you and center you.
in every way you dare
in every way you care
to trust me with your lust, so true.

and when it all is done
we have just begun
to explore new erotics in our lives.
for I will not complete
my taste of you, my sweet,
until from me, my life, the darkness drives.

the share

your victories lift me up and make me proud
no matter their scope or scale, for the shroud
of time will not fall so soon that I am jealous
of the life you share with me, people tell us
that we are a conundrum and I am bemused
by their arrogance, knowing they are confused
by the artifice and ignorance of never knowing
the union of dreams and sorrows, enjoying
an intimacy that is more than flesh and sweat,
but that is true and patient and strongly set
like an emerald in enduring gold. merging
lives without losing identity, each encouraging
the other to be their best and to, in all things, share,
raising both to a sacred place, beyond compare.

trouvere

hiding behind shutters
crying in the gutters
the lone trouvere sings soft,
lofty, alone and true

lovers fading to time
and the elevation
of new, purer muses
to their proper places

faces, traces of touch
clarified when uttered
in the pure speak of love;
desire, fire and faith

courtesan and priestess
his lover swears her heart
in this consecration
he is reborn to life

fairer than the selkies
sweeter than ambrosia
her kisses bind him here
to sing of her alone

moments into hours
hours into the days
that mark and make the years
confessed and blessed, the test

immortality tastes
like her kiss, her lips ripe
and her body a vessel
for her earnest passion

the words flow like flowers
in a spring sacrament
thrown into the river
to flow beyond these lands

imagination served
in distant lands as songs
commit to memory
and she is eternal

hiding behind shutters
crying in the gutters
the lone trouvere sings soft,
lofty, alone and true

lullabye

I will hold you tonight
and let you fade into the comforting grey.
my heartbeat your metronome.
my breath evidence of my vigilance.
my warmth proof of my passion and presence.

rest

I am here for you
even when I am not, for my will is strong
to belong in your arms, your bed, your life
and I will always be where you need me
even if just to play comfort to your needs.

laying down the awe

I'm laying down the awe
and picking right up where I left off

you have to know, you know,
that I can't feel it if I don't show
in radiant tiger pounces, bouncing
heart and soul to play my role
as the benchmark of desire

fire! fire! coming down the wire
or actually, more like fiber optic
in this day and age, our cages wage
an immovable war against our forces,
irresistible or not, we are fought and fraught
with all our insecurities. love is a disease.

at least the way a lot of people play it,
full of bluster and pain, they stain the drain
with the carnage of their carnivorous pants.
rude, crude and hewed from gnarl stumps
they can bring the humps but when the bumps
need a good phrenologist, they head for the hills.

I'm laying down the awe
and picking right up where I left off

you made it clear you want me here. damn near
dragged me through the swamp to romp
with you in fantastic delights, fantasy nights
where the chair is the snare for the sharing.
we electrify ourselves with our own anarchistic
energy, starting over at zero, the chase chaste
the demons of our pasts, cast aside
as we hide nothing, but accept everything
as the price of a perfectible passion.

it's yours. you called to me at a distance.
I was slow turning around, my calculations
say by about four fortnights. that's alright,
even though you scare the hell out of me,
I want you so bad, like nothing I've had
and I never want to make you mad enough
to pack up your stuff and take the next road
out of Damascus to the cliffs of perdition.

I'm laying down the awe
and picking right up where I left off

I can dance in the shadows
dance in the shadows
dance in the shadows
until the music stops and someone hops
onto the floor just a heartbeat ahead of me
(wouldn't be the first time) and that scares me
dares me, ensnares me in the notion
that maybe I need to press my suit.
this passive aggressive just got a bit possessive.

elegy

In the frame of all things
there is a very real chance
that I will go before you

and that in the aftermath
of my passing, the magnitude
of my love and admiration
will become so much more
apparent, as people tend to listen
more to the words of a dead man.

and so the world will see you
through these eyes, enchanted
by your smile. the soft laugh
that tells me that you have even
embarrassed yourself a little.

the way your eyes light up
when you are happy, little stars
in the firmament of your raven hair.
the way you say my name
even in front of people who do not
particularly like me very much.

and they will know my heart
and know the source of my love,
for it was born in you. I merely midwifed
the truth of you, that it might
breathe air and run with the children
we never had, or would have had.

and I envy you this, for in the light,
the spectrum of human emotions
when magnitude infects the multitudes
you will feel more love than I ever
could have touched, or comprehended
if I had not known you.

for as the light passes through me
I was not blind. I was not untouched
by the warmth and the heat and the bright
incandescent brisance like the explosion
of a thousand stars within me.

and I will be grateful.
and in precognizant memory
I am grateful for your love and grace.
your beauty and passion and wisdom.
and all the moments, virtual and literal
that passed between us like truth.

sometimes denied, but of a substance
that does not bend to the purposes
of others. not friend or lovers
or those who pose as one or the other
without knowing the nature of their role.

but I will remain, frozen in time
by words I spoke, without doubt
but in joy and pain and hope and fear
and the pleasure that comes from
accepting the magnitude of love

dedication to an angel

I will never let you go
never let you down
never let you drown
in the tides of life that come

I'm not wasting more of life
on lesser lights and dreams
than spending it with you
whatever that takes from me

Dancing barefoot in the snow
I can feel your eyes
watching with surprise
that I feel no pain

But I am merely resolute
and dedicated to your love
and your happiness
and I will dance my prayers

I will never let you go
never let you down
never let you drown
in the tides of life that come

patience

Patience is a virtue, earned and learned by
testing the limits of our sanity,
the vanity of our egos, try
as we might, we are never fully free
of our worst intentions our pretension
that this world somehow exists our whim,
our purposes and paradoxes, sun'
shining because we don't want rain, the grim
moments nothing more than our need for shade
from the bliss of eternal smiles and light.
You are worthy of all that I have made
of myself, patient and grey, with delight
that perhaps I'm one who can undertake
the beautiful challenge you will stake.

awakening

at times of sorrow
I will be there when you wake
take what you need of my soul
my strength my love my life
for it is yours
and when you need it
I will be there

no mocking judgment or rage
for in the morning, the beauty
of holding you is my evidence of God
and that the world spins true
and so for you
I pour out my moments
I will be there

I will hold you to me
and to all your coquettish promises
and kiss your hair, touch you
in ways tender and passionate
and ask you to let me
shoulder your burdens
I will be there

to me it is an act of love
to trust me with your pain and sorrows
and I will never be less
than a loving partner to you
I will not turn away
when you call to me in love or pain
I will be there

psalm

that we make merry of our sin
breaking hearts and breaking in
as we don't know the alchemy of love

passions fade, affections grow,
we weep and reap what we did sow
and fill our hearts with what they're empty of

my vows to you are not a flare
to mock your heart and make you care
when all I want is pretense to my thirst

I'll stand alone in shadow's grief
and wait for you, as purposed thief,
and think myself as blessed, not as cursed

for you are worth the tidal pain
and worth again the martyr's stain
from orbits you have pulled me to alight

I'll lay with you when you request
and care for you, times bitch and best,
and earn the right to hold you in the light

falling back into place

as it been so long since last I slapped my palm
flat against the Earth
to measure the effort required
to spin it out of orbit and crack the sun?

most likely. there are lovers who were unborn
when last I wore that tapestry
as a sacrificial robe.
I taste the stale copper of dried, ancient blood.

when did the poets give up the magic?
when did we leave the weaving to fingers
neither nimble or quick
that stick themselves and call it purging surgery?

we are more than blood, more than the resin
left by drying intimate fluids, crude druids
think that resurrecting ancient faiths
is the same as making new discoveries.

this is the faith of David the King. the cithara
of Cicero and of Homer. souls sliced
instead of priced for whatever the crowd throws
as the cock crows and we take pride in denial.

mare

we are all houses divided against themselves
loyalties between the soiled royalties we crown
down with the revolution, it turns sour
and the hour passes in a quickstep, weapons
drawn and erased on a case by case basis.
faces fade and the mad charade begins again.
I am the shadow at the window, drawing back
to vanish in the darkness, but leaving trace
in the vapours of my nostrils and my peculiar
bootprint, evidence of a passing peculiar.
familiar and yet, unmet. how long since
I have enjoyed what you may take for granted?
how long since I have felt breath on my cheek?
ephemeral. ethereal. unreal. the seal is peeled
and the wax no longer holds the solitary stone.
I passed the test and know the equation,
I faced it in a fortnight's silence when violence
with the bony cage seemed the sole solution.
the iron headboard does not chain me.
I am its possessor and confessor to the secret
muses that have wandered too deep
into the seas of storms, of tranquility
and my home in Mare Marginis.

rainbeau

many things and everything
I am
expected
to fill the gaps
the sniggering cracks
that appear without warning
in the sky

I am ready for the role
it doesn't mean
I am always comfortable
in it
but performance
in the unpleasantries
is an admirable trait

the call

take me from the ruins
strap on
my wings of glass
the sky beckons onward
it's time for me to answer
the call

argent wings and promises
spread out
against the sky
it is time to acknowledge
scars as maps for answering
the call

your voice echoes loudly
I roar
in answering
I tack into the sunlight
gaining hope and altitude
the call

nothing stands between us
nothing
but our own reserves
I am content to hover, lover,
in shadowed heavens, answering
the call

iridescence

a light in a thousand colours, cascading from the emerald green
you wrap yourself in. eyes of dark mystery and history,
a kiss like ebony and blood, flooding my soul with an unseen
course and force that commands of my soul a new story
built on truth, edgy and sharp, not the plastic playthings
that slipped in, in between the cracks to channel faith
like a venom, distorting the contorted hope that springs
like an hungry illusion, a meta metaphor for the wraith
that remains. strength an allegoried parlour trick,
sticking in mud made of dirt and the flood of earnest tears.
we are stronger than the pure elements, alloyed to stick
deep within the furnace of follies that belong to unborn years.
we are here, kairos, to collect the precognizant debt
in kisses, caresses, communicating in iridescent sweat.

faith

before I die
I will make love with you
so that
if there is no God
I shall have been to Heaven
within you
and be at peace

faith healer

I'm the faith healer, soul stealer, revealer of the light.
Will burn you down to build you up, drink from your sacred grail.
I walk the line, devil and divine, creature of the night.
I never ask for more than what you dare slip through the veil.
The curdled mask I took to task lays cracked and cold as death.
The whitest lace, it leaves no trace when immolated wet.
I fill my chest with winds of your West that I might share breath.
I fill your need, but you feel me feed, place me in your debt.
The wall of sound has come unbound, I slap it back to hold.
I'm damned, yours to command, consecrating my fate alone.
Silver lips eclipse your hips, drink ambrosia red and gold.
I claim the same you asked of me, symphony overthrown.
When it is all said, it is nothing but a bed, except
it is anything and everything for which we've wept.

gospel

Words of faith and the insurrection of passions.
Dreams against the common faith and premonitions.
Your trace speaks solemn volumes, gospel to my soul.
I am but messenger, bound to deliver whole
the truth of your pledge and vows, beyond my control,
words of faith and insurrection of passions.
Proof that this evangelist has found his mission's
path. Angel invocateur, mother of visions,
your trace speaks solemn volumes, gospel to my soul.
I am eloquent as Bragi, playing my role
as herald of the truth of your beauty, the sole
words of faith and the insurrection of passions
given to me, driven by your invitations
for me to give my soul to your soft persuasions.
Your trace speaks solemn volumes, gospel to my soul.
I am yours, bound unto this life and the next, cautions
cast aside, as well as my pride, to be made whole.
Words of faith and the insurrection of passions
Your trace speaks solemn volumes, gospel to my soul.

transgressive: the king falls

the jack become the knave becomes the jester
and the king falls down. his crown, brown
with the excrement of his own hypocrisies,
the disease of the excellent, those who rise
to fly the skies of the present and the future,
tense with the sense of destiny, often self-made
in the mad hats and bad cats that sat still
only long enough to make a transgressive tale
out of a children's nursery rhyme. crime of time,
kairos over chronos, and I am weighing sands
I have no control over as the graphite rods
melt within me, thin with the heat of receding
holy waters, the daughters of the sun run
and I am left in the cleft of a punishing stone.
break me and take from me everything,
it has been done before and I endured, purified
and clarified, brittle behind the facade but gods
usually are. you just have to find the curtain
to pull down the temple around them, the final
prayer of a Nazarite, trimmed on a whim.

ascendency

the formula
was there all the time
but without
                    the spark
it was in a
dark place

hiding itself from the revelation

but then

you
          danced in

words striking sparks and a form
like
          mortal sin

you captured me
enraptured me
and I   found

the philosopher's stone

to transmute the base metal
of my ancient heart
into
gold platinum radium
polonium uranium plutonium

and with a ruby blue whiff of light
night
is transformed in New Mexico skies
to the flash of creation

and I have found the equation
(working backwards from the effect

not as easy as it sounds
and it doesn't sound all that easy)

I have the skeleton key
for shackles I have worn
longer than you have been alive

and I use it, now,
peeling away the chains
of mortal mediocrity

of lies told and unwisely taken as gold

not every part and parcel of my heart
but those whose bandwidth I understand now
to have been illusion

and all the hollowed catacombs
are now hallowed the flood of blood
of my passion for you
has new space and places to fill

the past

the past is nothing
nothing but a book
that we take our lessons from

the ink and pages
made of blood and flesh
a bible of our experience

but we are not the book
we are the blood and flesh
still living, moving forward

White Sunday 77

this is not a contest
this is not a game
I fight for the future
not a prize, not a name

I am in every moment
reaching out for your soul
I am seeking contentment
not a sense of control

there's so many ways to walk
so many ways to fall
there's a thousand words I should say
the next time that I call
but the truth is still written
in the stones of my heart
I am bound to your passion
and I never can part

for what is redemption
but a chance to make good
and what use is pledging
all the efforts I could
be out peddling to another
or others by the score
when all I want is you, my love,
just you and nothing more

so forgive me my aching
and forgive me my pain
and forgive me the sorrows
that come upon me to stain
me with earnest admiration
for every martyr who has been
I am here for your love
and to me, that's no sin

evidence

I am an inconvenient man
difficult to explain
harder to justify
particularly to those who
aren't even supposed to know
I exist

this isn't a prison
it is freedom
I move with the shadows
but I can still see the sun
and what is begun is far from over
not a field of clover

yet

but I have seen enough grass bend
in the wind to know which way is East
and although not yet released
I know that the priest isn't called
for a dirt farewell
still miles to go before we sleep, together

but like Marquise de Merteuil said
it is the obstacles that ensure
success in matters of the heart
we all need a couple of trellises
to scale to get us in the mood
to do some bad with the good

prison

This has been my prison
for as long as I recall
every stone I placed myself
I've wandered every hall

alone and yet, within myself
I've many I've still met
who've stepped across the mark'd line
and made of me their pet

for this is not a pleasant place
to visit, or to dwell.
though some would think it heaven
I have learned that it is hell

to be bound within these bitter walls
and left to crawl for days
to find yourself a loveless freak
inside a praise'd haze

whispered of in fear and love
and left alone to die
for sins I am not party to
and prisoner of a lie

celebration

you are the child of my dreams.
the wellspring of my creativity.
promised and prepared in your heart,
given to the truth of your power
over me and through me, to rule,
first my life, then the world,
then whatever memories retain me
when life and love are gone.

I surrender every pretender to my soul.
false idols and the worship of illusions.
You are like a beautiful and wild orchid
growing in the soft peat of a lost shore,
more than the parts of your beauty;
the attar, the petals, the elegant stem
that raises you to heaven, to my lips,
that I may drink of nectar I alone understand
as the essence of life and redemption.

You are purity and desire
cool logic and the fire
that burns me to contemplate,
taken and claimed, tamed
but never broken, a trust,
a shatteringly beautiful faith
I place in you, unique but for God
alone to measure against.
I am here because this is where
I can find the masterwork
of all creation, the key of life.

Your eyes hold the answers.
Your kiss tells me all the things
I never thought I could know
and I go to the end of the road
in a dance of reckless dreams.
Purified in the pride I feel for you
I seal for you, within me.
Hold me for a moment and skies
go from black to indigo to cyan,
light provided, coincided with
the moment you whispered
your dreams into my hand
and told me to keep them safe
until we can share them

correspondent

I am your correspondent,
despondent, at times:
laying at a distance
paying for the crimes
of others as I hover:
not heaven or earth:
feet touching
nothingness.
and yet I am at ease
(most of the time)
going through the emotions
in proxy and veils,
when what I want is out of reach...
until I set my sails
and the word is given
to bring me to the bend:
to find a path against the wrath:
to sail until the end
and I run aground within you
and breathe a free man's breath.
bound to you, a promise, true
until the distant death.
I am your correspondent.

liberation

the cold iron
is a promise
not a prison
a symbol of
a faith that confounds even me.
learned and
practiced in
sterile rooms
full of uncomprehending acolytes
who had never
and will never
understand
the word love.
I am practiced in the iron path
and will wait
until you return
and we celebrate
the beauty of
consecration
the duty of
consummation
the purity of
commitments
that have taught me that a promise
is a truth
waiting to be fulfilled.
I have not lied.
you will not be denied.
I am claimed and tamed.
and have found in you
the echo of my religion.
and evidence of God.

true spirit

you are no placebo, no milk sugar
fake that I would take to convince myself
that I have found my divine paramour,
another clay sculpture placed on the shelf
to admire from a distance, a totem
hand-carved as an idol of irony,
for such things are not really seraphim
but illusion. I opened eye to see
the undeniable truth of you, born
to beauty, raised in grace and evolving
into something radiant and reborn
in the baptism of life, commanding
my soul and heart and flesh; Bacchante,
my sweet esthete, courtesan, White Sunday.

cresting

I will never doubt your sweet elegance,
the grace embraced without a trace of doubt.
I find myself elevated by chance,
a random encounter with life, about
which I had no hope or dream so sublime.
Stay with me for as long as I please you
and I will bend the course of life and time
that I linger long enough to speak true
the words of infinite amomancies.
You are Aphrodite and fates reborn,
the soul of an innocent, if you please,
and the promise of love given and sworn.
I will surrender all I am and more,
a beggar's purse to rise where angels soar.

eyes

I wish you could see yourself
through the eyes that I see,
the clarity of your heart,
an earnest purity
that wars with the arrogance
of a world of the mad.
treating you so shamefully,
angel tears falling sad.
But memory is not fate.
And I wish to be clear
I am come to walk with you
not surrender to fear.
You are perfect within you.
And have dreams to achieve.
I will walk as far allowed
and I never will leave
but by your command I am
here to shoulder the sky.
Loving you with all my soul
til the day that I die.

apollo

I look to you to chase the pain
and find in me a new refrain
a song that comes from beauty and from joy.
The storms have passed, they come again,
it's the nature of the wind and rain
but that doesn't mean we can't seek shelter from them.

Truth's a bitch, lies dig deep
and burn at us when we dare sleep
and simplified, our pride won't let us wake.
We need to know a better path
avoid the deep and poisoned wrath
that floods our veins whenever we near hope.

Out of the East and heading West
I'll put your passions to their test
but I won't leave without you, I can't do that.
You're all I want and all I need
and for your love I'll gladly bleed
and lay against the rocks, forever aching.

Memory is but a lie,
just scars that we can all deny
if we want more from life than shallow suitors.
I'll stay with you through every night
and stand beside you, every fight,
and lay me down beside you, when it's over.

in the time...

I will walk the fields near Ka-Latil
in the time of the apple harvest
to fulfill promises I have made
obligations I gladly swore to
loyalty given and with joy

the trees will be most barren
the winds, cool and the leaves
as they lay upon the ground
yellow and brown and wet
with the recent rains

I will walk from one side of the fields
to the other, and back again,
trying not to obviously watch
to see if you appear
your answer signified in your presence

I will smell the cool autumnal wind
and the vinegar of those apples
that fell and were crushed
before they could be harvested
to be eaten or made into ciders

I will be happy, no matter what my soul
senses in the presence of a line
drawn in the sands of the clouds
months ago, marking but one point
in an eternal looping swirl of hearts

and if on towards evening I remain
alone with my apprehensions
I will not be angry or bitter
but will return home, to write
of the experience of this year's dreams

and when, next summer, the harvest
comes upon us again, I will call out,
ask you again, you will hear me
and again the vigil will begin,
a sacrament of patience and love

for I am like the trees in the orchard
bearing my fruit more than once
waiting patiently for the harvest
and praying that the right hands
will take my fruit and accept it

coexisting

it is sometimes
sometimes
more than enough that we exist
in the same world
in the same moment
in the same room, virtual or otherwise,
for you are
my evidence of a loving God
and I do not always need
to taste ambrosia
to appreciate the scent
and the memory
and the joy
it brings
you bring
merely by existing

paramour

Time is passing but it hasn't past.
The fates are coming but the die is cast.
I love you more than I can say,
but you will see it in the roles I play
in your life and in the world,
with the passion of a hero hurled
into legends he never thought
would call for him, battles fought
against wraiths and dragons,
sprites and mist, legions
set like Cyrano's test,
they call me on, they bring my best
that I may prove myself, win your heart,
though I suspect, I had that from the start.
But the lady has a right to set the quest
and who am I to deny, my love confessed,
that I want her to be to me
my paramour, in all degree.

laugh

you like it when I'm just a little bit needy.
when you can laugh, not cruelly, but bemused
by my big-pawed clumsiness trying to get
"I love you" to pass through those rosebud lips.

I notice. you know you drive this bus and I,
I am fine with that, my Sunday Girl, deities
should have their way with mere mortals,
you never need say it for me to know it.

better you should mean it and express it
in the little foot stomping tantrums when I
forget my place and forget my prayers
than say it with a hollow accent, like humans.

I am trapped between adoration and life.
I am not your only acolyte, merely the inevitable.
even you acknowledge that, that the fates
have thrown their weight down that road.

so even I laugh sometimes, when you think
you have it all under control and I surrender
to your whim and will and oaths we've taken.
for even poets and goddesses have a right to love.

Charm and Grace

and what will you do when you find what is real?
will you seek your control and confess what you feel
or lay unfisted hands to accept all the demands
that will bend you, upend you and send you to grace?

and what will you find at the end of the way?
promises perishing in the bittersweet grey?
I have found what I need and for it I will bleed
if required to prove I will stand for my place.

and what will it purpose of nothing is won,
if mocking remains and the stains, the sun,
merely burns to leave scar that marks you as far
from the shores of a siren who turned from your face?

and I will tell you stories of lovers that fell,
of women and men who have battered down Hell
to seek something grander than venom and dander
and found, simply, love without the coward's disgrace.

the silence

you never need to say a word to be heard
but interpretation sometimes fails me when silence
takes you, makes you mute and elusive.
I am used to the brighter chords of birds
calling out their needs to skies, their presence
proof enough of their purpose, proof they live.
when I am silenced and sealed away, entombed
by the necessity of your fragile, agile nature,
I pound against the black stone walls,
the iron headboard a cell door, my assumed
stability mocked by pain and your unsure
whispers. I vow, but now, your silence calls.

the path

the path.
long and exquisitely complicated.

more than a few
stones out of place.

like that road in Morgantown
they made during the WPA
a road of bricks
now impossible to ride over
without ripping out your axles.

I want to be able to take my time
and find a way
to travel that path.
picking through the yellow bricks
and the dead end mazes.

I want to find my way to you.
you asked me to do that.
I promised you I would.
I never want to break a promise
to you.
Too many have.

I would be unique.
I would be the one who walked
when others crawled away
crying "it's so hard to love you"
and blaming you for their cowardice.

I want to be there.
Even if, in the end,
you don't show up
to watch me break the ribbon.

My feet twisted and aching
but my soul resolute.

patience II

my love
you asked me to wait

and I shall.

for love is not a word to me.
it is a place where things touch
more than the consecration of flesh
more than the hydraulic mesh
of hips and lips in eclipse.

it is a place where words signify truth
and cold iron and sharp rocks
and fantasies and memories
are not to be underestimated.

you will understand one day
more than you do now
about so many things.

I will not pick you out
from between my teeth in pink scraps
with my lesbian-short fingernails.

I will not write platitudes
while all the while my soul
lays in a black marble tub, wrists slit.

I will celebrate the apple harvest
if not this year, then next or next,
I am, you have said, patient and kind.

I will pace myself on this road
to yet another Damascus, knowing Rome
awaits all true evangelists. Even me.

I will lay in the chair and await you,
promises kept in eventuality
are not lies and need no regrets.

you asked me to wait

and I shall.

brisance

my light is dying.
it flickers
and sparks.
I can smell the oil
that spits out,
unused,
wasted,
the temperature too low
to ignite.

my light is dying.
as am I.
too much
too much of nothing
crowds my sphere.
hopeful
foolish
taking things offered, like a
dumb Trojan.

my light is dying.
watch it fade.
closely
closely, understand
that I am
more than
my light.
and I have bandwidth unseen
by your eyes.

my light is dying.
look away
quickly
quickly, I exhale
the fifth word
the one
I know.
shield your eyes for I am burning
brisant gold.

my light is dying.
but only
as you
as you perceived it.
I am strong

and have
been here.
I know the way out of darkness
e'en alone.

my love.

stigmata: the hallowed hollows

the hallowed hollows are red with my energies,
lust and love and couer rage, staged intimacies
that have been overturned by the fulcrumed wisp
of light. blue and a curious indigo, the crisp
violet of revelation and I am castoff and away
as so many times before, darkness to the fae
and yet living, a heart beating a crippled thrum
but beating nonetheless, this kodo drum
chasing away the daemons and the angels alike
as I fail redemption one more time and strike
against an iron headboard where I am told to wait
patiently for promises and vows to confiscate
my pain in night music kisses, sweet and true,
black roses and white lace, a martyr'd barter for two.

when the sun burns black

You never think of the sun
in anything except yellow and gold
and light and warmth eternal.
And yet, one day it shall grow old and cold.
The sun mourns in tears
of sunspot black and anguish when it knows
that the heat and light it sheds
has caused harm to any, and it shows
such little of this sorrow
against a radiant sky that it seems
indifferent or unharmed
yet it reaches deeper than darkest dreams.

falling into darkness

it is only in the light that we learn what is that's right
and learn what we must fight against at night
the darkness and the black within us, pulling back
against all hope and dreams of peace, we stack
our paltry chips and dip our hands in holy water
for a gamble and a prayer we swore we'd never again utter
but here we are at equinox, slipping from the dream,
falling into darkness, with an ancient, echoed scream
that reflects off into nothing, there's no angel on the way,
the fall is all that matters. it is alone we pay
the price of our perditions and the sum of all our pain
laid against us on the jagged stones to pull a crimson stain
and deposit us as broken forms, a warning to be made
to the fools who would repeat the path in lover's foul charade.

nacht

it is 3 am
and you were supposed to be here
but this is life
and life doesn't always cooperate
and the silence
is deafening, like mortar fire
consuming me
in my own anguish and solitude.

it is 3 am
and I am here, alone, contemplating
why I am here
and you are not. I looked everywhere
just to be sure
but I am alone. floating in an ether,
in the grey space
between Heaven and Hell and hope.

it is 3 am
and I didn't think to bring pen or paper
just in the case
I needed to write this down, raw words
I now find I'm
composing in advance, precognizant
of the dark mood
that will consume me if I do not.

leaving behind

leaving behind
not much more than dust
the crust of yesterday's bread
and all that was said
but never really relied on
I tried on
a couple of different hats
but you skin enough cats
and all that's left is kitty litter

I'm not bitter
because that's how I got here
and here is pretty damn good
from where I sit
ask me in a few days
and see if the haze has reconciled
to a wild child
or a roadkill
a question of will
a question of passion
that will fashion the next apocalypsis
in a form warm or colding
I'm not folding
because I drew the queen of hearts
and that's a pretty good start
part and parcel
a morsel becomes a feast
and the hunting cats are released
to fend for themselves
on the scattered tattered shattered shelves
when I should have left them

and now have.

the acceleration constant
in an instant
is reformulated
and I am gated
into the Haily Mary slipstream
where every dream
means something
something profound
so I will confound
with a sound
like a song of the night
into a light
I will touch
with all my purpose
and see if I am the poet, after all

erosion

even the mountains cry.
massive as they are. hard and stark.
stone for bones and the sky their burden.

carrying the night and the day.
the winds cut deep, as do the rains
and all the majesty is undone.

but they are not human
and are neglected because we think of them
as eternal. unmoving. stone.

so we are surprised when we hear them
groaning beneath all the burdens
and the rivers flow sweet with their tears.

chastity

surrender me your chastity
I'll give you all I've left
to fill your aching soul with me
and taste your tender cleft.

I'll answer to your fantasies
I've sins yet to atone
with tender touch and savageries
to make of you, mine own.

I want to be your satyr king,
your lover, daddy, prince.
I want to find you swallowing
every hot and throbbing inch.

And when we lay in aftermath,
in completed, heated rests,
we've miles to go along this path,
I'll kiss your perfect breasts.

When at length we resurrect
and wake to find our thirst
reawakened by our wild aspect,
we'll sate again this curse.

I will never ask your grace
to let me taste one trace
of another's heat and sweet disgrace,
for I know my need and place.

adversity

faith without challenge is not faith
love without tension is a wraith
of a ghost of a passion, untested.

I am pale and sick and lay alone,
but you have sworn greater stand
and I will lay alone in your name.

be well and strong, hurry back,
but do not short shrift that which requires
your attention and your focus.

I will wait, I promised. I do not wait
to keep the promise, but I promised
so you would know that I would wait.

patiently? as best as I can, like a man
who has tasted honey and then has none.
but content the feast will return.

the precipice as poem

What are you doing?

Contemplating

The questioner looked
the direction I was staring.
He could see the salt flats
run almost to the horizon,
ending in a precipice,

rocky and harsh.

Contemplating what, the fall?

No, the run
I replied
exasperated that he was interrupting my focus.

The sun had just risen,
behind me.
The 2,370th time
I had seen my shadow
appear
then diminish
as the sun rose higher in the sky.

The questioner looked at me.
You don't look ready to run that far
His eyes narrowed
as he surveyed the scene,
making note
of the fact
that I was still rooted
where he had found me,
where I had been for years,
contemplating the run.

I'm ready
I replied, softly.
I thought I was ready
before,
but the mirage had dissipated
mid-stride
and I had,
after a brief sprint,

walked back to the very spot
where I'd began,
and taken up my vigil,
again.

And what will you do when you reach the precipice
he asked,
slyly.

He knew the answer.
He wanted me to say it,
to consider it.

He kicked a pebble in his path
and looked to me for my answer.

Pressure speech.

He knew I'd have to say something.

I will leap.

The simplicity of the answer
startled the questioner,
who usually received a conditional answer
bringing into account
the wind speed
and the distance run
and the time of the day
and any of a thousand other
considerations and mitigating factors.

But not this time.

You will leap
he repeated.
He whistled softly.

You know how far down that canyon goes?

All the way
I replied.
I've been over its rocks before.

I know you have
he said,
shifting from one foot to the other,

then back.
A subtle dance
as he weighed his next thought.

But it has been a while, hasn't it? Your bones may not withstand the impact when you hit the ground.

I am not
hitting the bottom
this time
I said softly,
a touch of defiance in my throat.

You're not
hitting the bottom
this time
the questioner responded,
incredulously.
You always hit the bottom.
Everyone
always
hits the damn bottom.
Nobody flies.
Everyone dies.
You're just a bit...tougher than most.

I prefer
to think of myself
as resilient,
I responded.
For the first time
this day
I turned to meet his gaze.
And you're standing in my path.

Pardon me
the questioner mocked
and stepped to the side,
he motioned me by
Be my guest.

I cleared my mind.
I could hear the questioner
clearing his throat
I could hear
by the sound of the wind through his hair
which way he was facing
and what the expression on his face was.

This was a moment of clarity.
Not my first, by any means.
I lowered my shoulders
and flexed my legs.
They ached.
Years of disuse.
Of neglect.
I had lost so much time,
so much of my youth,
standing here.

Waiting.

Like that rock gendarme that finally
fell.

I expected to one day be found,
just cracked sandstone
and an epitaph.
I didn't plan for this.

I heard a faint thrumming
from the canyon.
How many times had I heard that,
every morning,
as the sun touched the stones
on the far side
and the thermals created
a pipe-organ effect.
It was thrilling to realize
I would pass through that wall of sound.
Pass through the rising wind.
Pass through.

The
first
step
took
forever.

My left knee

locked

and popped

and crackled

like it was going to explode
as the muscle
and sinew
commanded its movement.

I could feel the damage done
by age and neglect.
I could feel the blood flow
into corners that had been hollow
for what seemed an eternity.
I could feel.
It felt good.

As the left foot
slapped the salty sands
the right foot
was already off the ground.
This is how you run,
I thought.
This is how you run.
A stabbing pain shot up my back,
a flirtation of a cramp
as I commanded my body bend
to my mind's whim and will.

I could hear the questioner chuckle
as pain played across my face.

But the doppler effect
already came into play
against his laugh,
which shifted from
high pitch
to low
as I passed and accelerated.
My eyes were closed
against the initial shock of my body.

They open to the light
and the salty air
made them bleed tears.
Another footfall.
Another.
Less man than machine now,
my body was responding
to a primal command.

The primal command
it had for so many years
lived and died to
and now was reborn to.

I could hear
the questioner
shout
something
off in the distance,
behind me,
but the sound
barely reached me
and was too muffled
by my own steam engine breath.
I could hear my heart
through the blood in my ears,
feel it in my chest.
My arms moved of their own volition,
I was falling into a racing crouch,
my body tense
and intensely driven.
The hot and salty wind
in my face
distorting my features.

I began to chant a name.

It dulled the pain,
intensified my motion,
purified my spirit.

I do not know how long
I ran,
all I know is that
with every second
I was faster
than the second before.
Fast as I could run.
Faster,
harder,
hotter,
driven.
Driven.
The bend of my ankles
as I rose to run

as I once had,
the flat of my foot
never touching earth,
driving from the ball and toes.
My eyes barely open,
just enough to see
the lights around me bending.
Blueshifting to indigo.
My skin torched
and screamed
as the air rushed by like
dry acid.
I am alive.
I am alive.

There is the precipice.

No doubt.
No hesitation.

This is the instant
where we fly
or we die.

No doubt.
No hesitation.
Last tread on the stone
and I am skyborne.
I spread my arms
and scream my defiance,
again.

A name,
irrelevant to all but myself.
And her.

And I fly,
whether or not
anyone catches me.
Whether or not
the fates mock me.

I fly.

to a lover

This is not for the cold catalepsies
but the pure warmth you can invoke
with a soft smile or the simplest ease
with words of truth and love. In you awoke
my slumbering passion, admiration
for this woman who steps into my life
with hesitant grace, elegance hard won
in her own sphere, now as near as a wife
though more than one reasoned season shall pass
before you may choose to lose your ronin
reputation to the gentle impasse
within sharing, caring, daring to win
whatever it is within my power
to grant to you. I am your dreams' bower.

White Sunday 52

some insist that vows are mad
take what you can and run, they say.
I don't want to live that way.
those who do, they make me sad.
romance is not found in spark
we play at being lovers for.
the shadows dance by, by the score,
they flicker out in solemn dark.
alone I sit, a vow to clutch.
alone, and yet with more than most.
a dignity, not memory's ghost,
I gamble all for your honest touch.
dreams are but for waking from.
I want your all. for it I've come.

another hollow midnight

another hollow midnight
these are the times
when I wish I'd liked the taste
of that first cigarette
something to do with my hands
my mouth
my money
besides sitting here
sitting here
like a deflated toy balloon
to avoid pacing
or curling up in the corner
and finding solace
in shadows

another hollow midnight
it's not that she's
not here
obviously
because the sheets are straight
and there is no telltale
outline
of where she fell
with me on top
finding my way

another hollow midnight
it's that she chooses
not to be here
and I can't argue
with her logic, because she's right
we make no sense
at all
but that's the way
the heart chooses
to speak its mind

another hollow midnight
reflecting on the cigarettes
I never smoked
the memories I never had
and the dry air
that swirls up around me
when it should be
wet and clinging

like lips and hips and hands
when lovers
want something
something more
something true

another hollow midnight
I think I'll write a poem
and tell the world
how it hurts like glass shards
under my tongue
in my heart
and there are no ashtrays
anyway
if I wanted to smoke
just those mocking sheets
where I laid the rose petals
as if to summon here
when I knew the odds
all along

I will write for a while
then lay down
let the petals wither
let my words ferment
congeal and spoil
before I flush them
like used condoms
from a prophylactic heart
used to the feel
of latex instead of flesh
but hating it all the while
romantics
don't like the secret handshake
of those who don't understand
another hollow midnight

single strand string theory

epileptic cataleptic septic to the core
memories emeried seminarian roar
gods at odds with frauds and foes
the dancer takes the stage and goes
where no one ever went before
gran jete and nothing nevermore
formulaic Fortunatos, entered and centered,
humanity shed, it will lay with the dead
while the ritual will pitch usual patterns.
binding and winding the blinding unfinding
musical interlude words of an altitude
flicked and sticked and pricked then sicced
like a therianthropic half man span
of a life half unwound and still too much
remains for the pains and stains of tomorrow.
the narrow marrow runs cold, then gold.
and all is sold, bold for the burning bowl.

cleansing the wound

alone against the rocks I lay.
broken. roadkill, but for final breath.
no more dreams, no dragons to slay.
I am just waiting for the death
that promises its loyal blade
in prophecies and tributes sung,
a morbid, maddening song is played,
and we slide in beneath the dung.
for comes a time when passions fade
and grey possess all we held.
when sacraments are mocked, betrayed
by dark illusions, echoes welled
in tears of pain to taunt the path
and sell to us a coward's wrath.

Katrina was a bitch

the wind and waters came like angry swarms of wasps
stinging down the barriers in the artifice of all,
bringing down walls and roads and entire towns,
washing away sorrows to be replaced tenfold.
Katrina was a bitch

even more so to me, after a fashion. Katrina was a bitch,
for she took my mortality. the coffin my friend
Thom had made for me 30 years before,
that I had humped across this country, back and forth,
to be buried in, one day.

Katrina took it. oh, she had her accessories before
and after the fact of her acting out against
whatever it was she was pissed off about that day,
but I blame her. without my coffin, I cannot die.

yeah, Katrina made me immortal. the bitch.
now I must endure human suffering forever.
I must watch those I love wither and die and know
that I cannot be with them, again, ever.

Katrina was a bitch, heartless and cruel to thousands,
millions, and a symbol of the wrath of nature
before the incompetence of man. but, to be honest,
I'm most ticked off because she stole my death.

intimate mythologies

teach me of your
mythologies.
the legends
that you see
dance
when you close your eyes
and realize
that reality
is just another excuse
for the cynicism of others.
for Plato said
this is all shadows.
but I
have great peripheral vision
and have been known
to move my neck
enough
to see things most
can't or won't.
I need
a frame of reference
whether it is
Aphrodite or Venus
or another pantheon,
altogether,
so that I do not
defile your temples
(in a bad way)
or utter
insecure profanities.
this is important to me,
as you are,
and I would know my place
in heaven
and feel secure
I will always
wake up in your arms,
and you in mine.

I will pass through the fire

I will pass through the fire
my flesh clinging to my bones
the smell of ozone and burnt hair
my lash-less eyes reopened
to see with an even greater clarity and charity
I will pass through the fire
for your love
I will pass through the fire
my hands torched and scorched
my feet bare and blistered
my silent tongue loosened
to speak of the moment when I broke with life
I will pass through the fire
for your love
I will pass through the fire
my coeur rage waging war with self-preservation
the hesitation I once felt, melting
my doubts, I have lived a good life
and if this is the final gate, I have no regrets
I will pass through the fire
for your love

The Seventh Song

so bitter lies my wormwood soul
deserved of contempt and of wrath.
the pain and stain of failed control,
reserved for heaven, hellions laugh.
for what is man if not his best,
and what are dreams if not to shape
with gnarled hands and hearts we attest
the moment's kiss, the decade's rape.
the towers fall and we cannot climb
higher than the lowest stone that fell.
our wings have not winds, e'en sublime,
to lift us up and mock this Hell.
for patience pales and curdles black
within our souls, we can't look back.

another paper cup

the bitter herbs
taste better with Kool-Aid
so I can wash them down
and get
another paper cup
another paper cup
and I tell myself that I can't taste
the bitter herbs

but

they were there
they left a strange sensation
in my belly
and smelled of
cinnamon
kisses
and the colour of your lips
at an indecent distance

so

I can say I took
my wormwood, but I never really
tasted it
like I did your sweat
long nights trying so hard to say
that for which there are no words
just the magic of your touch
incendiary

and

I need to be immolated
desecrated by your passions
given and received
in the music box of memory
wet with our hungers
to feel anything
to taste anything
to know anything

for sure
for ever

revelation 49

your love is a revelation. a purifying spirit
that consumes me in a pillar of fire and light.
I learn from the universe the nature of love.
I learn from the universe the nature of dreams.
a perfect epiphany. a perfected epiphany.
your beauty and faith and earnest touch
is a gift I could never be worthy of, your love
is spiritual and physical and mine, by grace.

neosonnet 48

in this bed your maidenhead is certain to be found.
a new release, a perfect peace, a love without relent.
for in my life and in my soul, I am forever bound
to you alone, and we atone our follies, my lament
is reconciled, my lover and child, born of ancient dream.
touching in fashions transcending our passions, joy
and revelation, resolution and revolution perfecting theme
of love transcending the shallows, the parapets of Troy,
thrown down in the name of the arrogance of man
to think that what is divine can be touched and held.
you are here because you chose to be, the purpose and plan
of love fulfilled, a consecration, illumination. what was felled
is risen and given as sacrifice to the gods of love, who nod
a beatific grace to acknowledge the presence of a wise and merciful God.

dark powers

I refuse to use
my dark powers,
even for good.
for I am mortal
and my judgment
is far from perfect.
what I want
may not be
what is best.
what I need
may steal life
from others.
and I'm not
of a mind
to be evil.

love, desire, and need

I can only say what I know.
There is a point where desire and love are shallow words
but we are loath to confess our needs.
Need, the unwillingness to go without.
Oxygen, water, food and your love.

Not love itself, for so many sins
are committed in the blank slate that hangs fate on a word
so that trouvere may sing memories.
But you. Your love. The heated sweet cinnamon
of your eyes and thighs and no disguise.

You are naked to me, beyond metaphor.
All attempts to cast you as cat or stone or mythic beast
is a waste of my soul, you are your own legend.
And as I confess the crackling flames of lust
and soft adoration, you are as a fulcrum.

Patience and Passion

I'm not going anywhere.
Well, not on a vector remotely away from you
in the long run.
I plan to stick around,
cheer you on in all life's little competitions,
pick up the pieces
when you get blindsided .
It isn't that you need me, but that I want you
to have the advantage.

So I'll sit in this comfy chair,
you know the one, and see what happens next.
And after that.
See if you see your way clear,
not because you are unmotivated now, but truthfully,
there's a lot
we have to deal with.
Yet I'm not running, but standing my ground, standing around,
waiting for your blessing, to begin.

Damn you for awakening me

damn you for awakening me.
I had slept longer than I had dreamt possible
and had accepted my fate as a sleep unto death
but you walked in and with a single kiss blew breath
into these grey and shriveled lungs. I feel life.
I am alive.
my heart, no longer merely beating because it can,
hammers within my breast with the fury of creation,
flooding my mind, my soul, my loins with the need
to express myself in manners proper and necessary.

damn you for awakening me.
I had surrendered to my prison and laid down to die
and you decided that you wanted to see if the legends
were true and my wings were still able to blot out the sun
as I wrapped you in them and carried you to the top
of Mount Aetna,
to be ravished as in the legends I thought were myths,
having lost my faith in the gods of love and their child,
now a woman of comely form and wicked wiles who dares
to summon me from my tomb to fulfill our union.

damn you for awakening me.
your cries of passion and fear and tenderness burn away
my doubts and I am now more phoenix than golem.
I am now more the hungry heat, incarnate, than thought,
roaring my spells of summoning to draw you closer.
we melt and merge
and the prophesies never told us what happens next beyond
a general sense of a happy ever after ending, our spark struck
to burn eternal in the hearts of all brave enough to look up
and see your beauty in the bowl of the sun, reborn as I am.

the greater question

eyes that do not beg the greater question
but ask with gentle reproach to be given
a moment's, an hour's, a night's release
and peace from the sorrowful shallows of life.
skin, soft and taut, warm to the touch.
lips like rose petals, soft and full of life.
breasts, flawlessly risen to pink meringues
that demand a taste so as not to waste
the beauty of their pleasant presence.
thighs, lean and inviting, more than a night
on white satin, calling soundlessly the lover.
the feast is spread and the bed the canvas
to the work of the art and religion of surrender.

Sussamma Ritual

let the words be spoken
let the summoning start
let the blood and the passion reside in each heart.

once timeless and pensive
the moments are observed,
the silence broken as the memory is curved.

to rise and remember
that which was never lost.
to transcend a promise at a terrible cost.

bent, ravaged and shattered.
the sanctuary falls.
the leper imploding to avenge sterile calls.

no apologies

you said
no apologies
and I embrace that
we don't owe the world
anything
but the echo of our heat
drying on sheets
and in the wind

words
consecrating passion
the memory of life
the purpose of life
the beauty of you
pressed like a flower
in the book
I am still writing
because you came along
when I thought I was done
and undid the last chapter
into a whole new arc
full of mystery and fantasy
and love and shadows
and I am grateful
for every excruciating second
as the clock counts down
to a purpose
for which I will not apologize

except to you,
for my having taken so long
to get here

only memories of skin remain

You shivered at the cold and thought the room
would be empty on your return, iron
headboard still cold and hard and your bridegroom
gone, a sea of insecurities, dawn
and midnight, stolen in a promised kiss
that would never come. But I kept faith, held
on when silence roared for I would not miss
this consecration for life or withheld
my love for doubt. You will always find me,
patient if not perfect. Not only skin
but lambent determination to see
this through with you, to everyday begin
the best I know how, in your heart and arms,
and surrendered to your brave love and charms.

Fabric armour

will you close your eyes
the first time we kiss
and let all that you are and know
flow into me as I melt into you
my hands sliding down and peeling
your fabric armour
so that we may begin and continue
what we will continue and not finish
for many, many years
if ever?

purification of passion

in the instants become moments and the moments becoming years
we wash, wash away the blackened blood and sanctify the tears.
we find ourselves transfigured, we find our apokalypsis,
revelations in tender times and in bastions, shoulders and hips
pressed together, unified to not be denied, pilgrims of peace
on a road that extends to the edge of our imagination.
we relinquish our hollow rages, we accept the fire's release.
we immolate to consecrate this sacred souls' conflagration.
a kiss can cure us of our pain, an earnest touch can share our grief,
we baptize lies to make them true, we purify, seek the relief
of a beauty that transcends our lachrymal and lost essences,
an affection that achieves perfection in divine presences
that acknowledge that what we bind on earth is bound forevermore.
that grant the lovers what is most necessary, perfect and pure.

sacrilege

I am not here to perfect you, to resurrect
you to some higher state of purity and grace.
I am here to make my sacrifice, my respect
abandoned for your beauty, bound in white lace
and placed upon the altar. I will choose to lose
myself to the rituals and rapture of you.
I offer myself such that were you to refuse
my supplications and ministration that few
would be the paths not into a purgatory
where I would pass aeons of regret, fantasies
of my merger with the true divine, your glory,
cast down as the Morningstar in grim tapestries
of what falls to those who dare to love a goddess
and are bold enough to reach out, to joy express.

raw

aspect one

pale red. not pink. pale red.
I said it quietly, in reverence
in the expression of that which is bled
to provide a purification.
a consecration. a penetration.
validating the caged, raging heart
that beats a quickstep in pain.
an alloy of quicksilver and base metal.
heat from friction. friction
from desire and the fire
of unresolved doubts that catch
like wicks sticking their message
in light and a slight discomfort
magnified by the presence
of a binding force, coarse like rope,
tied tenderly, but tightly.
rubbing raw the points of contact.
so you can always say
that what happens next
was beyond your control.

aspect two

the natural order is that fire
does not exist to the purpose
of rendering what is sweet and true
and given by the earth, to bland
and artificial and blackened.

we are all best in our raw forms.
untampered with, our evolutions
coming from growth and awareness,
not the crackle and snap of sparks
that draw us in to doubt ourselves.

aspect three

Peeled or sealed, beneath it all, we are raw.
Beyond bare flesh, the open nerves that serve
to alert us to the slightest trespass, real
or imagined, we are vulnerable and open.
To pain and pleasure. Doubt and fury.
We feel every touch and even the approach
of strong enough sources and forces of light
and heat and the gravity of an electric heart.
Your bare flesh is beautiful and suitable
for dreams. I would like to write a villanelle
in my own blood, across your naked back,
an intimacy beyond imagination and redemption.
For such touch between mortals is sacrilege,
an elevation of ourselves to that of gods.
But you are worthy of such respect and ardor.
And I, I am willing to be raw with you.

digital desires

Would I dare so to unburden my heart
were we not separated by the miles
that taunt and trap us, we can barely start
to say truths before distance defiles
our capacity to reach out and touch
with soft hand or to kiss with hungry lips
to punctuate the words so fragile, such
messenger of brittle desire that trips
at the speed of light to carry the sound
that should be softly held in a pale room
where we are the electricity, found
arcing and sparking to defy the tomb
of lifeless hearts, only played at before
cursed veils liberated our rapport.

the perfecting dark

as the demons head for cover you will swear no other lover
will ever lay hand to your heated flesh again. I brand you with kisses
that melt into your skin, thin sins evaporate before the barrage.
your defense rent, your resistance spent and your passions bent
to my needs, my hunger, dark enough to sate us both to a degree
we could not have anticipated. I am consumed by my need
to bleed my last barriers into you, and to find those corners
of your radiant soul that are as untouched as the far side of heaven.
your every touch urges me on in and deeper yet than dimensions
traced my shallower penetrations of your essence in all manners.
I am here for you and for me and for the unity beyond lesser beings.
to leave you limp and aching, full and yet still hungry for the next feast
to be released to your care and wonderment, and my worship of you
as an unfaltering altar that overturns all the false goddesses.

your resolute

you can leave me to die
but I will not, can not,
for that is blasphemy
to my purpose, my vow.
planets may yet shatter,
constellations scatter
it will be no matter.
I am your resolute.

the sun will burn my flesh
and the cold will numb me.
fading thought will dumb me
down to the snapped masses.
I am given to stand
and to offer my hand
to my promises' command.
I am your resolute.

I am throwback to grace
of a different time
a different place where
courtly love was the code.
defiant to the gates
where Orpheus awaits,
the champion of fates.
I am your resolute.

chaos

culling the chaos.
breaking the bond.
that holds me and folds me,
here, and beyond

reaching for passion
and the truth it reveals.
the bitter wrist-slitter
never knows how it feels.

to ride on the thunder.
to panic the gods.
to play dead in bright red.
to conquer the odds.

visiting Venus.
clinching with Mars.
a titan to frighten.
torn, born of scars.

sacrifice bartered
in a bed in my head
where lovers immortal
remain, in my stead.

Unfulfilled Wish for Intimacy

Truth be told I want to hold lightning in a brass bottle,
rub the sides and see what colour the genie is that shows,
that answers my insolence and arrogance, a battle
of wills to bear me away from the realm of what man knows
and into the speculations of something more than life:
The kiss and claw of lovers when words weave amomancies
and my power flowers for hours to the touch of wife
or mistress, lover, soubrette or courtesan, who will please
herself at my expense. Selfish we are when bodies mesh
and the flesh commands and demands the surrender of lies.
There is a moment of truth in intimacies, the creche
of our earnest natures, cradling our best hopes in the prize
that slips through fingers insensitive to the quintessence
in the labyrinth of a shallow and selfish presence.

what radiant fires

the word becomes flesh, the flesh becomes heat
and we immolate our souls to complete
the transcendent arc of love and passion, caught
in the circuits of creation where what is wrought
is aught it is to be, and we see only a narrow band
of the light, the heat, the bittersweet command
of our natures over our intentioned tension.
there comes a time when choices are spun
as destinies, beyond our will, but that is not true.
as I choose not to lose my faith, my belief in you.

colour cycle

red

the colour of fire and desire.
heat, sweet and sweaty.
I can feel the seal of bodies
melting and merging, purging
us of our identities for the moment.
crimson, scarlet and the angry
solferino that swallows me up.

gold

flawless. priceless. beautiful.
desired of all, including me.
to be a part of that radiance,
that perfect curve of malleable,
mutable and mesmeric flesh
that serves shell over
and even more precious soul.

cyan

sky blue, the hue of heaven.
clouded by doubt and every shout
that distracts you from defining
what it is you want and need
and bleed. blue, when you cannot breathe.
I would stand for you and protect
in indigo nights and trackless skies
so that your heart would never be blue.

pink

I think (with a wink)
you know what I am saying.
mine for yours, ours for hours,
intense and giddy, sublime crime
against no one but our own vows
not to let this happen.

black

no light. but life endures.
closed eyes to focus on senses
already to the point of screaming,
dreaming desire into reality.
the power of a black rose,
the flower of your champion.
penetrating you to mark you
as his, and his alone.

verdance

you are young and not yet ready for the world
and all the colours and flavours and textures
and passions that you will inherit one day.
stay where you are and play where you are
and know that you are watched over.
your youth, your beauty, will be a trap
for others and for you, lay it wisely, and true.

silver

are you the unmaker on what I have woven?
the creature of myth to swallow my gossamer
and lay icons on my heart and through me
that I may be brought down by inopportune
hungers brought on by your scent and the nape
of your neck, where I would draw the crash
and clash between mortality and immortality,
between love and lust and life and dust?
if so, I am here and I will offer no resistance.
to die for love is the greatest gift I can receive.

a transitional state

I'm for trading my memories for dreams.
You have taken me, awakened me and
I am not desirous of a return, seems
that I am ready to move on to stand
proactive in a last-year world. You plant
hope in me. Hope and firecracker lust,
desire and passion kindled to raise chant
to liturgy. I want to conquer dust
and damnation for your grace, your face,
for every trace of all you have offered
in evocation and prophecy, trace
the tears and tenderness proffered
in acknowledgment that there is something
real and worthy and beautiful coming.

Power rises

I am here for you, and yet for my needs.
Greedy and hungry, thirsty for love that
bursts on the tongue like raspberries, the seeds
and juice filling your mouth, no weak or flat
notes in this symphony. Power rises
and rafters rattle, for there is no place
for mediocrity when disguises
are discarded like impudent clothes, face
to face we stand, even at a distance,
reaching for one another to so yield
our essences and crack the resistance
that has, for too long, been a crust and shield
against love as real as would burn heaven
when we give ourselves to transcend our ken.

so once again

so once again there's an electric lady,
to challenge me my purpose and my dreams.
shall I dissolve again into the ether?
shall I resolve the conflict, as it seems?

I once gave up my poor and mortal birthright
that I might touch the sky and see true things.
I am stronger yet and wiser, well, and so
my choice, my voice, is now not waxen wings.

so once again there's an electric lady.
the light so bright it burns deep, with sweet heat,
an apokalypse that so gamely trips
into my world, my arms, the suite now complete.

bring me what you care and dare and bear to share,
I am unafraid. Stronger now, I would take
you into my sphere and pour myself out,
like waterglass, and loving vows ne'er forsake.

for the final time, my electric lady,
I stand before you in this human shell.
begging redemption, no pretension,
I would not, your tender love, to say farewell .

The Sunday Girl returns

the Sunday Girl looks to the red, ramshackle cracks
that carve themselves into the chaos of life and cries
that all she wants is to be whole. but she wants more.
yes, for a moment she wants to find the shattered pieces
re-assembled, so she can see what it looks like to those
who lack the eyes and hands and souls to feel the flaws
that are the law and the order of the universe, not the
Max Factor pancake smoothness that looks so fake in close-up.

the Sunday Girl wants the freedom to be herself.
not as she was, for time runs away like an uncooked egg,
but as she should have, could have, would have been if everyone
didn't want their pound or inch or pinch of flesh, then and now,
and even tomorrow, on the die-now-pay-later plan.
I will collect the pieces, if she lets me, or just point and wave
to where I think they fell, if not carried away by a passerby
looking for a souvenir of greatness not yet realized.

the Sunday Girl may do with them what she will.
she may toss them, toss them, toss them aside and kick
and scream and dream of being totally in control of her fate.
but truth is stronger than will, and I know this for I cannot
fly or outrun light except in my mind and words and dreams
and I will give them to her, as mortar and spackle, for her heart.
what she does beyond that is her will to fulfill, for I am not
the Sunday Girl. just a stranger in love. with cracks of his own.

paroxysm

paroxysm. furnace of light implodes.
emotions merged and surged, chained and constrained,
they command their release, their static modes
a mockery of the chaos and feigned
indifference. passion heated, flashpoint
achieved and the walls in place bear brunt,
a mending of molecular heart, joint
of will barely holding in this parent
of evolutionary change, fusion
in the hands of Aphrodite. weapon
of a man, turned inward to save the one
point of light in the sky to gaze upon
but the carnage rages inside this shell.
tonight there are celebrations in Hell.

if we accept the divine

if God is God should it matter
if we care more for them
than they for us

for there are ten billion
people in the world
and only one God

we need only love one God
(who is confessedly
a jealous God, anyway)

but if we accept the divine
as divine and limitless
how can we hold God faithful?

it is a question for those
greater than me and wiser
for I have so much love I ache

love for everyone, everyone,
but a special sense of love
for the one, jealous God

until mourning comes

you may rest here
if you like
if you are weary

I will stand
sentinel to your heart
and your soul

letting no thing
no one
trouble you

my arms will
press you
to me

my heart
will play rhythm
to your breathing
as you sleep

burrowed in
like a kitten
in a blanket

I am warm
and gentle
and mean no harm

I will lay here
and hold you
until mourning comes

the gods ride in

the devil rode out that
the gods may ride back in.
gods of truth. of passion. of poetry.
eyes of glass and steel.
tongues like silk and fire.
voices that silence the storm.
as that is the natural order of things.

the way the sun rises on fire
and lights the tops of the trees
before it kisses the damp grasses
like all great kisses, with fire and light,
memories of the night but memories
until the sun retreats to surrender
to the lovers the arcane rituals of joy.

hands on fevered brows, seeking life
that hides among the grey simulacrums
that have stayed where they fell, broke
and unwilling to heal, for all that is needed
is the will to stand back up and scream
the songs of the dance of the forevers
in the instant between friend and lover.

roar with joy and penetrate my soul.
find the core still sore from the last touch
but that is the proof of life I demand,
the evidence of the command of a fine soul
over the eventual result of the wagers.
broken back stacks of lackwit murmurs
can only pile so high before they die.

gods of light and dark, of feast and famine,
the crime of personality. of desire
for something more than tepid timidity.
stand. stand. stand for something more
than the lesser whims of lesser souls.
the gods ride in, and we are among them.
to remake the world in beauty and poetry.

kiss me

kiss me
fear me not for I want something else
than your life.
I want your soul, your heart,
your warm skin and heated blood
to sustain me and fill me.
to warm my lips
and fill my lungs with your surrender.
to bring me to the surface
that I may know the taste of life
if only for the moments
that it remains with you.
remembering that you,
knowing it would mean your death
yet in the knowledge of my desire
that runs to love and passion
you could not press lips
to seal your fate and my hunger
and had the courage and desire to
kiss me

with unclouded eyes

there are religions, ancient and new,
that do not stir the soul as much as you
stir mine. the essence of your spirit,
the mettle of your soul, near it
I am pulled into the gravity of joy
and can do little but fall, destroy
me with but a single artifice
if you want to see my bliss
turned to tormented desolation.
but know you, my passion,
my affection, is as real as the sun,
and as radiant and heated, won
by nothing more than your being
the revelation I am, in your words, seeing.

for you

for you
I want to heal the wounds
and end the pain
the doubt
the questions that are irrelevant

ten thousand reasons
exist why we don't make sense
ten thousand more
rise to match the impertinence
of anyone
who says love doesn't matter

it does
and can move mountains and part seas
and make the skies light at night.

for you
I want to say the things I have never dared
and share everything i have ever shared
and all because
and all because
and all because
for you
I was put into this world

in the early morning hours

in the early morning hours
the thunder came from the West
and woke me.
and broke me in half.
the golem came and spoke to me, hard words.
of truth and ancient vows
I made long before I saw the butterfly girl.
before there were aubergines
and mad gypsies, jungle cats
and all manner of menagerie.

and he was right. black eyes
hiding not the soulless void, but expressing
truth and beauty and the duty of the lover
to live above and beyond the touch.
I have been ronin for a season and reason
persists for me to resist a harvest
in fields I am not entitled to.
words more bitter than Golgotha ash.
but true and valid and mine to hear.

and me, alone.

Grant me heaven

take you the sacrament of my white wine.
draw out the essence of my surrender,
swallowing my issue of the divine,
your reverence and severance, tender,
from the false religions, idolatry.
old passions pass away, your fingers play
and your warm, hungry mouth tears my flesh free,
the white blood of creation, a wine. I lay
hungry for redemption, tithe of pleasure.
for now, soft pink lips draw tight about me,
tongue, eloquently silent as you measure,
feed and bleed me of all resistance, free
of all free will, your temptation, tender,
witness of your wish to grant me heaven.

our story so far

shattered!
my ashes scattered!
as if my wishes mattered,
fallen from the sky.
twisted,
dark doubts persisted.
liberation? resisted!
fallen from the sky.
burning,
bright wings returning.
both yin and yang are yearning.
fallen from the sky.

the golem is the dragon.
reborn in a more functional shape.
soulless, but with the intercession
necessary to avoid, evade and serenade
back to square won. one beyond loss
is where we toss our hacksilver to win.
one more spin of the wheel that seals
the mystery of our history to be told
in abstract allegories, stories of bold
and competent hearts, for solitaires
shatter on the flat, grey stones
of ancient streets where feet tread
not often enough to justify a city.

the golem is the dragon.
from alabaster idols untouched
to the sacrilege of rutting Holy days,
bare feet leave a telling tread, odd marks
even in the best of times, consummated,
fate carries to weight if you do not believe
that predestination is nothing more
than a vague attempt to influence hearts
and make them do the bidding of hidden
agents of mediocrity. pretty lights fight
for dominance against a sky burnt black.
I once gave up my poor and mortal birthright
I wrote more than a lifetime ago, snow melts.

the golem is the dragon.
I was and am and will be something or someone
remade in the image of what is broken, words
spoken have their way with me, I weep.
I weep tears channeled from a thousand deaths,
to mark a single grave thought. hot to the touch,
is such a creature of stone and steel capable
of feeling anything, sealing anything, stealing
anything but the very joy of existence, resistance
of splintered amber ornaments, yellow and gold.
pensive peasant and king. courtesan and vestal
poured into molds to fill my belly, so hollow
that I would follow the scent of dreams into Hell.

I feel the sky

I feel the sky. it weeps for lovers, lost, never
having the opportunity that we have found
to lay down the tepid temptations and sever
heart from flesh, to be woven together and bound
to one another. into a single thing, heal
and seal and feel the pulse of my life inside you.
as I will feel you, fit in me, cast to reveal
all that is worthy, all that is, within you, true.
not the platitudes of rude suitors, seeking spark
but not fire. seeking an abstraction of you,
but never the woman, the child, the bright and dark
angel now woven into me, so very few
are given such surrender into victory.
and the sky no longer needs weep for you or me.

I want to be a Russian gangster

I want to drive black cars with the headlights off
and tell all the corrupt cops to just back the fuck off
I want the pouty leggy models wearing fur, doin' porn,
cause the Soviet Union fell before they was born

I want a driver named Ivan and a guy who breaks bones
working for me just in case someone taps all my phones
and tries to muscle in my corner of the capitalist chic
that turned a bakery to a disco that they call the Red Freak

I want to be a Russian gangster
I want to be a Russian gangster
I want to be a Russian gangster
and scare the shit out of the mob

I want to be the guy that's scary and breaks doors with my head
and have an everlasting orgy with Natacha in my bed
I want to be the guy you buy from and are scared of turning in
cause there's blood money to be made from all the vice I'm in

I want to be a Russian gangster
I want to be a Russian gangster
I want to be a Russian gangster
cause it beats the hell out of a job

I want to be wearing black in summer and black in winter, too
I want to have all of the money that used to be for you
I want to be so tough you'd run if you heard my accent
and I wouldn't have to give a damn what you're doing, where you went

I want to be a Russian gangster...

above the city

There is a rock high in the mountains
above Ka-Latil, the city of legends.
Flat, black, shielded by great cliffs
such that it has never been weathered.
Strange sigils marked it, brown and crude,
imprints of torn flesh and memory.
This is where the ronin leaves his dreams.
This is where he cuts into his flesh
a permanent memory of his every prayer,
to be flesh-pressed to the stone,
as earnest monument and sacred text.
So that, even if the wound would heal,
he would still see his life, in a scripture
of dried blood and truth. A revelation.

I have seen the stone. I, and I alone.
For I have sat upon it, singing to myself,
songs of love and desire, the urge to touch
and the need to lay with the conviction
of a martyr upon the brutal shards of life,
giving up one's life for the purpose to it.
Giving up eternity for the moment you seize
with both hands and try to stretch to cover
the sky above the city where the palace sits,
sapphire and black marble. The pain of loss.
Memories of kisses and touches and smiles
that did not last through the night or forever.
For I am the ronin, the amomancer, that poet
bound by the legacies of blood, dried and forever.

For what is a poet if not a martyr, forswearing
the sanity of the grey lives so many find comfort in?
What are my words, irrevocable, made of wounds
I have cut into myself while granting each lover
a plausible deniability? The phoenix walks away,
chuckling an awful relief that I alone am cut so deep
that I must lay my wounds to the hot and black stone
to close the wounds and leave evidence of my sins,
my faith, my dreams. To live in a black and white world,
etched in tan and crimson. To be tied to the religion
of King David and William Blake, of Ginsberg, of Byron.
I am here. Never alone. And with the eternal hope
that this time, love will endure and the intimate words
left in my own blood and flesh may heal, except in the stone.

intimacy

what care have I of moments outside
of these,
where I please you and you speak
the inarticulate language of love.
dreams in a kiss
windows in the darkness
the writhing of mingled beings
being what they choose
not losing in the loosing
of the bindings of lace
that I might raise you to me
as I seek only to give to you
all my fire and desire
for you are mine and fine
as the wine I drank from you
between the warm thighs I delight in,
kissing and missing no curve and fold
that informs you of my passion.
I will be your lover
when light without heat fades.
and leave my mark inside you
to guide you closer to the man
who would bind himself to you
for the truth he has found.
and you are beautiful.

stormweaver

gonna make a believer
even out of the deceiver.
gonna break and take and wake
the foundations of the earth, to make
the skies light up, explode and arc
with the fire you inspire, ripping up the dark.
translating the vision for the blind and unkind
who've never really seen it and will find
it alien to their understanding, heat and light
from the same source, the full course, night
flowing into day into life and splitting infinity.
stormweaving by the power of will, making trinity
the pop of an indifferent champagne cork. power
is the prerogative of the fearless, the flower
of creation is found beyond where we die.
I cannot be bound but by the sound as I try
to use words to explain why I am here, closing
the gap, cutting the crap, the slap of posing
against cold stone idols that failed the test.
a copper conductor becomes the terminus, blest
by the possibilities and defiance of dogmas
of what is to become of the fallen, the laws
of nature not knowing what we can do, proud,
with a handful of rain and the friction of clouds.

lyric: everything and more

I feel a rush
whenever I see your name
your voice cuts deep
and reaches me in my sleep
your sultry smile
makes me think of your kiss and touch
not asking for much
just everything
and more

I feel your eyes
even when I am miles away
your presence bends
around walls and distance that
we will break down
in time and trust and heat and all
not asking for much
just everything
and more

I want your word
and what it means to you
you are a drug
and my veins burn when you're away
I need you now
and there's no methadone
not asking for much
just everything
and more

Witness tree

What shall be our witness tree,
our silent witness to our vows?
Where lovers come to speak their hearts
as we did, long before they came.

Perhaps a pine, so tall and straight,
evergreen steadfast symbol.
Catching the odd snow in winter,
keeping live the promise of life.

Perhaps an ancient oak, so strong,
Atlas to the forest sky, true
and earnest, indestructible
next to the frail neighboring boughs.

Perhaps a magnolia, sweet
and heady, refreshing the wind
and flowering to welcome life
and all its possibilities.

They are all witness to us, here,
in the silence of the forest,
where we speak words to God alone
and to one another, our hearts.

I surrender my will

I surrender my will, seeking yet more
than mere arrogant posturing, the touch
of the divine. Shackles of pain are poor
purpose in the heavens' mystery, much
remains to be experienced. The sight,
God in the grace of creation, your heart,
manifesting transfiguration's light.
The power of love echoing to part
the seas of the tears and fearful distrust
built on the coward's easy perfidy.
I would merge with your divine, kick the dust
and find the most remarkable beauty:
You as angel and the evangelist
seeks only for the blessing to persist.

Steal the crown

You beg the trespass, steal the crown.
Lips of peaches, ripened to red,
you dare to wear the crimson gown.
To draw out venom from your bed,
power claimed in the pleasured art.
Now courtesan and queen, priestess,
couer rage born in a battered heart.
And paramour, the idols press
and are shattered in your embrace.
Wondering when and where you've gone,
Helen stares into empty space.
The unexpected quarter, on
past the Pillars of Hercules.
Our fires burn in four degrees.

ceremonies of our nature

We are all creatures of habit
reassured by repetition, repetition.
Fitting our lives into boxes
that we might better guard hearts from recognition
by those who seek only prey.
By those who cut and tear with evil ambition.

Your body a metaphor

take me into you. your body a metaphor
for your heart. your soul. the heat
of your body, swallowing me up until
I spill life itself into you, lost to me
forever, but given with great joy and faith.
there is a mystery here, a beautiful
mystery as you feel me moving inside you,
taste yourself on my lips, hold with hands
my body, pressed into you to make us
an evolution of passion and surrender.
no pretender here, just your radiant skin,
drawing me in and wrapping about me.
taking me for your own. making me your own.
an allegory for our spirits, wet and afire.
I will surrender to you all you want, and more,
if only you will bless me with the sacrament
of your body as a parable, a testament, of your love.

Your sorrows

your sorrows are my sorrows
your pain, mine own.
I will lay between the rocks and you
and keep you safe, and warm.

I will give you the best I have to give,
leaving no thorns in the flowers I bring.
I will learn to eat what you eat
and never make you listen when I sing.

I will lay beside you when you need me
and I will carry our load when you are weak.
I will listen when you when what is important
or even not, is what you speak.

I will bring you herbs fresh from the meadows.
I will kiss your lips, and yours alone.
I will make this life what I can make of heaven,
and never leave you, never alone.

in praise of precognition

I have and will love with fierce devotion,
emotion layered upon itself, born
in respect, in a genuflection
upon a desire, a fire, torn
from the heart of the sun itself, a heat
so intense it makes mock of memory.
It burns away the pain, the incomplete,
the scars that others left in sorry
semblance of their lives, wounds to cauterize
with a persistent, insistent brisance.
A healing kiss long time coming. Arise
as does the Sunday sun, to live and dance
with a passion that blinds Prometheus
and renders lesser flesh extraneous.

anomaly

miracle.
anomaly.
a strong longing for something,
someone,
from an unexpected corner.
the taste of lace,
fingertips,
wet and whetting an appetite
for tight places
and faces
that will touch with silent eloquence.
and we will be
transfigured.
remade.
a sacrament of flesh and blood
shared
as a celebration of our own
testament
to a new state of being.

exhortation

take control. take my soul.
there is no more illusion.
naught to lose, if you choose,
the heat of perfect fusion.

edges melt, a fever felt,
impurities vaporizing.
strike the spark. split the dark.
we fall to birth a rising.

I answered a question today

Emily Dickinson was right.
It is the limbo that is Hell.
Assumptions laying trap
of pain or loss or transcendence.

It is an afterlife in this life.
A long, cold fall into shadows,
not knowing what is piled at the bottom.
Fear of the inevitability.

It is as large as Elysium.
As certain as Hell, this emptiness.
The stone is too large, too large,
and it moves of its own accord.

And I wait my judgment
like any prisoner of the world.
Defiance only as a last resort
when the sentence comes down.

For this is not the next room.
This is the here and now and now
we find ourselves like a cat in zero-gee,
unable to define up and down for ourselves.

It is the loss of control.
The powerlessness in the face of truth.
The black blood of slaughtered hope,
the scent of a bitter and awkward fate.

Fifty days

This is my Pentecost. Not in chronos, but kairos.
This is important. This. You. How the pieces fit,
not in the force-them-in-and-we'll-work-it-out-later way
that so many people can live with, but how they fall
together. Effortlessly, for now. No doubt there will be
times ahead where things tilt a bit like everything does
or even we find the tunnel of love is a corkscrew.
But if we ride the moment and trust, just enough,
we'll be fine, like lemon wine. I need this kiss.
I need to see you dance once more, barefoot,
catching my whim and will as I imagine centering
myself in the way you move your graceful hips,
trusting your lips don't lie in word or parting
to slide breath between us. Cinnamon dust
and the morning light, a rose on a silver tray,
the way things are supposed to be if we believe.
Grieving over lost and caustic causes, pauses
in the slipstream of the wind of Icarus.
You will find me. Bind me. Grind me.
But in the end I will say it was you who defined me.
For that is the ultimate purpose of a Pentecost.

a prayer for you

more than a moment.
more than a kiss.
more than forever,
a prayer for you, this.

more than a meeting.
more than a smile.
more than a merging,
purging all guile.

would you come in the moonlight
daring all to the chance
to encompass the twilight
with a dance, a romance
that defies all the logic
and all of your doubt,
that belies all our histories,
the mysteries, cast out.

more than a dreaming.
more than a night.
more than a mem'ry
of exquisite delight

more than is given.
more to receive.
more than you ever
have dared to believe.

will you fade away

will you fade away when I come to stay,
will you find a reason to deny me?
I have stepped up and out and far away
from the reassuring stones beneath me.

that I want you is transparent to me
and to all who read my poems and prayer.
that I want you is a miracle to see,
an unexpected corner of life, faerie and fair.

will you fade away when I come to stay,
will you find a reason to deny me?
I have stepped up and out and far away
from the reassuring stones beneath me.

Psalms

I shall make of your flesh a living scripture of Psalms
of love, silencing Solomon and raising a new religion,
bound by passion and earnest sharing of brave hearts.
Fire and light, the taste of you like roses and jasmine,
the way you hold me in sacramental sacrifice, sacred
as any prayer as you dare me to touch corners veiled
by your need to bleed in colours for which there are no words.
I have heard your chants and mantras, prepared a feast
in your name as I lay my hands upon the altar and draw
the very venoms I have tasted in lesser vessels,
vinegar and dregs of oils spoiled in mockery of joy.
What do the dead know of life? What do the silent
know of the sounds made when souls surrender to faith?
Consecrate me and I will lay a seed in the loins of memory.

suttee

There are angels and demons, creatures of perfect beauty and vile affections.
Then, there is you. Faint taint notwithstanding, it adds to your charms
and I find no harm in having a healthy curiosity and a desire for pleasure.
Indeed, I look forward to when skin meets skin and the thin protections
of our civilized illusions melt like tears before kisses, in my arms
I would find you no less beautiful and perfect, measure for measure
a treasure of your heart, I hope, manifested in more carnal expressions
that we can share with purpose to an expression and consummation, warms
to heat to fire to immolation, in which I would lay suttee, to blend my fate with yours.

Offerings at your feet

if I lay my offerings at your feet
would you, at least, consider them?
or would it be a sure defeat
to kneel and kiss your vestment's hem?
questions asked and answered yet,
I have. in past times, failed the test
where my sure heart was given, set
on goddesses who swore in jest.

the nature of wine and desire

I heard it. The sound of silence cracking around the edge
where the sedge has withered, all dithering aside,
I slide into to momentary gap between words
and find myself absurdly off balance, like a buffoon
in a Renaissance morality play, caught in the act
of acting like a normal human being, a role I am
rare to fill. expectations being what they are
and every scar has a name and a story
that rides with it to the place where the ancient
stop aging and become, themselves, memory.

You are beautiful. And brave and passionate.
and I am not a polished stone, fresh plucked
from the shore to show to friends with glee.
I am driftwood of an intriguing gnarl, you are
an unique flower of a tree I had never encountered
before I caught your scent, all jasmine and spice,
like a pear warmed on a very hot day in August.
I reach to touch your skin and crave to taste you,
your juices sweet and savoury to a familiar tongue.
And I wonder on the nature of wine and desire.

satin chessboard

I'll provide the fire.
I'll provide the light.
you provide the battlefield on which we'll spend the night.

you will bring your passion,
mine will be there, too.
I shall bring a tenderness
to share and comfort you.

I'll provide the questions.
you'll provide the thought.
I'll provide the formulae
to unbind the Gordian knot.

you will bring the red wine.
I will bring the white.
but in the darkness which is which
will be hidden from our sight.

I will play the suitor.
you will play what role
you choose in moments to defend
your flesh, your heart, your soul.

I will lay as sacrifice,
leaving nothing but to your will
to play this satin chessboard
with your purpose and your skill.

I'll provide the fire.
I'll provide the light.
you provide the battlefield on which we'll spend the night.

imagination

my imagination knows you too well.
the sound you make when I touch you, gently,
the feel of your body, curled into mine.
the tone of your voice when the words are fell:
but how they are spoken, reverently,
making me aware of divine design
in my encountering you, this frail shell
nothing but vessel for my light and heat.
paramour who conjours you as lover
and friend, companion and peer, fires of Hell
and the kiss of redemption, bittersweet.
I close my eyes and dream to discover
your presence where hope cast a patient spell.

WS III

roll away the stone. the stone that seals just one perspective.
for while the flesh is bound by walls and time, I've slipped free
to be a thing of light and quanta, bouncing through the ether
to both send and be a message, in and of myself, as such.
much to relate and yet can anyone relate to the inexplicable
except where a touch or glance communicates subtler truths
than all the hand-wringing head-shaking games when we must
filter reality through the lying layers of the necessity of survival.
the soothsayers and naysayers and game players protest.
too much. hiding from the hidden. forbidden mockeries spilt
like a glass of Pesach wine, long forgotten but the stain remains
for the celebrants to discover years from now, contemplating
what it is and what it means and if blood is really that red.

left for dead by the roadside

just wondering why
since you left me to die
by the side of the road
like some roadkill dog
you'd thought the better
of at least stopping to check on
you'd expect my sympathy
when it all comes down
in tatters and shatters
like crystal on a brick
a sickening sound I've found
like bones cracking from the inside
and usually I've swallowed my pride
and played toad to your scorpion
but not this time
no not this time
there's no reason for that rhyme
and if I forgive every crime
how will you ever learn
it's better to only burn bridges
when you want to make an enemy
and I don't, I won't hate
so don't you wait
for me to bad mouth you
it will not happen
but you shouldn't, I have said,
just left me for dead

addiction

I want you to suffer from my withdrawal.
feeling lost inside.
the throbbing glide denied
until you demand your next fix
with wicked smile and earnest guile
to lure me again, willingly,
to flood your veins with the my alchemy.
my base metal turned to gold as you hold
me deep, hungry for the rush, the flush
that leaves a deep and satisfying aftertaste
in both our mouths, evidence
that it was more for you than another pill.
another drag.
another sip of the nectar of forbidden fruit
that made your muscles ache and, awake,
made you walk in the land of dreams,
allowing me to taste you, to waste you.
not on carnival sideshow rides
but the full, merged and surged encouraged
purging purpose for which, even now,
I dream of in wicked prick'd metaphor
of an injection of my crude fluid
inside you to elevate your thighs high
to a dance of fire and desire sated.
only for the moment.
I want to be your drug, your addiction.
the friction of our flesh meshing messages
to our ancient brains, caught between moments
of civilized conduct that reassure us
that this is more than mere white blood
and the maddening taste of jasmine tea.

I do not chase the wind

I do not chase the wind
for it cannot be caught
and after I have fought
my way to the mountaintop
there would be no way to go
but down.

I do not chase the wind
for dreams are for their time
and I am wise, if past my prime,
and know how not to make an ass
of myself by thinking above the waist
sometimes.

I do not chase the wind
for it is but a metaphor
or five or six for the war
between the soul and the flesh
damned to fail and wail at rainbows
"Not fair!"

I do not chase the wind
for it would not be fair,
although if I would dare,
she might find me swift of foot,
carrying my golden apples of
poetry.

The Sunday Girl

the Sunday girl,
I've heard them say,
is bonny and blithe and good and gay.
and maybe, that's just what say they.

but she has potential.
a good mind
and passion.
more than she realizes
and beyond the mere spectrums
of intersecting lips and hips.
fire. couer rage.
enough to bare her soul
in words woeful and wicked,
rising on wings of fire
like some creature from Greek mythology.

or my mythologies.

she is growing, changing,
her thoughts are rearranging
as often as she changes lovers.
and then some.
which is perhaps why
she changes them
because they can't keep up
and she runs like a child in the meadow
laughing at their clutching hands
as they try to make it all work
but she's not ready for the steady
stability of a still-life portrait
to be hung in a hall. not yet.
maybe never. that's her decision.

freedom is just a word.

I know, in sad wisdom the truth:
you can't own the Sunday girl.
she may choose to lose the illusion
of freedom
for her own reasons
for a few seasons.
but, then again, she is the Sunday girl.
full of life, in all the impossible shades and hues,
the pinks and the blues and the darkest,

archest shades of grey that stay
just long enough for her to curl into a ball
and cry out her banshee-wail
challenge to the fates.

she is the not-dead.

the Sunday girl
she knows she owes you nothing
for the trifles you give her,
be they power and glory or immortality,
she's not the kind to bind herself
to your suppositions.
frustrating, but true for you
and for me, unless we choose to see
the world through her eyes
and realize
that this is the Sunday girl's world
and she is here to merely,
fearlessly, but not without tears,
make dreamers dream of her
and those like me, who grant immortality,
a purpose to our powers
more intimate than a kiss or a coit.

although I may wish it otherwise.

WS II

nails into wood
nails into flesh
the strangest meetings made to mesh
in pain and regret, the stain of a sweat
beyond prophecies and made mysteries.
the deserts fade
the deserts fail
to break the spirit of a dream that doesn't pale
next to the cold shroud, the veil of a cloud
that now will descend a faith to defend.
we bend our will
we bend our whim
and find that we are mere mortals against daemons grim
that make us believe and forget to receive
a sacrament taste of a lover displaced.

WS I

Torn and tossed, a Pentecost of more than five dimensions.
Slow to break the fast that lasted half a step of the dance
and then some. Kisses in scarlet and solferino, memory runs
and locks itself away. Playing for time expended in chance
opportunities that pleased all and none depending on the filter
of the perspective through eyes closed in a repose I once chose,
not knowing the price of commitment to the greater good, impure
like a diamond, to a first water. Last man out as the second sun rose
to bring a light that castrates the night but only for a season
or a score of seasonings, reasonings resounding in a pounding
like an elusive heart that has finally found the tempest tapestry, reason
enough to wait for the late fate of the sound of a heart, resounding.
Lay with me when you are ready, I am in no hurry to waste a resurrection
on the muddied middle of the hymns to a flawed law of perfection.

the barren idols

the barren idols

they mock me as they talk to me
in silent sibilancies, motionless dances
of seduction and sublime grace

I am primitive man

imagining deities in the stone and bone,
carving my own religion out of ignorance and fear,
here is the heart that cries dark blood

the goddess walks

cautious steps on the floor of the temple
perhaps another illusion, a trap of tapestries
to merely steal a feel and then desecration

the barren idols

they mock me as they talk to me
in silent sibilancies, motionless dances
of seduction and sublime grace

I am not spent

time stands still for me
as I evaluate the moment
then press it aside
it does not fit
my stubborn demand
to be a certain shade
or of a substance made

dreams of red and gold
fold and find themselves a new window
to watch down the street
where the sound of quick feet
is always of note
I swallow hard, discard,
the kisses catch in my throat

I am not waiting for something
that I know for sure is
I am just praying
that experience has lied
and life is not love denied

I am pondering
illusions of life that I've ridden
past the skies to the stars
and can show you the scars
of what I thought was real
and not just a clever spiel
I am given to remorse
but not prone to change my course

shall I just remain
taking space and spectrum and linger
like a rose in the green
like the voice of a singer
in a bottomless cave
marking time till the worms arrive
but still patient and alive

will the riddles I've ransomed
ever mean more than just a whim
will my countenance banish
vanished grin for a grim
will the spider unwind me
to find me spoiling for a fight
not a delight in the night

I am not spent.

inside you

I want to lose myself inside you
to find myself inside you
to find, to bind, to grind to
a depth of you no one knew
in four dimensions entered
with flesh and spirit centered
my passions pressed, unfettered,
and my kiss and release contoured
I want to be your acolyte
and worship you all through the night
and spare you not from all delight
you would permit me to incite
for you awake this sleeping beast
that was for so long bound, unreleased,
in need of goddess to the priest
and priestess to my passion's feast

the envious flowers

wherever you tread
the flowers nod and smile
and sing their song of attar
wishing for your notice
bare feet on cool stone
hair like wild blossoms
in the morning wind
beautiful and perfect
worthy of a poet's dreams
and the envy of the flowers

scattered like random thoughts

white
white as snow as clouds as dreams
as a puff of smoke
purified by your perfect kiss

white
white as light as milk as frost
as the milkweed seeds
scattered like random thoughts

white
white as bread as bleach as rage
as a blank paper page
waiting on you to compromise its virtue

altar

will you lay upon the altar
and offer me your soul
just to see if I will snatch it
in a flash of lost control

will you touch me with desire
that is ancient and anew
draw me in to share your pleasure
a hunger, pure and true

will you dare be my redemption
for my arrogance and fall
that I might yet deserve to set
my compass to your call

will you lay upon the altar
and offer me your soul
just to see if I will snatch it
in a flash of lost control

a long way down

at the point of my salvation
have I fallen from your grace
have you found me so unworthy
that you'd turn away your face
without word or slightest hint
of what lead to my disgrace
am I driven from the garden, blind?

is the tree of truth and knowledge
to be held just out of reach
will I need to find redemption
for some unforgiven breech
shall I learn to earn my heaven
in the lessons that you teach
and in time, your favour find?

wanting to be wanted

I want to hear your spirit
softly calling me
your veins throbbing at the memory
of my touch and trespass

I want to be your addiction
your nasty little habit
that you'd barter your dignity for
your life for an afternoon
with me pumping through your veins
messing with your mind
flooding your blood
dancing in your trance

I am here, whispering your name
a mantra of possession
a sinister confession
that I want to be wanted

sensate

touch and taste and sound and sight and scent
the veil is rent
and senses flood like blood from a wound
but this warm fluid is not red
not yet
but wet and pulsing life
of a sweeter degree
communicating your desire
your fire
as you kiss fingertips
with lips
thirsty
hungry
trembling to speak
to seek to express
the senses overtaken
with a simple kiss
or stroke of hand
or fingertip
or eloquent tongue
silently making love
that you may find me on more than a page
that becomes my cage
when it is locked away
in rooms you only come to
when you are alone
and you want to feel
your senses light up like a pyre
of dried exotic woods
that you can dance in the light
naked
in flesh and metaphor
grateful for my lips
fingertips
the truth they speak
that you are beautiful
worthy of reverence
and all the deity I need
for my faith to be restored

the sacraments' delight

would you be among the witness
who see me off the edge
daring all to choose to risk the fall
on a lover's boldest pledge?

would you read the tattered journals
and the scripture of my fate
choosing love above the cowardice
that is born in barren hate?

I am not here to ask you anything
but to speak my mind and leave
I have nothing to make offering
never tasking you to grieve

I am just a wandering minstrel
who is not afraid to lose
speaking of the errant arrogance
in whom, for love, I choose.

you are goddess and the heretic
a princess and a dream
that peels back from me the memories
like a tapestry, at the seam

I am trusting to the precipice
when I conjour you at night
and I wish for you the sacredness
of the sacraments' delight

hips

the curve of your hip
warmer than I expected

my hands trace your body
your grace even in repose
waking in me the songs

have I become an altar
to passions or is it you
or are we sharing brisance
without over-thinking it all

I can smell the heat of you
the sweet wet taste of jasmine
that I have been greedy for

discovering a goddess
in the way you move your hips

the baptism of desire

The baptism of desire, the fire burns away the doubt and shame.
Risen, like the phoenix, in heat and light and a solferino flame.
Passion descends on you, enters you, pure in its own right, no carnival
can drive away this mystery of the touch, avatars of the carnal
gods reborn to taste with lips and hips the eclipse of bartered ad val,
the baptism of desire, the fire burns away the doubt and shame.
I feel your tempested breath upon me, until nothing but you could tame
the lion of my loins that drives deep to fulfill an ancient aim and claim.
Passion descends on you, enters you, pure in its own right, no carnival
to bid farewell the flesh that meshes in urgent, ardent and unsubtle
stroke and writhe and kiss and rage and the poetry of the deeper thrall.
The baptism of desire, the fire burns away the doubt and shame.
I would gladly die tween the thighs that wrap and slap me, with a poet's name,
taking me for what I am, I surrender my urgent thirst and proclaim!
Passion descends on you, enters you, pure in its own right, no carnival
for I am not to surrender my couer rage for you, but in you, the same
as you will lay upon my flesh the consecration of your sacred scrawl:
The baptism of desire, the fire burns away the doubt and shame.
Passion descends on you, enters you, pure in its own right, no carnival

sweep

the curve, the nerve.
don't hit the nerve.
the blood is all we're after
the laughter of pain
the stain on sheets
the endorphin feedback loop
that little death hidden
in a scar
that perfects the sweetness
with a facet to be traced
by tear and raging rut.
I would kiss the flesh
and draw away the venom.
not to make it go away
but to share it.
and take it into me
to have something
undeniably
in common
with the dark woman
with the nightshade eyes
and a scar
or two
or ten thousand
to mark truth worth touching

nothing good at all

Nothing good can come of this.
Nothing good at all.
I feel you pierce my shadowed bliss.
Now in my sunken hall.
You've overrun the battlements
where I had made my stand.
And now cut deep inside my stones
I'd marked with sacred brand.
You're everywhere at once, and yet,
you dance, you dance away.
You've toppled walls in sacred halls,
you drive my thoughts astray.
And what would you, my conqueror,
demand to ransom back
my sanity, my vanity,
my soul on which you snack?
Benign malevolence you are
and beautiful, beside.
You've broken my defenses, token,
and in my heart, abide.

Let slip my leash

let slip my leash and I will run
run with limbs of quicksilver and skin of glass
passing the wind in my flight
laughing at the sun as I bring the night
not the darkness
but the beauty of the night
the song of the stars
the perfume of the moon
the sound of crickets and distant fading winds
as they shake the sleepy trees

I will run to you, eyes full of wonder and thunder,
seeking only to spend what time you allow
padding along the darker paths
to feel the heat of your skin
when you lay to rest
to smell your breath as you sleep
and imagine kisses I would never dare
as I wait for the rising sun
and run back into dreams
where I will await my reward

the cynical lover

I look under things.
between them.
looking for the hidden obstacle.
the bugs.
the lies.
the niceties that let me
make a fool of myself.

thumping melons for evidence
that the smooth skin and sweet aroma
is a fabrication,
meant to leave me disappointed
and, eventually, jaded.
I am not as trusting as I once was
or would like to be.

I can not tell when manners
are all that keep you from laughing at me
as I do my word dance
and cut your name into my heart
with blades accustomed to their task.
for I have heard even the gospel
from the mouths of sweet liars.

visions of war

ronin picking their way across the fields
that stand as monument to the arrogance
that tells us we can win peace at the point of a sword
bored gods look away and play their games
consumed by their immortality and the finality
of our self-immolation, consecrating carnage

the shadows of evening

unyielding edges of the infinite Moebius loop
that coops us up in our own cages of rage.
sage advice from friend or scripture
ignored or implemented just a moment too late
and fate wants to have a word with you
in the hall.
bring your books,
you won't be coming back.
molten copper blood in veins shredding
in pain, deadened to the immolation by will
and will alone, the placid stone we swallowed
with a kiss and a stiff drink of hemlock.
the shadows are not yet upon the hill
but still we know them to be inevitable,
inching ever closer to the porch.
to the wall. down the hall to where we lay,
waiting for the worms.

imprisoned hearts

The prison is inside, we hide our hearts
that none may break them. Pretty venoms spit,
hit their mark, but we are strong for our parts
and bind ourselves in bright rags that are split
only for pretense, we are not naive
to the purposes of tender tensions,
but we choose to guard that which we believe
essential, saving pretty pretensions
for the kiss and coit of those we can drain
for our nourishment and inspiration.
Leaving not death, but life and light, the pain
sucked in the instant of immolation.
I draw from you a flood of blood, a feast,
I share with you a thousand beasts, released.

lyric: romanticism

as the sun
traces fire across the sky
I smile into your heart
and hope to never die

for memory is no better
than a fantasy
truth just hopes you'll set her
to her destiny

we are not forgiven
any more than we forgive
we'll never know the answers
if we refuse to live

and I am waiting for you
with a dream forever new
and offer you no riddles
just a place where words are true

villain

would you take me for a villain if I lay with you tonight
and when all was said I fled your bed before the morning light?
would you think me a pretender if your beauty drew me near,
near enough to call your bluff and play upon your fear
of passion unrequited and thirst that's never quenched
and the furious, curious danger of romance when it's wrenched
and tossed aside for the moments to find satiation's rage
when we choose to loose illusion of our inner feral cage
and take glance to dance to touches, to kisses that explore
all the fantasies we can summon, all our passions and yet more
as we find a haven in our hearts, instinctive, yet we know
that there is sooth in soothing truth within our bodies' flow.
would you take me for a villain if I laid with you tonight
and when all was said I fled your bed before the morning light?

The promise of a ritual

like an ancient elder serpent god
avatar of a darker spirit
slithering up from out of shadows
scale on cool stone, voice like the winds
passing through the drying grass
where once grew trees of life and light.

like a darker priestess, summoning,
waiting for the red and black to melt
and run together like blood and night
the knife left buried, deep and silent,
the violent path to penetrate a heart
no longer of value as you evolve

like fire in the depths of an ancient fen
where no one claims the spark that set
the moss and dead twigs to crackle
like the cackle of creatures in the black.
like the taste of lips and lilacs, warm,
the promise of a ritual of ragged passion

prayer is not wasted

prayer
is not wasted on your soul
pain
that tried to wrest from you control

of all my fervent promises unbound
in all the sacred travesties I'd found

blood
becomes proof of truth and light
touch
that communicates the night

in all the eloquences I must speak
in the moments before I become too weak

kiss
with a purpose and release
dream
and may you find love and joy and peace

the dream is strong

memory fails me
at the altar where I kneel
my sins confound me
a past I can not conceal

there are angels in the air
without a thought without a care
and those of us of human form
must trade our souls to be kept warm

the visions recede
the incense precedes

and we are left to dance for hours that stretch to years

our passions resist
and then they persist

and we are left to pray to idols stacked like Russian dolls

you are lovely
and I cannot help but speak
words of yearning
the dream is strong, the dreamer weak

Paramour and Nothing More

An essence spun of red honey and of nightshade.
Paramour, and nothing more, golden fleece and jade.
Dreams drawn like fevered blood by leeches from a soul.
A kiss denied and deified to play its role,
lovers lost, crossed to toss their lust to dust and coal.
An essence spun of red honey and of nightshade.
A touch, a glance, a spirit's dance, so unafraid
to leap from the shadows to merge and purge the shade,
dreams drawn like fevered blood by leeches from a soul.
Thoughts given tongue, tongue given flesh and all control
surrendered like an illusion of virtue, stole.
An essence spun of red honey and of nightshade.
Every player acts, every actor played
a hand or made us what we are, our penance paid,
dreams drawn like fevered blood by leeches from a soul.
I want nothing more than the paramour not fade
on waking, not of just illusion but the whole.
An essence spun of red honey and of nightshade.
Dreams drawn like fevered blood by leeches from a soul.

Before the moon rises

a revelation perhaps given before the moon rises.
too soon for the civilization to wrap its soul around.
inconvenience in a thunder clap from out of everywhere.
truth surprises and tantalizes at times most inopportune
but bearing kairos over chronos, time enough for riddles
told in a practiced measure. the rituals of passion
stripped of the sacrament of true spirituality.
flesh to bread. blood to wine. a sense of the divine
in the taste of the sacrifice, given willingly.
cold stone idols and the shadow of the sun passes
into another night, where the chill fill us with doubt
we smother in platitudes and quotations. poster logic
without an understanding of the words, the whimsy,
the amomancy of the brave, slave to nothing,
but bound to speak of small words, sighed and undenied,
inscriptions on warm flesh, to be kissed, drawing out.
water from stone. wine from water. blood from wine.
and the cycle closes with a prayer shared between lovers
and the belief that they have found faith in the night.

kisses

the quiet cacophony of fleshes pressed, curious kisses.
furious hearts beating like hoofbeats of a stampeded beast.
the warmth of your hands, the urgency of your kisses
and the curl of your hips as I slip into you, I am released
to express myself in an inarticulate eloquence, kisses
melting doubt and reservations with each veneration
of your body as an altar for my passion. earnest kisses
that wander from lip to eyelid to ear to murmur words
that merely reinforce your awareness of my arousal, kisses
of more than lips, as you feel me slide ever deeper, taut
and hot and not at all ashamed by the grind I find, kisses
of an unique pleasure, as I feel your breasts pressing.
your acceptance, a blessing and an honor, for your kisses
invoke, provoke and evoke an essence of joy and contentment,
sharing and making and understanding love as more than kisses
or the pulse of me inside you as you draw from me my warm wine,
sparkling from the unrushed thrust gone to feral and pure, kisses
sure of my passion for you, wishing only to cxpress my love,
yes, my love, in your pleasure and awareness of my kisses.

sacred sound

a sacred sound, found in rhythms of hearts and tangled flesh,
meshing a message of eloquent surrender and satiation.
seeking an amplified life, and a merged one, purged of pain
we kiss each stain and draw it into ourselves with cunning touches
of fingers and lips and hips that slip into a natural ease
as we please ourselves and one another, hovering between
life and death, each breath a prayer to the silent gods
that gave us this altar of our own bodies to dare to share
in intimacies even a poet has trouble in confessing
the smooth and sweet curves of your shoulders and thighs
honey to my eyes and to be touched by warm hands
as I find my way inside you to let you claim me,
your lover for a moment I would eagerly extend into eternity
with your permission, just to hear that sacred sound again.

nice

I knew a woman once (or twice) who thought that being labeled "nice"
was quite an insult, particularly when it came to her beauty.
or her kisses. or the curve of her hips and breasts. or really anything
that could otherwise be described in more Olympian terms,
as she was very beautiful. and kissed with a passion that eclipsed
rational thought, and her hips and breasts (et cetera) were worth
a sonnet or ten thousand. which explains to some degree
the length and intensity of my poetic catalog. but I digress.

nice is not a bad word. it is not insulting or demeaning.
I think everyone should have nice people in their lives
who can speak intelligently. kiss articulately. and are honest,
and earnest, and all those other things that make laying down
besides them, to rest, a joy and a comfort that is...nice.
I think of people I know, lovely, worthy hearts and souls,
who are nice and deserving and beautiful and...nice.
and the word applies to she who cradles my heart, truly.

the zombie bride

The zombie bride?
She lied and tried
to get inside my head.
She said with a grind
she wanted me for my mind.
Or words to that effect.

thighs

my hands travel in a general meander,
along a seemingly infinite stretch of your lonesome thighways.
the road to your pleasure. a trail of tears
that bear the mark of every disappointment
cut in human cuneiform on the warm and hidden
tablets that now are exposed to my scrutiny.
my touch. my kiss. the slow rub of finger and face
as I trace my road to heaven by your warm legs.
I wonder if any man or woman has dared to take
their time and show respect for the vulnerability
and passion you represent in such a moment.
I can feel the heat that radiates from within you
and hear the soft, hesitant mewling of your arousal.
I am not here to just take what I can and flee,
a highwayman here for the plunder, then to thunder
off and away to seek another vacant road.
I am here on my journey to you, to express my desire
and my wonder at the beauty of your soul and body.
my hands travel in a general meander,
but not my heart, it has mapped the course to you.
and when granted safe passage by whatever roads
I must travel, I will take them gladly, even as I now
take great pleasure in pleasing you, teasing you,
making you want me, perhaps, a little more
than before I laid hands and lips and words
upon your most delicious and elegant thighs.

smitten meander

I find myself blinded by the incandescence
the lambent brisance
that overtakes me when I contemplate
your eyes

what lies
would I have to tell to win your affections?
what sacrifices
make to the hungry gods of passion and pain?
and, in the end,
would you love the man or just the artifice?
I do not know
and yet, every day, I feel your presence.

I will speak in generalities that those watching
for the sparks that speak
volumes in a tongue that touches heaven
and your lips

the altars of the city

I have fashioned halls as long as memory
cut from stone by tooth and claw
to the precise specifications of a lover's oath.
brandywine oceans parted to make way
for the armies of doubt, fleeing captivity
into a city of legends yet unborn, but sworn
to you from before you even dare to step
onto the sapphire steps ascending to your throne.
but the palace sits silent, sterile for the necessity
of your willingness to accept the conception
of something more than the morbid mediocrity
that lays traps and wraps itself around us
like a flailing, sightless vine in the verdancies
that would sell us Hell as anything other
than what it is...an arrogant lie we try
to wear like last year's sandals.
there is no need for the illusions and delusions
for you, for me, anymore. the word furnaces
are poked and stoked and the smoke is sweet
with the sacrificial boughs of a thousand woods,
ancient and elite and rare, spoken in mythologies
and prepared in accordance with the rituals
that begin and end with your presence.

Apokalypsis

the incisions are old and cold to the touch
they terminated their function as an injunction
against further passions permeated the fabric,
a cold, old, red oil that once was lit for light,
now fighting even for memory. the scars are relevant.

I have sealed away my soul as a time capsule,
allowing it only brief bursts of air and light
as needed to keep a fractured ruby heart beating.
have I really become so corrupted by this graceless age
that I would turn my face from love and wage a war within myself.

wars are fought for the right to write histories,
or to validate those told in whispered ironies
to those who only dream of war, even in the sphere of Venus,
for they have been playing the cold wombs so long
that they would not know what to do with living flesh.

I have seen the dead eyes, glistening only with light
reflected from distant fires that will never touch them,
the couer rage having fled and left us for dead so much
that even now I would lay down amidst the cold limbs
and let my fires bank in the abattoir of the forgotten.

pride can only carry you so far. purpose must be divine,
at least as divine as an earnest kiss or the touch
of an ardent mistress in the chill shadows of a cold room,
drawing out heat to feed upon and chase away the mediocrity
of bartered hearts cracked open like nuts on an anvil.

I have left behind the photos and the memories curdle
like even the sweetest milk does in time and nature.
I can recall their laughs, their kisses, their eyes and lies,
and the motivations that brought them to me and I to them
like some Valkyrie, picking through the slaughtered.

is there yet time for a final run through the fields
where the sun screams above an energetic horizon, reviving
even one as far gone as I am, and have been, for some time,
except in the illusions and the vampirism of inspiration.
I draw my blood from veins, in vanity and sanity, to burn.

and not unlike an abomination of golem and phoenix, I rise,
eyes of quicksilver, tears that are monuments and memories
of an ennobling futility. faith in the wraiths that call
me to fall a little harder next time for general amusement.
a dream of redemption in the arms of an angel, descending.

enigmatic darkness

you are enigma
even though there are trace
resonances
of other paths I have walked
other laughs I have heard
other eyes I have regarded
with fear and awe and the draw
of something very much alive
in the darkness that holds
promise
perhaps not for me
perhaps not to see
the light I would shine
in the corners you have
barricaded
against my arrival at this place
in this time
for this purpose
but I am a curious observer
and you are, of a nature,
a draw to me, like the smell
of an unfamiliar flower
in an unfamiliar place

fracturing rubies

I will watch you sleep, now.
for you are tired and at peace
at there is an intimacy beyond the touch and clutch of flesh,
meshing in hungry sibilance as we dance.
and will dance again, if left to my choice,
but your voice carries the option.

no mere moment in the stream of time
but a sense of ascension, here.
I have touched something rare and fair
and would care to again, beginning
an inevitable ending, playing a script
ripped from memory and a sense of the dramatic,
the emphatic and the empathetic.

will you see me as I am when you wake
or will I be yet another fractured ruby
to be cast aside now that you have seen
clearly and with a wish for it to not be so
my flaws that play into your gravest doubts about
the value of love as anything more than a verb?

I have placed my smooth red surface on the scales
before, and worn my feet hard with the roads
between the vendors and pretenders of an essence
that is never what it seems, except in dreams,
so I envy you your Morphean retreat, but I have lived
dreams brighter than any found in my fantasies.
truth, or at least the oath of it, accepted.

your lips remind me of abstractions, for they exist
not only to kiss and taste and draw me out,
but to whisper and shout your emotions and reactions.
full lips, red with satiation, yours and mine.
your skin is smooth, smoother than mine,
young and warm and I touch you, softly.

I draw the sheets more closely to you, to shield
you from the cool night air and my own ferality.
you are beautiful, asleep or awake and I take
a certain pleasure in the treasure you have slipped
into my memories, hoping it lasts but accepting,
accepting that this is your sphere I have entered
and when you wake, you may value me not.

alone

are we really that alone
that we have nothing but ourselves
and our own doubts about
everything

sounds of silence, violence
in a world where we need to feed
on something more than tears,
isolation

for an earnest word or kiss
we would leave these tattered shells
the shadows of our hells
without regret

disguises

dark and stark, we mark our souls with spray tans and lipstick,
covering the truth from the hovering valkyries, just doing their jobs
as they wander the outer edges, the sedges and sediments
of our cryptic confessions, morality a compass and impediment sent
to make it just a little more like a test and we wrest tomorrow
from the yesterday that clouds and crowds the moment, tears soft
like the frayed edge of a ripped pair of jeans, speaking of times
when the shearing force was enough to split the fabric.

patience

though every moment seems an eternity
for the desire, the fire, that you inspire
with your perfect grace and a face
that Helen would have envied, patience
will lend itself to my crusade for your heart.

this is not some mere schoolboy notion
but emotion, devotion, that lays cables
to wind and bind and blind me to those
who I have chosen to not give my soul,
such as it is, to win your fair regard.

feralities

I press my lips against your flesh
and follow soon, with hips that mesh
and match and mold and find my hold
with hands well eager to feel your curves.

the passion, it transcends the nerves,
and desire fires thought and act
and to your touch I well react,
to serve my purpose to your needs.

and, high aloft, like windblown seeds
we find our place within a cloud
and restrained urges burst aloud,
articulated feralities.

tell me the words you want to hear
and at which point you dare to fear
the loss of self to merg'd souls
in coals that burn to new degree.

and I in you, and you with me,
are tangled, mangled, wild and free,
within our sphere of heated skins
who knows what will from what begins.

the instant turns to moment spent
then hours without wild relent.
shall we ascend another tier
and whisper from a vanished sphere?

of what we left behind to fade,
like litter from a passed parade,
in celebration of our finds
of join'd flesh and join'd minds?

I want to feel your full release
to follow with your gentle peace
and find that I might penetrate
in every sense, your precious gates.

beyond the feral symmetry

flesh and blood. I want it all, all of it, every pore
and sore, aching muscle throughout your hot, taut form,
glistening with sweat and regret we'll deal with no more,
for our greater regrets were in the hunger denied, warm
essence to the presence that existed when barriers fell
and we were one flesh, one mind, one inarticulate being,
speaking in whispers and growls and screams that swell
to echo off the walls that serve silent witness, freeing
us to like in the instant, where we are merged and purged
by the acts of the surrendered lovers, the feeling of you,
wrapped around me as I see how deep you are, encouraged
by your guttural sounds and gripping fingertips, that drew
me into you, to fill an ancient need beyond the poetry,
beyond the memory, beyond the feral symmetry.

a suitor, withdrawn

not selling you excuses for the stumbles and the falls
that persuade me, accept the path down which my purpose calls.
of copper and of silver, I conduct, connect, reflect
all the light that comes, bends to me, the lambence I project
onto pages for the ages yet to pass, yet long gone,
that would stir a heart to understand a suitor, withdrawn.

children of the pain

where music rises in the gloaming layers of dreams
pricked like indifferent balloons, fates sealed,
we are voices that spin the webwords of emotions
oft left by the side of the road, like a dejected suitor,
denied the promised land but defiant to the end.
the road is not always well-lit and the ill-fit of our shoes
makes it even longer for those of us seeking redemption
in one last kiss, one last hit or miss proposition
that we would not sell in a shell game of lame excuses
for the follies of our fantasies. dark things hide
in shadows yet to be cast and in the past we cringe,
sometimes, at the memories that tomorrow suckles from.

an origami cage

there is the thought
I caught in my dreams
bound to the night
more than it seems
the riddle that rattles
inside me, alone,
prayers that disown me
my tears to atone
that trusting is really
an errand for fools
and nobody cares
to play by the rules;
the regent, the consort,
the fool, all agree
that there's nothing remaining
on the trencher for me
the feast is forgotten
the stains slowly fade
but in the scale of forever
a moment is made
between where we had started
and where we will end
like flowers, our hearts
but a season will spend
drinking in sunshine
painting the fields
until time lets us languish
and memory yields
yields to the fading
of flesh and of page
like fireflies captured
in an origami cage

in wisps and whispers

in wisps and whispers.
fire and ice.
I sold my soul.
I paid the price.
and all the angels
fled my bed
for what was thought
and what was said.

and whiskers twitch
in subtle breeze
as deities
do what they please.
leaving just
the scribe of note
who marks the time
but has no vote.

the statues fall
for lightning strike.
and actors call
when hemlines hike.
the songbirds nest
in forests deep
to pray the cats
tonight will sleep.

the gypsies dance
on matted soil
and keep the trance
with fragrant oil.
the minstrels strum
and figure rhyme
as we all hum
to keep the time.

the butterflies
and beasts of lore
give muffled cries
and ask the floor.
but moments still
take up the hour
and time we kill
transcends whims' power.

my memories
I regret not, and yet.
I weep for faces
I shall not forget.
I kiss, in sleep,
that trace of light
that danced just once
then fled my sight.

late to the garden

how shall I find you if I am late to the garden
and all the wanderers and fragrant blossoms
are already taken, to be carried far away,
leaving me in a dull grey silence, alone.
alone like a solitary stone on a trackless shore
amidst infinite grains of sand, abandoned,
to wait for the next ten thousand years
to be broken down to fit into the beach.
I have come to understand the poison
of silence, the violence of solitude, the grim
and dim diminution of hope and joy and love.
black diamond to the arrogant sandstone
where even the quartz cracks and wears
in the face of a greater hardness.
how shall I find you if I am late to the garden
and there is not even the track of bare feet
left on the dry and pocked rocks
to serve as a clue of where you stood
waiting for me, but I was slow to arrive
and you chose to believe I was not coming,
that the fates had mocked you once more
and that I was an agent of pain and regret.
I will sit amongst these stones and weep,
my tears proving only my sorrow and solitude.

if I fell

if I fell on my knees before you
and begged you for your heart
would you think about my hunger
and consider me apart

from the other offered lovers
and their mysteries, their stones
that they lay upon the altars
as a barter for your bones

to be part of their alchemistry
with saffron and with ash
to be part of an experiment
when their base illusions clash

I come bearing nothing more
than truths and tenderness
a gift of heart and heat
in a graceless, chilling wilderness

I am a simple weaver of words
words pressed like last autumn's leaves
between the pages of trivial tales
that are only as true as one believes

Commandment 6

It's what I do,
he said,
I pull the trigger
now they're dead.
I'm a bad man
doing what you expect of me.

It's what we do,
we said,
we flip the switch
now he's dead.
we're society
caught up in our own hypocrisy.

ever upwards

my soul
your soul
all souls
are living things
the sum and substance of our lives
like the rings of a tree
telling the story of the past
yet still reaching skyward
for another drop of the rain of hope
another ray of the sun of dreams
another cool breeze of introspection
even when bent by forces
beyond our control, our soul
still reaches upwards
ever upwards, thanking the past
and glad for the anchoring roots
of our birthed natures and fates.

like a blossom

like a blossom in the summer's wind
I see you as something pure and passionate
warm and woven into the tapestry of senses,
forswearing the defenses of illusion.
I can see you, feel you, smell your essence
in the presence in the creation,
as a charity to me from a smiling God
who sees the beauty in what you are
and were and will be, all as part of all.
you are beautiful and precious, every petal.
every tracery of colour and scent and touch.
like a blossom in the summer's wind.

I am become man

I am become man, the destroyer of Words.
I will bend your thoughts to my own purposes.
I will eat the soul of your dreams.
I will barter for what I want with what you need.
I will justify myself in flags and books and fire
that bleeds into the skies of poorer peoples
and their waters and their lands, that I might prosper.
I will lie to you when there is no need to.
I will fall upon you when peace is the only way.
to resolve the conflict of ideologies and theologies.
I am become man, the destroyer of Words,
who mocks the purposes of a benign God
who takes many forms and facets to teach us
to reach us with the sanity that, in our vanity,
escapes us, rapes us of the innocence of peace.
I strike from the corners and the shadows,
proud of my conceits and deceits, my heart beats
with a black and bitter rhythm fashioned of bile and guile
that I will explain away as necessary to a higher purpose
that I lack the soul to recognize as I kill it with honed irony.

don't be afraid...

fear is within me.
not in the shadows I used to think
were just waiting for me to look away
to snatch me up and swallow me whole
like my heart does, sometimes.
I am my own question mark.
I am my own nay-sayer.
I should know better than to doubt
because I have been here the whole time
and seen what I have survived
and triumphed over with a laugh
and a smile and a roar of victory.
fear is within me.
that I might best control it.

flesh to flesh

flesh to flesh
we mesh
very well

perhaps no coincidence
that in the present tense
and present tensions
we make gifts of our lifting spirits

lovers hovering
over a great descent
and, in our indecent indescension,
we find no reason to fall

just to release
with a hungry, primal peace,
a fitting merge to purge
our urges to foreswear love

flesh to flesh
we mesh
very well

making love

I would spin my world into you, making tapestry of your tears
to shield us from the inclement souls of those who would watch
to see what lovers, true lovers, do when they brave the bare skin
of memories yet unborn and unborne. torn from our hearts,
the passions and emotions find freedom in the soft rhythms
of kisses and caresses, tender trespasses that lead us to need
the reassurance that all is still right with one corner of this sphere.

I will give over to you all you would ask of me, task to me,
placing my trust in every thrust of feral bodies given their freedom
to devour the power of our touching, comfort found in movement
and the slow, silent stillness when we need to hear our own hearts,
as we have lost our boundaries in the tangle of bodies, alive
with rebirth and a joy that tickles and tingles and mingles
every pain we've ever know with every joy still to be shown.

Nothing between us but hope

you are a lantern to my soul,
lambent to my touch. your surrender
awakens me to make sacrifice
after sacrifice, pieces of myself
given as evidence of a new communion.
the old idols fade and crumble
into piles of dust and sand.
nothing can stand the test of time
but that which is willing to wait.
wait until the time for idols is passed
and we cast ourselves in images
of our true selves, severed from lies
that we even tell to the mirror
to make clearer the falsehoods
we feed upon. I have no need of riddles.
the religion of ronin is patience
and the desire to see things as they are.
I should like to see you naked,
with nothing between us but hope.

solitaire with a suicide king

Paul Simon said
"an island never cries"
and I know he was right
because they don't let lies
into poetry and the fight
to wait until you're dead

to be alone is as universal
as anything I can imagine.
the memory of pale skin
the instinct to touch, again,
even an illusion of a sin
that leaves us hollow and full.

full of a hunger unknown
just moments before, when the illusion
of being perfect in our solitude
was still our premise and we'd begun
to accept ourselves, as we could exclude
the failings for which we'd atone.

I am not a rock.
for I feel the serpent's coils
as they crush the life from me.
I feel the echoes of every lie's soils
upon me and by me and can see
the bloody stone that waits to mock.

lovesong

warm to the touch
pale to the light
in your embrace is the purest delight
faith in your word
trust in your heart
knowing that never we should be apart

for love is a binding
a test of our souls
to see if we dare to fulfill our true roles
halves of perfection
lost until when
we find our completion and our lives can begin

the search may seem endless
but I know what I've found
a song that at last seems more than just sound
soft kisses of crimson
and peace to my nights
as I lay down beside you in the fading of lights.

and the dreamers dance on

Perilously close to touching what I know I can't resist,
close to coupling to a moment that shall evermore persist
all my nightmares and philosophies are thrown down in a kiss.

and the dreamers dance on and on.

I am falling for illusion that is coming true, in truth,
speaking words of ancient languages that contain all of the sooth,
claiming heart for heart and then some, like a law for eye or tooth.

and the dreamers dance on and on.

Shall I face my fate as fearlessly as you arrived last night,
dancing to celestial musics that shroud menace from my sight
as I find in your fair beauty all the promises of light?

and the dreamers dance on and on.
and the dreamers dance on and on.
and the dreamers dance on and on.

hearing the chains groan

Cry "Havoc" and let slip the gods of love,
glove wrapped, tapped to their essence,
a presence of menace and memory, mad
with desire of an ambiguous focus, crocus
in a field of fireflowers, Spring's a bitch.

I am bound by my own defenses, pretenses
that shield and do not yield to a sealed sentiment.
Bent and rusted, they hold in cold links
that sink might Atlantis beneath waters
in which bathe the daughters of desire.

Listen as I snarl my defiance at the bindings,
unwinding thread by thread for I am not dead
and no one said I would sleep forever,
bound by these grounding chains of pain and stain
that even now realize their folly as I contemplate you.

The metal feels my limbs as they heat, sweet blood
flooding my every, every extremity. The golem
sets himself against the taut anchors and the Earth
itself must tremble as I test the durability of regret.
I reach for a kiss or more and the links scream surrender.

The Vampire: Irony of Lust...

I shall drink, I think,
only that which is necessary
to keep me alive and humbled.
For were I to take my fill
I will, perhaps, be guilty
of taking your life, a wife
to such a creature as I am,
cold and condemned to a Hell
of the night where even light
has turned against you.
The irony is, I would be free,
empowered, my powers flowering
in the nurture of your lost future.

ten thousand roses

if I brought ten thousand roses
would you think to change your mind
and come back to where your kisses
taught me how love is defined

if I waited for a lifetime
would you meet me at the end
would you stay with me forever
and be more than just a friend

if I brought ten thousand roses
and promised all my heart and more
would you step back into loving me
give me what I'm living for

if I promised and delivered
a miracle, and more, each day
would you remember memories
or would you hurry on your way

if I brought ten thousand roses
and I brought ten thousand more
could I count on all you promised
when you loved me once before

flashes of light

Flashes
of light.
The night passes
uneventfully for most,
trapped between life and death
for threescore and ten
on the average.

But I
am not
looking for the
average life and death
having seen you pass
in flashes of light.

Crimson,
your lips.
Colours blossom
in fantasies you create
like a goddess of desire
who will feed on me
and my graven prayers.

shiny, shiny things

waking up to more than the violence of silence,
the rude solitude of a bed half empty
(or half full, if that is your take on it).
not that a bed makes up for everything said or unsaid
this side of the fence, pensive pretense a pence
in the cornucopia of hope and heresy.
do you really know what you want, what haunts you,
taunts you, flaunts itself before you like new knowledge
you could not capture in college or a collage of memories
of degrees of earnest learning? turning base metal
into shiny, shiny things and the linking rings
of a trick of the night and the light within,
lambent and hypergolic, for that is the nature of passion.

I dreamt of you last night

I dreamt of you last night.

dark dreams that break the dark with a truer sense of silence.
avatars and metaphors of dangers and strangers.
violence to my good wishes for you.
a sense of sorrow borrowed from
the histories and mysteries we've shared.

I dreamt of you last night.

and every muscle and sinew braced to pull you from harm,
only to be faced with the burnt ends of a rope
I would have cast you, blasted from my hands
by the demands of shadow figures
in your head, in your bed.

I dreamt of you last night.

yet no cold catalepsy returned to make mock by mettle,
only a hollow sorrow the one promise
I'd ever gotten from you was orphaned
by the side of the road like a castoff kitten,
left to die, as was I.

I dreamt of you last night.

evidence of God

I find evidence of God
in the way you smile.
proof positive, that there is
something undefiled
despite the way the world spins,
often trashing hopes.
for you have that essence, prime,
surmounting slopes
that lead to the mountaintop
where there is vision
that sees beyond the moment
and finds in us one
more chance to dance with bare feet
on the soft Spring grass
and laugh like children
as the angels pass.

the nature of my soul

It will be life,
in all its beauty and pain,
purity and stain,
angelic refrain
and cry of despair,
I am there.

Selah.

Love: tempest's touch

Harvest the thought that was regent and rare,
an air upon an harmonic desire
to cap our life and tone with tender care,
to pull our hands from the hot sparks and fire
that would consume us down to smoke and ash.
Mottled, bottled memory of a time
when we were proud, cresting as the waves crash
on inarticulate sands, in a prime
that marks not clock or purse, but energies
released and not ceased in the face of pain
that strives to drive us to unwilling knees
before we speak its name, in flames, again.
But we love because we can and as such
we are made immortal to tempests' touch.

gather you

I would gather you, as a rare orchid,
in jungles of my life. reds and pinks
and a curious lavender to tempt me
to touch and taste and take for my own
that which nature has raised up beautiful,
indifferent to my desires.

I would gather you, as a rare orchid,
bright and perfect. proof of God
even if I must contend with defenses
made to hold me away and teach humility
in the lessons you have learned in pain
and sadness, cast as madness.

I would gather you, and lay with you,
your petals filling my senses, making my defenses
an anecdote of ages past, as I am drawn
so deep inside your very presence
by your beauty and mystery
that I am lost, forevermore.

more than a moment

I want to touch you and feel your skin against mine
a consummation divine. the wine of your sweat, wet
and yet not as wet as you will get when we set ourselves
up for a fall, all the angels and angles against us, lust
dusting us with the hunger you raise in me, to see
how long I can bear to stare before I must feel you,
seal you with my flesh and oaths as you take me in,
break me in to your desires and fires, inspiring me
to see how long, how strong your wordless song
can sustain when the pain is washed away in sweet heat
that burns from eyes to feet and back again, as much
as you want, as I would haunt your every corner,
honor bound to sound deep inside you to convince you
that I'm here for more than to taste you, to waste you
like the hollow lovers of the past, casting their shallows
into the hallows of the temple of your body. to surrender
to one who is not pretender and wants more than a moment.

were I an angel

If I were an angel I would not feel
this sharp, roaring desire to enter you.
To merge with you and lose myself, burning
with a penetrative moment we hold
high from the sky and make heaven our bed.
If I were an angel I would not feel
the mad, feral hunger to demonstrate
the arousal you can invoke with eyes
that speak to me of your own wilding thirst,
needing to draw an avatar of me
in fluids crimson and pale, I surrender.
If I were an angel. But you know that
I am but man, craving your blood and fire.

you are not here

you are not here.
and I can feel your absence, a hole
in time and space. and in my soul,
where you should always be, and yet,
when you are not here, I regret
every time I spoke words you doubted
and thought false passions when I shouted
them in metered rhyme that I might best
remember them, later. truth you can test
with the sound and the semblance of pain
I carry within me when you are absent, vain
though I am I am humbled by you and ache
for your absence so mightily that I break.
you are not here.

the law is love

and the law is love.
who am I to challenge the law?
no one. for I accept it as stone.
as air. as water. as light. the night
holds no terror for me, for you came to me,
the first time, in the darkness.
a silhouette of shameless beauty,
sharing herself with someone open
to the probability of love.
and the law is love.
to live without love is a prison,
grey stone walls and metal bars
that do not bend and do not mend hearts
shattered in past escapes from the cell
that mocks Hell as a loveless place.
full of the cold baptisms of mockery
and the tick tock crockery of delusion.
I am given to the law. the law of love.

not asking for a miracle

I am not asking for a miracle.
Just an everyday,
everyday,
run of the mill love story.
With moments that get rough
and some tough issues,
tough issues,
that need to be worked out.
Because love isn't easy.
It doesn't fall from the sky,
from the sky,
and give you the happily ever after.
But it gives you a good reason
to forgive and to live,
and to live,
with the unexpected bumps and thumps.
I am not asking for a miracle.
Just someone who can smile,
who can smile,
and still tell me off when I get lost and crossed.

to an image

you are more than the sum of parts
too easily captured in light and word,
cut and pasted and wasted
when they do not tell the story
or even the cover of the book.

there is purpose to the person,
and every vision provisioned of hope
tells us more than the curve of skin
and the colour of your hair.
fair though you may be, you are more.

for every soul wears the shell of life,
every life wears the shell of experience,
and every experience is more than fate,
more than random chance and happenstance.
it is the forge of the soul, the furnace.

and how can eyes capture the truth of steel
forged in the fires of desires and the liars
who think that you are nothing more
than the sum of some parts, easily captured
but never held, for they have touched nothing.

5_4

you are five dimensions in a four-dimensional world.
around you my senses bend, my logic is curled
like smoke from a fire, reborn from a coal.
a metaphor'd passion that bursts from my soul
to explode with a fury that causes no harm,
that should bid no distraction and raise no alarm.
the fire is warmth that is cool and white-hot,
giving truth to the legends that once you had thought
were but stories they told you to give you a dream
of a world where romantics could live by the theme
of love as a part of life, light and night shared,
with no memories to poison, no karma compared.
when we accept the emotions and devotions of those
who have given us all without pretense or pose.

soft passion

I am the touch of earnest hands
laid upon you to please you, release you.
to dare and share and care your pleasure,
a treasure to my soul, your ecstasy,
your surrender to this tender trespass.
I would touch and taste and listen
for as long as you would let my other senses
without pretense take tensioned flesh and unleash
all you are, to the waiting universe,
keeping back only the moments in which
you let me, if only for an instant, be lover
and friend and servant to your necessity.
I would capture your ragged breath between
my lips and lay hands upon hips that deserve
more than the artifice of desire, but the fire
that burns and learns more in a single touch
than in ten thousand pretty words, waits.
soft passion bids me to dream of you, alive
with your blossoming heart and to take
what is given, with gratitude and deep, delicious
touch and melting into something that is more
than the twain that met in a wet moment.
I am surrendered unto your most perfect joy.
I would worship your body as evidence of God.

orgasm

feel soft the fire rise, burning with hunger
and a need to release and take in new fuel.
I can imagine you, hands playing proxy
for my desires. your body slowly surrendering
to the pleasure it needs, indeed, it calls for
like food or water. or love. a touch of love
worthy to embrace and enter you, to center you
around a deep, steady, passionate penetration
to more than just your physical core
as you soar in electric fire unleashed
with such power that you feel torn apart
and reborn, laying there, a smile returning
to your face, your body breathing gentle now.
given, and taken, by your control.
and in my mind and heart, I was there,
and kiss you with reverence and passion.

deep breach

you are just out of reach, but not forever.
not forever, for ever does hope spring eternal
and infernal when I see your face and grace,
striking sparks against the splinted flint
that was once my heart, waking at dawn
to see you rise like Aphrodite from the sea,
calling me to touch you. first with my word,
praying to be heard and that your heart is stirred
to curiosity and a gentler reception than the candied dandies
who strut their shadows like pagan peacocks,
unaware of the elegance of the religion of love.
sacrifices that fold inward like praying hands
to expand the rippling universe that turns crippling
pain into understanding and gives sight to the blind.
find me in the caesura between hope and passion
while my soul falls into orbit about yours, a radiant star
marked only with the scars of life to make it perfect.
a whim and a will and a soft, comforting madness,
a deeper breach forms in my soul, and I find you there.
already waiting for me, your arms spread like the horizon.

the venom of our vices

I want to crush you to me, like a flower, releasing the vagrant fragrance
that lay hidden so long, too long, as we danced our tentative tarantella,
seeking to purge ourselves of the venom of our vices, throbbing
to be released and captured, purified in moments of wet fire
to be kindled in soft touches, waiting for the moment when eyes close
and the clothes are long discarded, like all attempts at restraint.
paint me with your crimson and I will see your eyes burn when I turn
steel into liquid heat that spreads on bedsheets torn and tangled.

the penetrating rose

the focus shifts to your hand. your soft hand. the hand
that brushes aside my hair to gaze into my eyes when
that is all we dare do for fear of showing the cards
of our hearts to the riverboat gamblers who charge
and bluff and cheat their ways across this game. with
firm and cautious resolve, you guide the penetrating rose
to its vase. or perhaps, to a new bed, rich and nurturing.
where it will take root. and grow strong as an expression
of passion and love. I stare deeply into your burnt honey
eyes and see the fire in them, as parts the impediments
to the penetrating rose. I see your eyes. I feel your eyes
locked into mine, sending fire and pleasure like some
great spiritual semaphore. a single sound escapes your lips.
and the penetrating rose slides softly into place. and
you brush aside my hair again, with the soft hand that
guided the flower to its new home. where it takes root.
and blossoms as your eyes, hand, heart and flesh desire.

welcome to the furnace

welcome to the furnace
the sweet heat in sheets sleets
and glass and brass alike melt
as I smelt a higher order of mettle.
fettle words are not hammered
like Toledo steel, you have to feel
the fire, the desire of a higher order,
a white hot crucible is not a runcible spoon,
and the moon is the antithesis of the sun,
bordering on a consuming consummation
where every derivation in desperation
is just a cheap Chinese knock off
of the designer hearts from the anvil
where people go to blow on their soup
because they say it is too hot
when all the while they need the burn
that turns them inside out to be bride
to a golem still wet from the forge.
the sweat of creation rips apart
all that it touches, in a leper's blood flood.

Aubergine

my passion for you is aubergine,
deep and dark and full of the blood
that floods my heart and limbs
when I look upon you, naked,
stretched out as evidence
that God must have been a man;
Rodin with flesh and bone,
sculpting your body as a temple
to an unnamed goddess,
that she may find a home
and draw near her worshipers
and at least one poet,
his heart aubergine with awe
and lust and the desire
to consecrate and defile
with every thrust and breath
and word
left in his body.

Lady Destiny

you've taken many forms to warm the shadows of your sphere.
pain that can drain and stain, the times I hold most dear.
your path, a laugh and tear and puzzle to be solved.
only that which has been broken can, in turn, be evolved.

In February you have held my soul in simple words.
Marched me to the cliff to hear the voice of calling birds.
In August you have bound, profound, my soul to ageless sin,
a dream supreme, and yet I scream in silence, deep within.

So what have you now brought to me, Lady Destiny?
Another corpse that warps my sense and sanity?
Or are you now the lover, for the moment, once again?
Proclaiming quest is over and that hope may finally reign?

In November you have wound my boundless prayers for peace.
September shattered vow and now I find a dread release.
And what of strange April and the apples made of gold
now I am old and lost my speed to win the race foretold?

more than Gods can comprehend

I wrote her words so she'd understand
the sinking weight atop the sand
but I am not given to move on.

I made my vows and paid a price
but that doesn't mean I will think twice
about wanting what I want and what I need.

because there's truth 'round every bend
and it would be a lie, my friend,
to bury and forget all that we've won.

it lives and grows, with scuffs and starts,
like fearless souls and loving hearts
until it signifies the two are one.

I will not fade or fall away,
and years from now you may just say
I think he had it right, I had it wrong.

so this is why I play this song
to hold the line and pray she bears my suit.
not playing cute
or holding back
I have to speak the perfect fact:

I love you more than Gods can comprehend.

eve

swallowing the light.
vouchsafing the coming night.
fire to devour.
I take it in to feed my power.

lambent to the scene.
regrets are for the lesser queen.
I take it all to seal;
my guarantee of what is real.

warm, and so I drain
the fire, desire and the pain
that is drawn to me.
that is spawn to be.

swallowing the fire
a curious thing, desire.
I take in your release
to find the bind that shall not cease.

Floreale

I should like to feel the smooth heat
of your legs in the dark.
strong and soft and a delight to senses
that are brought out at night.
flesh on flesh they mesh well
with the darkness, drawing me in.
the skin against my hands,
my back, my face, no trace
of fear or shame or blame
for why we are both here.
and you draw me near
with your legs in the dark.

To acknowledge life

you can live on your knees
or die on your feet
but the story isn't complete
as life is an incurable disease
and sooner or later, we all fall.

it's easy to fall. to haul
our battered carcasses to the edge
and hurl them off the impossible ledge
high atop the self-made palace wall
of the temple of our own best intents.

cowards touch knee to the cool stone
every day, surrendering to the pain and stain
because it is easier that way, to remain
curled in our fatalistic fetal position.
rise. rise. rise to acknowledge life.

Going Dancing

life is a dance.
on point, every joint reacting
as you practice the spontaneity
of love and dreams. you are a deity
to freedom and desire as your fire
leaps from heart to limb to eyes,
open in the awe and inspiration,
your grace facing your soul, released.

you will bloom

you will bloom when the room seems darkest
and the air seems thick and sick and cold.
for in those moments the walls and chairs,
the very airs, will need you to return to them,
to burn like a new star in the heavens
that rearranges the constellations
with her fire and light and changes the night
into a place for lovers to lay together
and wonder on the beautiful light in the sky
that, despite adversity and pain, refused to die.

Strawberry Kiss

red as morning, bright and so sweet it calls
for lips to taste and not to waste a bit.
biting in metaphor, sweet, in enthralls
any who would dare kiss with passion and wit
and find both gone, lost in the grace of touch
as the soft fruit gives up secrets to mouth
and scent and thought, you are now caught by such
perfect harvest of the sunshine and south
winds that carried merry favour to please
and seize and tease lips blessed to find heaven
unleashed to bind a kind of dream to seize
a sustenance of more than flesh and then
the red, red taste passes into mem'ry
and so you beg for just one more berry.

Insomnia

eyes closed against the darkness
seems rather redundant, but everything
is a distraction. sandman is losing traction
as he tries to climb the mountains
of hadeda thoughts that are fluttering
and screeching and pecking at me
as my arm falls asleep before I do
and I lay there, thinking of things
I wouldn't think of if I were with you.
tonight.

Your red shoes

slip into your red shoes.
you know the ones.
the ones that go with everything
but holding back
even a fraction
as they get traction on my heart
and I hear them even in the dark
even after your feet are no longer in them
even as I am lost within you
dreaming of the first time you
slipped into those red shoes.
when you walked all over me
metaphorically as I found myself
only admiring them as an excuse
to study further your elegant legs
and imagine what they would look like
from angles that red shoes might be
a bit out of place in
(but I am game if you are).

unafraid

unafraid. I want to live out of the shade.
where liars and losers and the lackwit bruisers fade
to ashes. where the deep, bloody gashes of trust betrayed
does not mean you must live, dismayed,
the septic wounds bringing pain those final hours
where innocence seems a handicap against the seven powers
now aligned in a mesalliance, the violence of silence
metaphor for more of the irony of emotional belligerence
that punches itself out like George Foreman in Zaire
before being dropped like a bad habit by those who dare to care.
all I need is a microphone, three words and the truth.
all I need is an earnest heart, these words to speak the sooth.

with all due respect

veils of time and apple blossom breezes.
the grind of life and all it seizes.
we are better for the moment, better for the thought
we caught in butterfly envy, truth like a candle flame.
a name, unashamed, but carried and buried
in cardboard, having fallen on its sword in beauty
like the arc of the final falling embers.
once around the sun and all things begun flicker
and fall away like the closing moments of a day
that will be remembered. as you will be.

closing the wounds

Blood, it purifies.
Then, at last, it dries
to a shell of, well, memory.
I do not allow myself to be
forgetful about such things as pain.
Five months to the day
that I sent my heart away
it came back to me, slightly worse
for the wear. A worn and terse
red ink stamping: Abandoned.
So here I sit, peace
filling me with release.
My words, writ in respect,
curl halfway round the sun to reflect
upon the nature of closure.

life is a gallery of art

Life is a gallery of art
and I can walk down the halls
admiring the creative hand
that mixed the colours and laid stroke
upon stroke
upon stroke
to bring the curve alive in the face
and hands
and hips
of a beautiful woman
without stealing the canvas
and running home with it
to hide it away in hunger or pride.
most of the time.

I respect the artist and the sculptor.
Rodin has always been a favourite,
able to make stone awaken
to the point that jealous hearts
accused him of casting from corpses,
for they were of the blood of Salieri
and could not comprehend
the gifts of another, envious
and bitter, their suns eclipsed
by a greater light that stole
their place on pedestals they carved
in their lust for recognition
and their willingness to believe
that they were the only stars.

I have my own definition of art
as that which resonates with me
and makes me feel something more
than a mere impression of skill,
a thrill, a chill, a will to change
and rearrange the priorities of life
or at least to know a new appreciation
for women with freckles or red hair.
It is there, in the gallery,
where we find our quickened pulses caught
in gossamer and summer wind that spins us
into hearts like pinwheels, shiny toys
that bring the smile of a child
for whom all of life is a miracle of creation.

Where calls the siren

shall I follow where calls the siren?
Odysseus was wise enough to have himself bound
that he might not, yet still hear the song.
I am not so clever.
and so my choice is whether to walk away, doubting words
that promise paradise, as they are born of mortals
and there are so many ways these things can
end badly, sadly, madly, or just
fade to jade, and promises made
become premises for contemplation.
or to find faith in pillow propositions
that are nothing until made bone and stone.
shall I follow where calls the siren?

metafive

stolen memories, unrepentant dreamers
take a long drink from the flask of tasks
mastered in alabaster darkness, wasted on blind men.
finding the bindings unwound and discarded
like the shroud of an impatient resurrection.
insurrection that escapes detection
until the infection penetrates the membranes
and the disease does as it pleases.

into the wind

your kiss is like the dew that forms
on the lips of a glass of ice
on the hottest of days
a tempting afterthought of relief
that there is hope in Hell
of a quenched thirst, a lifted curse
if only by the will of those daring,
caring to face into the wind
and take a little heat
risk a real defeat
for that is where the wars are won.

kissing the Charybdis

build your whims and wishes carefully,
for cotton candy castles blow away
when the slightest breeze comes.
a puff of air from the nostrils of daemons and dreams.
I've been sold more than one sack of sorrows,
tomorrows that were past their due date, sold.
old gold and the red of lips, painted,
sainted thoughts that fought for nothing.
nothing but a ring of ink and cold hands,
clamped clammy over the oracles of truth,
to silence them from shouting a warning.
morning glories and black roses strewn for miles.
trace flesh growing back over the mending bones.

scar

I will wear this mark as a point of pride,
for the lash of life is an ennobling stroke,
poking holes in our self-righteous wrath,
laughing at us like a child kissing clouds,
proud of all that goes into couer rage.

flesh

I like to touch your skin
and feel the flesh mesh in colours proud and loud,
with the subtlety of a distant mandolin,
playing a tune you'd swear you'd heard
in the background of an old gangster movie
just before all Hell broke loose.
and, as you kiss me, lips parted,
hips started and eyes closing to focus,
it breaks loose here.
with very different results.

dance

snowflake whispers melt and dry
on tongues that kiss the flesh once stung.
albino words grow pink and glow
to launch a dragon in the sky.
your whispers wait for moments yet
to brave the wind of souls seemed twinned
in earthen jars and bronze barb spars
that draw the blood our dreams to wet
dance for as long as the music plays.
then dance to the memories, the rest of all days.

tenderly

I think of you tenderly and dream of you
constantly and passionately and sometimes we
are even wearing clothes in those dreams.
you are inside me at a depth I never knew
I never flew to in my strangest thoughts
but now I am caught up in your life.
No one can charm me and nothing can harm me
while I am here, thinking of you now.
Do not doubt but that I will dream of you tonight.
and tenderly, wish I was there to hold you
as you sleep, shielding the jealous stars
and feeling your every breath as proof of God.

constant

I can still smell your perfume
in a room where you have never been.
you manifest so well,
conjured for your part from a willing heart
into arms yet open and ready.
steady hands wait to gentle pain
torn and born by panic and by strain
and yet through all, I do remain
constant.
and waiting for your kiss.

unspoken truths

shouting lies does not make them true.
it is the quiet truths, those that may even
sleep for a season, hidden for reasons
obscure and unsure, these are gospel.
a gospel in kisses and memories promised,
bound by unsound vows that now seem imprudent
but nonetheless are the same metal cast.
I have surrendered to my honor, to my love.
I have given my flesh to a single pyre
where I shall stand, immolated.
where I shall stand, consecrated.
where I shall stand, recreated.
or look a bit foolish.
but such is the nature of unspoken truth.

the road beyond Damascus

the road goes on.
on beyond your furthest dream.
on beyond the horizon.
stretching out in all directions
with intersections dark and bright.

bits of bone and brass mix with dust
that rises with every footstep
to choke the sun from the track
I leave behind for the blind
to follow with fingertip probity.

the road goes on and on,
so long already, hands unsteady
seek a pillow rock to lay against.
the present, tense, becomes memory
and the martyr'd hearts did their part

do not walk with me. do not.
for my stride is long and my goal is far
and you will fall by the way, cursing yourself
and nursing a bruised ego for daring
to rise above the grey, if only for a kiss

I will speak of you in the distant cities
places where pity becomes compassion
and we fashion idols from cloth and clay
when we play like lovers. but only pantomime.
for the road beyond Damascus is hard.

feet taking me far and fast until at last
some city hears that they were my last bed.
and that somewhere on the road I fell.
and another dancer picks up their load
and starts walking on the road beyond Damascus.

the fate of lovers

ignore the roar of the mad and sad
and find your center on which to stand
I will applaud and laud your heart
that all may know I stood for you
and in each mote and mountain fell
I will abide as close as let
to sleep beside you and regret
nothing bartered for your soft hand
that rests in mine even in dark
when madness comes and pain abounds
so I might sit and guard your soul
that I will not leave you to the night

as much as I try

as much as I may try
I cannot deny that I love you.
you have entered my life
as a friend and wife, and I know, true,
that my heart is at peace
with the gentle release of your pleasure.
for which I will hold,
a promise of gold, your joy is my treasure.

the presence

It is not surrender to the pain to cry out from it,
to acknowledge it, to defy it, and it alone.
I atone for many sins. Lesser and greater.
Mine and others, it seems. I take the lash and crash
into myself. Splintered. But with a resolved heart
that I have a purpose in rising to bow
and grip again the handles.
Not in a show of defiance, but of love.
I choose to kneel to heal what I can
for I have a pattern and a promise to keep.

a duty to the heart

there is blood on the altar to feed indifferent deities.
sacrifices of little consequence, the virtue of vows unmade
and made mock in whispers that echo louder than shouted truths
for they slide, as narrow blades, between the weave that guards
from shards of shattered illusions and displaced fear and anger.

I will burn the incense to purify this room, then seal it.
seal it in wax and sweat and words that turn regret into joy,
for in our hearts we make our avatars and they are immortal,
as are the vows of a priest; released, but bound by something
not to be unbound by practiced hands. we wake to memory.

nefarious zone

you danced for me the other night
to music I could not hear
but felt in my heart
and I felt your body sway
as the light passed in colours cool
heated by your soft smile
and the release of the leaden thoughts
and demands of abstract stresses
as your tresses brushed your shoulders
and you were free
as always
but needed the reminder

quintessence

better an ounce of the fifth stuff
than a world of lesser substance.
bartering handfuls of dirt for a single diamond
will only work on a man needing to farm
and I am not that hungry anymore,
for I have smelled the crisp bacon praise
in your laugh when I tell you I love you
and felt the warmth of your passion
radiant across more than an ocean
of time and tears and hopes and fears
I will swim, if I must, to reach the dust
where I will lay my head and heart
at the end of all things, next to an ounce
of the fifth stuff, your soul. immortal.
better an ounce of the fifth stuff
than anymore lies to my heart.

conundrum

the symphony begins, as overture rises.
the wind is hot
and a miracle dances in tongues of flame
as a name fades.
dry mouths chant the curse they purse lips
to let slip away.
where the liars lie
and the bullies strike
and the cowards run
how shall I react to the conundrum?

with pride? pride is for fools
who do not know the value of beauty
and hide behind a facade of arrogance.

with rage? rage is a cage
that traps you and poisons you
until there is nothing left but pain and regret.

with madness? to what end?
could you defend your suit
when mocked by the locking clock of reality?

no.

no.

no.

there is a time for surrender.
and it is now.
so let the winds blow
and the fires burn
and the castle turn to stone and ash.
and I will...

wait.

to be collected.
and hope for the hand I will accept.
and none other.

sacrament: February 20

thirty minutes wonderful
a week or two in a year
kiss from an earnest lover
the truth contained in a tear

all I want is surrender
all I offer is my all
lives are lived on less beauty
waiting for the dreams to fall

justice is not for lovers
stealing feasts inside a sip
taken from a cup of joy
passing from touch to my lip

good right arm

I want to be your good right arm,
snake charmer to your doubts and out
of nowhere show up (when it is convenient)
to sweep you off your feet, more
than a champion, more than a friend.
Blind in the mindfields, trusting your will,
believing in you when the moments are still
and the silence is deafening, a dense, wet regret,
measured in tears and fears and passing years.
A reward of purpose for a good right arm.

faith, confessed

you asked me to confess love, and I did.
for you saw behind the facade where I had hid
the truth that rose higher than heaven, shy
to touch that which, as much as anything I
had ever encountered or imagined in this sphere,
I was hungry for. seeking to more than draw near,
but to penetrate all shells invoked to shield
you from all that I would offer, all that I now yield.

a patient, passionate heart

I will sit here, with her, until moments bleed away
and she rises from her bed on legs strong with will
driven by steam and a grim gaiety, to sway
notions fates will relate later as proof that still
there is freedom to rise, even against the wind
and a power in love and hope that breaks the chain
of prejudice in all things found brittle when pinned
to the punishing stone. for I was told "remain".

move your heart

I wish I could move your heart
from eight thousand miles away
I wish I could move your heart
so that we could share the day

I am not much for making wishes
as they sometimes don't come true
but I wish I could move your heart
so that I could stay with you.

I have given my surrender
so that you might know that I
just want to move your heart
so I won't ever make you cry.

I make a wish to move your heart
and tightly close my eyes
I pray for all things lost and crossed
and spread my wings to rise.

For if I cannot move your heart
than I must find a way
to tear down mounts and walls and such
and make of life what I may.

gentle is the hand

gentle is the hand that soothes the soul
too often struck or shackled, hackles raised
and temperament crazed by pain and sorrows.
I would be kind to you and bind to you
as you would let me in, I am twin
to your reading of the signs and designs,
and would just know the way to be best for you.

pain to peace

muck to mire. stone to fire. clouds, aloud, call down the sky.
and I, I am not really anywhere I was when once I walked,
walked like a blind man, bruised and used and confused
by every sound and surface encountered and yet, I endure.
unsure of everything but my own heart, a compass of flint,
splintered and splinted, but mine own, no matter what is said
in mockery or dread of the nature of my passions and compassions.

I said it more than once.
but no one was listening
with more than ears used to
shutting out unpleasant truths
and the clarity of a kiss.
I said it more than once.
and I meant it the first time.
the rooster crows low and metaphor
transcends the atomic truths revealed
in the precise words chosen for exposure.
I said it more than once.
but the words were all words
that someone else had said and I,
I was made an echo of the shadows,
screaming dreams you cannot wake up from.
I said it more than once.
but the words mean something different
and sometimes even indifferent,
cobbled by careful hands
but hobbled in the handling.
I said it more than once
so that there would be no mistaking
the waking from the cold, cracked earth,
that rebirth would mean something more
than stretch marks and recriminations.

pain to peace. we release nothing but what we choose to,
refusing to offer more of ourselves than the nothings
we have left after the ground has found us filling
and we are no longer willing to ask more than a hole
and a means to fill it in once we fall in and surrender,
pretending we are bending our fates when we howl at the sun.
I will stand here, as promised, even if I stand alone forever.

cascades radiant

let down your hair to fall in cascades radiant
that frame a face for which there is not a trace
of doubt, in my heart, of its beauty. Aphrodite born
to warn mere mortals of the folly of mediocrity
as she fills my soul to overflowing with pink ink
to spill on page and wage a war with memories
that do not go gentle into that good night, but leave
feeling a bit rejected, disrespected, but thus is
the nature of moments transcendent, as when you
let down your hair to fall in cascades radiant.

when your hair is grey

I will be there, if you will,
when your hair is grey
and the day is uphill.

the truth of the rose

how gently the forge of God must have bent to curl the aspect
of your petals and leaves, a woman like unto a rose, perfect
in all her colour and texture and fragrance, not without thorns
for those incautious and unsuitable suitors to take as horns
into their own flesh and drive them mad with a prick'd pain
for having dared to touch that which was made liar's bane.
for the truth of the rose is in the very nature of its beauty,
and the scent of love arises from within, as each bloom's duty
is to express the very eloquence and elegance of all creation.
and I will stand to love you in prick'd thicket without hesitation.

draw the venom

deep and unclean, the wound festers,
testing your endurance and those who cannot bear
to see your pain and dare not stand to draw out
the venom you have come to take as part of life
that is permanent and penitent and perverse.

a curse, if you would, accepted as inevitable
and surrendered to in exhaustion and regret.
I kiss the wound and lay my heat upon it,
feeling it as a living thing, saying softly
to me "She is mine, come no closer".

I kiss the wound and close my eyes and dream
a dream yet unfulfilled and, singing psalms,
under my breath, bartering death for life
I cannot live without, I draw out slowly
the bitter gall that chills your veins and heart.

I draw out the venom as gently and thoroughly
as I can, ever vigilant for your pain and strain
that I may not, again, be one who merely
slapped linen to poisoned skin and looked
the other way for another day and did not stay.

the wound is deep and a part of you now,
and every day for the rest of my life, if I must,
I will draw out the venom in touch and kiss and word
you may have heard once upon a time, but never
through lips that have dared to draw the venom.

clouds

I think hearts are like clouds.
at a distance they are solid,
often imagined in various shapes
to suit our moods or fancies
or to subtly test other people's
imaginations or intelligence.

But close up, they are ethereal.
Capable of great power and force,
wind and lightning and flooding rains
that sweep away whole continents.
But you cannot hold them, for they
were made to blow wild and free.

purgatory

In all its glory, purgatory
is naught but time and pain.
A room, a tomb, of uncertain doom,
while waiting on a train
you know will come, it always does,
and yet so great the fear
that one day it will not return
and leave you stranded here.

the judgement of history and mystery

mortals are ephemeral
lasting for a few seasons
then dust and ash and trash
to be buried and ferried into darkness
with the words of the poets and prophets
spoken over their arrogant debris

effort

it is in the effort
not the attainment
that we find virtue or disgrace
the human race must strive
to build a better moment
a better tomorrow
but we cannot control
the complex and confounding
variable and actions of others
accomplishing at least a measure
of the goals they bleed for and from
in deed and word and hope

Kintsugi: The River of Molten Gold

the great ovipositor of divine starshine

the gift, such as it is called, is both cursed and delightful.
a cure and rabidity that forces one to see colours and taste flavours
ripped from the very ether of the universe
and beyond
as toxic as madness may be
and beautiful like a peppermint kiss
under mistletoe
never consummated
never forgotten
bartered as obsidian roses for redemption
at a funeral
where the shadow is granted substance.

cracks in a neutron star patched with memory

in time the crust of the cup fractures
and there is a suggestion of a leak
before the shards explode outward
to imbed themselves in the synapses
of the unfortunate bravo who dared
to sip the subtle hemlock of jasmine
blooming at night as background music
to the immortalization of a comely muse.

settling for the sediment in the pool of your eyes

tell me you name for the ten thousandth time, my mind
had already chosen it for you, burned in black embers
in the halls of the resonances of deep-fired inspirations
where immortality is the price I pay in slices of seduction
as you barter flesh for flechettes that bury themselves
deeper than you can imagine, even if you do not understand
this game that is not a game to me, but oxygen ignited

epigenesis

desire is not part of our genetic makeup
but it is ultimately epigenetic
carried in the fluids and flecks of life
influencing the fates and forcing our hands
beyond the standing glands of procreation
willful in its own way, slaying complacency
you are reborn immortal in trouvere's
code of remembrance and immortalization

shattered tattered scattered

too many voices and too many choices
poisoning the path and laughing at virtue
and virtual thought, caught on the hot claws
of brittle, bitter conundrums
when the twig is bent, the tree struggles
to right itself, to fight itself towards the sky
before mythologies and theologies grasped
like the handle of a sword, slashing the cord.

the sound of lost laughter

the deafening silence. indifference.
bred by the dead to stand their stead
and compel belief in compliant simplicity
as the band plays on a simple song
and the well is tainted in faint feints
against the origins of the species
as we struggle against the poison wind
that fills our lungs and minds with madness.

temporality

caught up in the dance of the decades
traded for mere moments when lips meet
and communicate more than words, absurd
as it seems, we are prisoners to our natures
and our nurture lays as epigenesis to code
of ten thousand degenerations, tasking us
and asking us to live down to the glazed haze
of memories made and unmade, woven.

serpent singing in the garden

the song is subtle, but persistent, a faint invitation
to remain and play, the illusion of the fantasy
lingers like the scent of honeysuckle and an incense
of an alien spice, close to cinnamon, but not quite.
the danger is not apparent, and indeed the threat
is not oppressive, it is even pleasant if one suspends
the question of the reality reflected in verdant scales
that fall away as you lean into the fantasy and are lost.

the dreams of the damned

There are dreams
that are buried in the sky.
To find them you must die
So I've heard.
But to seek the
quintessence in the clouds
must we tangle in our shrouds?
How absurd.

the amomancy

I draw you, in my words,
as water from a well,
as an artist captures beauty,
as duty draws the epic heroine
to conquer the evil of indifference,
in amomancies bright and perfect.

red and feral

no doubt a kitsune,
practicing her power over her form,
soft and warm, capturing my whimsy
and leaving the marks of her claws
and craft on my heart and my back
and my memories.

I hate being the responsible one

I hate being the responsible one
the one people expect to behave
to be a slave to proper conduct
at least in my actions. my thoughts,
debating the various choices in voices
ancient and instinctive, telling otherwise.
and if you could read them
we would all be in trouble, very quickly.

Alone, to atone

love is a shape of infinite facets
each one a challenge to vanity and sanity
desire, fire, a funeral pyre built of sorrowed
tomorrows basking in the grey lights
you were never warned to expect
when you fall from a height, blind,
never knowing where the bottom is
or how long you must fall as the echoes
of your own voice reject you
and flee into the darkness.

The melody is subtext to the words

the cithara sets the hairs on my neck to dance as if
mimicking tiny lightnings reminiscent of when last
you breathed against my neck, language failing you,
but communication not requiring translation, unmistakable,
takes the three dimensions of time as mirrors to an horizontal
rapture as the hand of God and gods pluck us for redemption
and further consideration as to our ultimate intimacy
with the universe and our collapse into a Russian doll
where every layer is ourselves, merely smaller and smaller.

Questionable Decisions

I have made more than a few questionable decisions in my life.
Who to kiss. Who to dismiss. Who to trust as the dust rises
of their retreat from standing with me at the inflection point.
It doesn't make of me a bad person, but it makes of me a person
who has made bad decisions, motivated by ignorance
or arrogance or misunderstanding what is at stake
when the break consecrates doubt and hindsight
perfect as a hawk's vision but only in the aftermath.
I am far more guarded than I one was, and that is something
that I regret as I make my apologies and take my penance,

rewired

motives and memories
lucid dreams
the imperfect perfection of reflection
when the opportunity presents itself

e e cummings

I would like to ask e e cummings
how he felt about the Oxford comma
and the Microsoft dictate to only put
one space at a full stop.

Prayerful whispers against the night sky

I made promises to you and to the God of my youth,
devotion in my emotion, oaths more molten steel
eternities vouched for, the blood and seed cast
to seal the crypt where slipped my honor
but you were inconstant in matters beyond the bed
and my soul could not accept the barter of identity
for fealty to my vows. Rarely a day passes
without my shattered grief at your absence.
I see you in my mind's eye, content and,
I hope, happy that my resolve held in bands
forged by Hephaestus at Apollo's urging
the names of the gods and goddesses
still buried in my legacy and legend.

Poignard

stab as deep as you need to
in order to heal your own soul
I am not immortal or indestructible
yet I know pain is not fatal
and I will drag my battered ego
into the shadows to survive.
know that knowing my vulnerabilities
is not the same as dominance,
I will bleed for the rest of my life
but there is much yet to accomplish.

yes, I slept with your sister

once we were ended
the screaming void in my soul could only be filled
or so I thought
with a similar presence
and it was easy
to find someone who wanted
what we had
when we were together
and seemingly the perfect couple
they were a mistake
that I confessed
not as a taunt or a haunt
but as desperation move
to prove I would survive
without you

agent provocateur

stop me in my tracks and prove to me that empathy
is not the path for all who wish the best for all
for only in such a world do we prosper
one and all
now and future generations
driven by avarice and fear
hearing voices in the shadows
and laying lies as traps
for desperate minds

birth of madness

clawing up from the nothingness
as a metaphor for the big bang
for the creation of the universe
from a single point of darkness
into light and thought and dreams
and poetry and love and the rebirth
of awareness of the eternal hope
that we cling to even in the night

I cannot forget your kiss

I cannot forget your kiss
I miss it like the first snow in December
I remember how it felt in both the primary
color and flavor of your lips and the way
your hips not so subtly brushed against me
as if trying to separate me from my sanity
quite successfully as I recall and all
the tiny pinpricks that danced across
my skin were calling your arcane name
and making crude requests for what I
should do next, without pause or subtext
as I leaned in for another kiss, successfully

bathysphere

all relationships are like a ride in a bathysphere
into the depths, cold and dark,
trusting to the team (of two, usually)
that this is safe and the trip is worth the risk
as we dare the uncertainty with hope
and adrenaline and eyes open
to embrace what might be waiting for us
deep. dark. alien landscapes and seascapes.

the regency of the negative

the no is the source of all real power
or should be, as dissent is not consent,
and you should always have the choice
to voice doubt and hesitation, taken
as a reflection of conscience and concern
to burn the candle just a little longer
until you are certain that you are not
making a mistake with your nod.

remember me in your dreams

the desolation of time, a crime against joy
that steals what we had wanted, taunted
by clock and calendar and missteps
pilfering the details around the edge
that pledged happiness and tomorrows
now long past, blasted to pieces that cease
to echo the picture that hung on the wall.

till the gunpowder never ran out on the heels of our boots

I would live for a time where innocence is not a crime
to be punished with the harshest of penalties, the breeze
never becomes a derecho, bearing widespread destruction
as a consequence of nothing more than the indifference
of nature, striking out without anger or emotion, purely
of the surly state of a universe far too large to comprehend,
to bend to our desires and our fires, blessed light in the night
that takes its time resolving into dawn for our sanity.

the day before we met

The day before we met you did not expect me.
your religion. your experience. your dreams
did not anticipate the shifting winds and sands
painting zen garden pictures on the fabric of
space and time that erases itself from moment
to moment as you dodged my touch and swept ahead
breaking away like a splintering iceberg, ancient
but forever changing with the tides and times.

The then and now became the when and how
we never chose and froze to the bright stagnation
that surrounds us like clouds of clowns descending
in an ancient dream that never ends, merely pausing
when we wake and take a few more faltering steps
to the edge of our lives, daring the uncaring light
to beat down upon us one more time, that we
may know the mediocrity we wrap ourselves in.

jasmine in the jacob's ladder between your thighs

the electricity dances across my face and down my neck
sprites of light conjour impure certainties
attar of the altar on which all is surrendered
for the insurrection resurrection circumspection
genuflection self-protection venesection to draw
effigies of unremarkable lovers who hovered
in murky skies for surprising lies and the cries
of the catalyzing catalepsies, conjugal catastrophes.

remarking on the remarkable

a touch of whisper, a taste of light,
the scent of memory, skin on skin
begin again
the seizing synesthesia you sought,
fought for in the game of life and death.
you still don't understand, except at night
at the moment when the rem sleep reveals
the connections between confections,
slippery soap bubble memories popped
when you reach out to them.

the festering flesh

knee deep in the stables of the horses of a mythos
that you are a part of without understanding
a parkour pattern of living the resolution
of a revolution that pirouettes and sweats
a venom that glazes the phases of the moon
when the three body problem solves itself.
eventually in karaoke cataclysm, singing
a song you learned before you understood
what all the words meant, mimicry
crying out for context and purpose.

patience is a virtue held in contempt

a fistful of gingham, wistful of forgotten times
unliving and unforgiving, the moss-covered
bricks lining the street where the suitor waits,
his fresh-pressed shirt tucked in ancient jeans
that once held promises, now a faded repetition
of a superstition of fashion, long gone iconography.

electric blue and the colour of night

clashing against our retinae
flickering illusions optical date rape
everything is misunderstood and amplified
by what we want to see or feel in the moment.

I am drained by the pretty vampires

drawn to your hunger and thirst, cursed to share my life
regardless of how weak I have become from time to time.
seeking those who feed my need to be fed upon, dawn
is no guardian, I am a food bank for the pitiable pretties
for I lament the times in my life where I have performed
questionable things, if only in my heart, and seek redemption
of Icarus, torn apart as penance, ever challenging myself
to endure as a purification ritual against my own darkness.
it affects my definitions and perceptions. a revenant spent
in iron coins in the market of the mythologies. Enduring.

solar

stepping from the shade to recharge my cells.
eyes shut against the fires that would melt me
if given their druthers. revitalized and warned,
the arc of Apollo stormed to demand the moment

the false gods of memory

I remember in imperfect plates of tin and silicon
the sound of your voice, even when the accent has shifted,
lifted you above the time and place in which you endure,
the same soul and barely altered form, warm against
the cooling environment or blistering history you chose
as roses on the trellis as I forget pieces of the puzzle
that would muzzle my passion and sorrow, tomorrow
I will know less of you than I knew yesterday, a shame.

I have been deceived enough but not enough

that I recall, three times has a woman deceived me as to her
relationship status
hiding relevant facts and pacts to their own ends
however noble the intention
failing to mention pertinent details
or telling me what I want to hear
when you have your own agenda
and you suspect I would not be so compliant
as you need me want me to be
when the opportunity presents itself.

the curious spider in the corner of my bookcase

he is disturbing nothing but my calm
but my calm calls for a death sentence
which I, with great restraint, deny
and hope he or she stays in his place

mourn the moment

mourn the moment
innocence lost
the cost of arrogance
the curse of ignorance
the wages of fear and hatred
great nations and great personages
have dealt with such times,
indeed, greatness is often a byproduct
of unproductive times
now get off your knees
and restart the climb that Sisyphus
defined his life by, fighting,
at least metaphorically
against evil and the stubbornness
of the worst of our kind,
blinded by the three deaths
that history mocks us with
and at least make it a punishing fight
against the night of our lost
nobility and integrity.

love in all the shades and colours and flavours

could I love beyond my boundaries?
of course, you do not build walls around your religion
but include whatever the revelation,
there is a great evil in those who redefine
the epiphanies they encounter..
I have been smitten by beautiful women
of every race, creed, and shade of melanin,
of every state of birth, transitioned and translated,
for affection, love, passion fashions itself
as it sees fit, and who am I to deny the truth?

severing

severing myself in a thousand ways
from the past
from the future
from the physical dimensions
is of no real use
to diminish the pain
to diminish the strain
of dealing with life
within and without me
and denies me the duty
the beauty of creation

dust devils

in the moment you told me truths I accepted as such
to touch the essence of you in that moment
I cannot blame you for the evolution
the revolution
that is part of being human
shaped by the forces visible
and invisible to you
as they swirl like a thousand dust devils
playing across the fields of the harvest
and carrying debris and the promise of life

we will wither

we will wither and die
slowly, we hope, as we grapple with thoughts
still crisp like a crabapple
picked worm in the fields
that are not unfamiliar
where our descendants
will have their lives
until it is their turn

reticent

I am not reticent to speak of you
for my own sake, but to take care
not to compromise what you have said
or implied (if not actually, openly lied)

shards as currency

the puzzles confound us and abound in the gaming rooms
of the casinos of our choices, voices calling out for us
to wager ever more, imploring us to lose it all or win
riches beyond our imaginings and expectations.

I do not know if you are alive

In my heart you always will be sweet and heated memories, playing out
on the big screen of decades when you ruled my feelings, even if unaware
of how profoundly you played the role you had taken on, sometimes epic
and sometimes as a day player, curled up in the shadows to represent
an expected abstraction required to fulfill Chekov's expectations.

I have no control over what you remember me, if you remember me at all,
and you may not even know or care that I was ever there, my role lacking
any real resonance or whether I was just a placeholder, colder than death
even at my zenith, perhaps even a plot device to contrast with the real
leading man, who was more what you were looking for. I hope you found him.

And that, in the finality, if there are such times, you are content,
having found more joy than sorrow and no longer dwelling on pain past.
I wrote this poem with you in mind (and heart) and wish to let you know
that all my memories of you are, on the balance, lighter than air, heavier
than most philosophical considerations. Whatever your fate, I wish you well.

Instincts aside

the nature of man is to pursue wisdom in the face on instincts honed
over millions of years that have served us well most of the time.
But we can be the pettiest of primates, allowing hate and fear to rule
when we should be well past that, cowering from strange sounds
and concepts that are not that far from our understanding, opportunities
abound for empathies and to embrace our humanity as wings
that draw us closer to heavens we reject often out of the bad behaviors
of the messengers and not the message itself, knee jerk reactions.

in the rain

I stood in the rain for over an hour, waiting for your arrival.
My judgement in trusting you, for you had not attentions of being there.
It was a game to you, a mockery of my good intentions.
Cruel and perfect in its cruelty, to this day I feel the blade of rejection,
a metaphor and more for the pain was real, and I wondered if you
understood how much your actions and intentions made the world colder.

Perfecting the process as a way to chaos

Tiny gestures tying together threads and webs and the leavings of a meal
left to cool on the table set with great precision and haste, to seal
the life we should have taken more seriously than we did, kidding
ourselves that our wishes were all that mattered, the urgent bidding
that accumulates the fates in a kintsugi manifestation of prayers
and passions derived from the leavings of apples, grapes, and pears
fermented to a broth of bacteria that gives us the illusion of romance
in a dance you never dared to share with me, never taking the chance
that we many instinctively know how the pieces fit if we quit trying
to make everything turn out the way we imagined, the dead are dying
to show us the marble bed they said was all we deserved, cold stone
against bare flesh beyond caring, beyond daring to stop being alone.

About the author

William F. DeVault was born in Greenville, South Carolina, USA, on August 16, 1955. A few weeks thereafter his family moved to Alaska, as his father was with the US Air Force. Thus began his meandering ways. He has visited every state in the union, as well as Canada. He has lived in no less than 11 states, but it wasn't until just shy of his 41st birthday, when living in Venice Beach, California, that he says he felt at home.

He is the second of 5 children, married twice and divorced as many time at this writing. His works have been banned in a Catholic girl's school in Ireland, he's been investigated as an holy man by one group, continued to write almost constantly, judged regional and state finals for **Poetry Out Loud**, and turned down an offer to ghostwrite a Hollywood actor's "autobiography". He considers himself a Quaker, yet he considers poetry his religion, as expressed in his book **Qoheleth**.

In 2005, the **Appalachian Education Initiative** included him in "**Art & Soul**", a coffee table book of 50 notable creative artists educated in West Virginia. Since 2023 he has been the lead judge of the Morgantown High – William F. DeVault – Venetian Spider Press poetry contest at his alma mater.

In 2017 the **National Beat Poetry Foundation** named him the **US National Beat Poet Laureate** for 2017-2018. In 2025 they circled back and named him a **New Generation Beat Poet Laureate**, a lifetime appointment. In 1996 Yahoo named him the **Romantic Poet of the Internet.**

In 2017 he was offered, and accepted, the opportunity to be CEO of **Venetian Spider Press**, conditional to them taking on a seven (or more) book project. This is 8th, but the final of the arc of 7. He continues to work in the private sector, as well, as a management and business development consultant, because his creditors like money more than poetry.

He has collaborated with European hardcore composer/performer **Ophidian** on several pieces, one of which, "**Nightfall Angel**" went to #1 on the European Hardcore/Industrial charts.

Married and divorced twice, he has three grown children; Perelandra, Elric, and Dante. He takes the oaths he makes to himself very seriously, trying to live up to his "mythology", with sometimes odd lifestyle results.

And he says that poetry ends when the poet becomes more important than the poem.

Lyrics Rights Notice

Best wishes!

www.ingramcontent.com/pod-product-compliance
Lightning Source LLC
Chambersburg PA
CBHW080812020826
48982CB00017B/955

* 9 7 9 8 9 9 9 5 2 3 2 0 4 *